Young People, Sex and the Media

Also by David Buckingham

MEDIA EDUCATION: Learning, Literacy and Contemporary Culture

AFTER THE DEATH OF CHILDHOOD: Growing up in the Age of Electronic Media

THE MAKING OF CITIZENS: Young People, News and Politics

MOVING IMAGES: Understanding Children's Emotional Responses to Television

CHILDREN TALKING TELEVISION: The Making of Television Literacy

Young People, Sex and the Media

The Facts of Life?

David Buckingham
Sara Bragg

First published 2004 by
PALGRAVE MACMILLAN
Houndmills, Basingstoke, Hampshire RG21 6XS and
175 Fifth Avenue, New York, N. Y. 10010
Companies and representatives throughout the world

PALGRAVE MACMILLAN is the global academic imprint of the Palgrave Macmillan division of St. Martin's Press, LLC and of Palgrave Macmillan Ltd. Macmillan® is a registered trademark in the United States, United Kingdom and other countries. Palgrave is a registered trademark in the European Union and other countries.

ISBN 1–4039–1822–8 Hardback
ISBN 1–4039–1823–6 Paperback

This book is printed on paper suitable for recycling and made from fully managed and sustained forest sources.

A catalogue record for this book is available from the British Library.

Library of Congress Cataloging-in-Publication Data
Buckingham, David, 1954–
    Young people, sex, and the media: the facts of life? / David Buckingham, Sara Bragg.
        p. cm.
    Includes bibliographical references and index.
    ISBN 1–4039–1822–8 – ISBN 1–4039–1823–6 (pbk.)
    1. Mass media and teenagers–Great Britain. 2. Mass media and children–Great Britain. 3. Sex in mass media–Great Britain.
4. Teenagers–Great Britain–Attitudes. I. Bragg, Sara, 1963–II. Title.
HQ799.2.M35B84 2003
302.23'0835'0941–dc22

                                                                    2003053686

10   9   8   7   6   5   4   3   2   1
13 12 11 10 09 08 07 06 05 04

Printed and bound in Great Britain by
Antony Rowe Ltd, Chippenham and Eastbourne

Contents

List of Figures

Acknowledgments

The research described in this book was funded by a consortium of media regulators in the UK, led by the Broadcasting Standards Commission. It also included the Advertising Standards Authority, the British Board of Film Classification, the British Broadcasting Corporation and the Independent Television Commission. We are very grateful to Alan Chant at the ASA, Sue Clark at the BBFC, Andrea Wills at the BBC and Isobel Reid, Jane Sancho and Sarah Thane at the ITC for their support, and particularly to Andrea Millwood-Hargrave at the BSC for her co-ordinating role. We would also like to thank Lorraine Miller and Tam Huggett at the BSC for their administrative back up.

The project included a number of other elements, which are only briefly represented in this book. In particular, we undertook an extensive review of the literature relating to young people and sexual content on television (Bragg and Buckingham, 2002). We felt that readers of this book might not be so keen to wade through our summaries and criticisms of other people's research before hearing about our own; and so our account of this is relatively brief. For those who are interested, the report can be obtained from the Broadcasting Standards Commission, most easily by downloading it from the website at: *www.bsc.org.uk*

We also conducted an extensive survey of around 800 young people's views on these issues. Again, we have drawn on this briefly in writing this book, although our emphasis here is on the qualitative aspects of the research. A separate report of the survey was published by the BSC in Autumn 2003; and further information about this can also be obtained from the BSC website.

This was an extensive project, and we have many people to thank. We are grateful to the teachers who helped arrange our pilot interviews: Tracy Glennan, Chris Reene and Mary Tomlinson. During the main part of the research, Helen Bridge, Carol Minkey, Jane Sweetlove and Kathryn Wilkinson went out of their way to ensure the smooth running of a major research endeavour, co-ordinating both the interviews and the survey arrangements on top of their existing teaching and management commitments. We are extremely appreciative of their efforts. We are also grateful to the heads of the schools who gave us access (Greg Deery, David Linsell, Martin Thorn, Frank Vigon), and thank all the teachers whose work was affected by the project, for their support and understanding.

We are also grateful to Chi Pang at the ITC for video reproduction; Sue Barnard and her team of transcribers at Academic Transcriptions, Cambridge, for always providing a speedy and professional service; Sue Cranmer for help conducting the parent focus groups; Josephine Ward at the BBC, Martha Stylianou and Gareth Nimmo-Jones for help selecting extracts for our video; Ryan Taylor at the ASA for providing copies of advertisements; and Briar Towers, our editor at Palgrave. Margaret Scanlon advised on the wording and coding of the surveys and Erica 'Wordsmith' Smith designed and illustrated them beautifully. Pat Van Breemen at The Poplars B&B extended generous hospitality during our stays in the north of England. Liesbeth de Block, Mark Erickson, JoEllen Fisherkeller, David Gauntlett and Peter Redman offered valuable comments on earlier drafts of the manuscript.

Finally, we thank all the young people who contributed to the project – those who completed our survey, and in particular those who agreed to take part in the interviews, on whom we made sometimes onerous, sometimes intrusive, demands. All of them taught us something and we are most grateful for their co-operation and insights.

1
Introduction

Children today are growing up much too soon – or so we are frequently told. They are being deprived of their childhood. Their essential innocence has been lost. Indeed, some would say that childhood itself is effectively being destroyed. For many people, perhaps the most troubling aspect of this phenomenon is to do with sex. Young people seem to be maturing physically – and showing an interest in sex – at an ever-earlier age. Even quite young children appear to adults to be alarmingly knowledgeable about the intimate details of sexual behaviour. Children, it is argued, are being prematurely 'sexualised'.

There is a certain amount of evidence for these claims, at least as regards the sexual behaviour of teenagers. The age at which young people first experience sexual intercourse has steadily fallen over the past few decades; while the number of young people – particularly girls – who are sexually active has risen significantly (Moore and Rosenthal 1993). Britain has the highest rate of teenage and unplanned pregnancies in Europe, which despite a fall in the early 1990s have now begun to increase again. So too have sexually transmitted diseases, including HIV, and particularly amongst the heterosexual population. In fact, many of these developments began in the 1950s rather than, as is often thought, in the 'permissive' 1960s; although they are now widely seen to represent a form of social crisis (Measor *et al.* 2000). Much of the blame for this supposed loosening of sexual boundaries and the subsequent 'loss' of children's innocence has been placed on the media, and on consumer culture more broadly. These arguments are traditionally the territory of right-wing moralists. It is perhaps not surprising to find a conservative newspaper like the *Daily Mail* fulminating about the media's 'sick conspiracy to destroy childhood', as ten-year-olds are apparently 'bombarded on all sides by pre-teen make-up, clinging

1

clothes and magazines encouraging them to be Lolitas' (24.7.02). Likewise, its columnist Peter Hitchens (2002: 49) paints a picture of a culture saturated and depraved by uncontrollable sexuality, most of it derived from the media:

> It is very hard to be innocent in modern Britain. Advertising on television, on posters and on the radio, is drenched in sexual innuendo. Television programmes rely almost entirely on sex and violence to raise their drooping audience figures. The playgrounds of primary schools echo with sexual taunts and jibes. Rock music, which is now almost compulsory in the lives of even the youngest, is full of sexual expression and desire.

Yet this image of childhood innocence debauched by media and consumer culture also appeals to more liberal commentators. Radio presenter Jenni Murray, writing in the Mail (30.5.02), recalls memories of her own childhood in the 1950s – 'I devoured *Bunty*. My chums and I read every word and then sat for hours in the bedroom discussing the daring deeds of the Four Marys' – and contrasts this with the 'obsession with sex and shallow celebrity' and the 'rampant consumerism' of contemporary girls' magazines. Here again, the media are seen to be guilty of a 'theft of childhood'. Meanwhile, Jasmin Alibhai-Brown of the Independent (18.3.02) laments her 'innocent' daughter's impending corruption at the hands of a 'sordid popular culture'. 'Powerful, immoral people', she argues, will 'manipulate her desires and appetites', pressurising her to transform herself into a 'sex machine'. According to Alibhai-Brown,

> ... the next campaign for British feminists needs to [be] directed at those advertisers, broadcasters, celebrity pedlars, newspapers, magazines, pop stars and others who have made this carnal hell for our young ones, and who still insist that this is nothing at all to do with them.

Fewer commentators seem prepared to argue that this development is in any way a positive thing. Some point to the levels of ignorance about sexual matters among the young, and to the inadequacy of formal sex education; yet few seem prepared to justify the availability of sexual information in the media on the grounds that it represents a greater degree of openness. Even liberationists like the gay activist Peter Tatchell, who argue for the importance of 'honesty' about sexual matters and advocate 'sexual rights' for young people, tend to dismiss the 'half-baked and sensationalist' information which they perceive in the media (2002: 70).

Childhood in peril?

In some respects, of course, this is an old issue. In 2002, Channel Four screened a series excavating the history of sex on television, which clearly showed how the same debates and anxieties have surfaced time and again in the history of this medium – even if what counts as 'explicit' representation has changed markedly over time. The concerns provoked by the sexual gyrations of pop stars in the 1950s – as in Elvis Presley's celebrated appearance on the *Ed Sullivan Show* – or by the steamy intimacies of television dramas like *Bouquet of Barbed Wire* in the 1970s may now appear merely quaint. Yet the arguments that were made then about their corrupting influence on children, and about their contribution to a more general moral decline, are very similar to those that continue to be made today. And of course, similar concerns were raised in relation to much older media. In the late 1920s, early research on the effects of the silent movies on American youth partly focused on the influence of sexual content, in the form of stars such as Greta Garbo and Rudolph Valentino – although this aspect of the research was suppressed at the time (Jowett *et al.* 1996). As Judith Levine (2002) points out, the notion that young minds are particularly vulnerable to influence in this respect is one of the founding principles of obscenity law; and she quotes a judgment about an anticlerical pamphlet which was banned in 1868 on the grounds that it might stimulate 'thoughts of a most impure and libidinous character' among the young.

Nevertheless, this debate about the dangers of sexual content in the media seems to have taken on a new urgency in recent years. The advent of new media technologies – video, cable, satellite and of course the internet – has made it increasingly difficult to prevent young people from gaining access to sexually explicit material. Yet the regulation of the media has also become politically problematic. According to many social theorists, we now live in more pluralistic, secular societies, in which there is no longer a clearly defined consensus on moral issues. The media themselves have also increasingly sought to address more diverse, fragmented 'taste communities'; and there is a growing political commitment to the principle of 'free speech' (Thompson and Sharma 1998). Whether we see these changes as evidence of a greater openness or as symptomatic of the rise of moral depravity, it is hard to deny that sexual material is now more widely available than it was in the past – perhaps particularly to children.

Yet what difference does this make? The recurrent claim that children are being 'sexualised' at the hands of the media obviously implies that they were not sexual in the past, and have now become so. Likewise, the view that children's relation to sexuality is being 'commodified' or 'commercialised' also seems to presume that there was an earlier time in which childhood was somehow free from commercial influences. As ever, we are encouraged to look back to a golden age of innocence, well before the media led us all to 'carnal hell'.

This narrative of decline is one which many historians of childhood would certainly dispute: the lives of children, even as recently as the nineteenth century, were far from insulated from the influence of sexuality, or indeed from the economy (e.g. Cunningham 1995; Hendrick 1997). The notion of childhood as an asexual condition was decisively exploded by the work of Sigmund Freud in the early years of the twentieth century. Yet the public visibility of sexuality in the modern media clearly undermines the separation between children and adults on which our modern conception of childhood is ultimately based. Children's sexuality – or their knowledge of sexuality – may be becoming visible to adults in a way that it was not in the past, or at least in the recent past. It is not so much that children have suddenly become sexual, more that adults are now being forced to recognise this fact.

As in many other areas, the notion of childhood comes to be used here as the vehicle for much broader concerns about the social order. As Philip Jenkins (1992) has argued, children are often used in a 'politics of substitution' which has been practised by moral entrepreneurs of both Left and Right. In a climate of growing uncertainty, invoking fears about children provides a powerful means of commanding public attention and support: campaigns against homosexuality are redefined as campaigns against paedophiles; campaigns against pornography become campaigns against child pornography; and campaigns against immorality and Satanism become campaigns against ritualistic child abuse. Those who have the temerity to doubt claims about the epidemic proportions of such phenomena can therefore easily be stigmatised as hostile to children. Thus, children's access to sexual knowledge is often regarded as part of a more general permissiveness, equated with a rise in violence, drug use and criminal activity amongst the young. From this perspective, sexual knowledge places children in danger; but it also makes them potentially dangerous.

To some extent, it is possible to distinguish here between broadly 'conservative' and 'liberal' perspectives. Thus, conservatives hold sexual permissiveness partly responsible for what they perceive as social or moral decline; while liberals argue that sexual repression leads to a whole range of social ills. Yet these views overlap in complex ways with different perspectives on childhood. On the one hand, children's awareness of sexuality can be seen as a healthy, natural phenomenon, which is distinguished from some of the more distorted or corrupted conceptions of adults. On the other, it can also be viewed as precocious or unnatural; and the acquisition of sexual knowledge can be seen to weaken the boundaries between childhood and adulthood, which are apparently designed to protect children.

Likewise, the debate about children's exposure to representations of sexuality in the media seems equally polarised. On one side, there are those who continue to argue that children should not be prematurely introduced to ideas about sex and sexuality, and consequently call for greater censorship and control. On the other are those who claim that children have a right to see and read things which may deal with their emotional needs and concerns, including those relating to sexuality. Yet both 'sides' in this debate invoke ideas about the 'natural' form of sexuality, and about children's inherent needs or interests; and in doing so, they inevitably define them in particular ways. While they may purport to speak on behalf of children, they also construct 'the child' in ways that can be seen to reflect broader social and political motivations.

Cause for concern?

Despite the range of views expressed in these debates, there appears to be some consensus about the idea that there is more sex in the media, and that it is more 'explicit' than it used to be. This is perhaps most apparent in the case of television. In the UK, both of the most recent newcomers to terrestrial TV have attracted criticism on these grounds. In its early days, Channel Four became notorious among more conservative critics for its explicit representations of sexual activity; and, more recently, Channel Five has been censured for screening soft pornography in late-night slots. It is often argued that sexual references and representations have become more frequent in mainstream programming – both before and after the 9 p.m. 'watershed' for family viewing.

But to what extent is this impression justified? Studies conducted in the United States suggest that there is indeed an increasing amount of sexual material on television there – although these studies rarely include systematic comparisons over more than a few years. One particular problem here is that researchers do not use a common set of definitions, categories or procedures. Only in recent years, in the work of Dale Kunkel and his colleagues (1999; 2001) have researchers begun to develop a more consistent approach. The most recent of these studies found that references to sex had increased quite significantly over a two-year period, and that sexual behaviour was either shown or discussed in around two-thirds of programmes. There is also some evidence that the range of sexual behaviours depicted or referred to has become more diverse in recent years (Greenberg and Busselle 1996). Nevertheless, talk about sex is more common than actual portrayals, and visual representations remain relatively rare.

US television is often considered to be less sexually explicit than British television, so it may be surprising to find that research in the UK has not reached similar conclusions. A report produced for the Broadcasting Standards Commission in 1999 found that less than one in five terrestrial programmes showed sexual behaviour, and just over one third contained verbal references, the large majority of which were fairly mild. Furthermore, there was no consistent increase in such material, at least over the 1990s. The report concluded that there was 'no actual evidence to support public perception of increased sexual activity' on British television (BSC 1999). The contrast between these findings and those of the US studies is quite striking; and while they may reflect differences between British and American television, they also reflect different definitions of what 'counts' as sexual content (for more detailed discussion, see Bragg and Buckingham 2002).

Yet even if people believe there is more sex on television than there used to be, are they really bothered about this? To what extent do the anxieties expressed by newspaper columnists and politicians reflect more widespread public concern? In fact, research on public attitudes suggests that most people in Britain are fairly relaxed about this issue. When asked directly, a significant proportion of people agree that there is 'too much' sex on television – although higher percentages agree that there is too much in the print media. However, attitudes towards sexual content do appear to have become more permissive in recent years: fewer respondents claim to find sex scenes 'offensive' or embarrassing, and a significant majority feel that they are acceptable if included as part of a storyline. As many as 93 per cent of respondents in one BSC survey expressed a preference for self-regulation, claiming that viewers could turn off or over if they were offended by what they saw (BSC 1999).

These findings are paralleled by a broader shift towards more 'liberal' or 'permissive' attitudes towards sex in real life, particularly in respect of gay and lesbian relationships. Over the past 50 years, patterns of sexual behaviour have become more diverse, and attitudes have become less prohibitive (Moore and Rosenthal 1993). Research by the regulatory bodies (e.g. Hanley 2000; Millwood Hargrave 1992; 1999) and broader social attitude surveys (Hill and Thomson 2000) have found that the British public is less and less likely to support a restrictive approach to public discussion of sexual issues. However, there are some important social differences here. In general, men and young people are less likely to say that sex is an issue of concern; while women and older people are more likely to say they are 'offended' by sex on screen, or that there is 'too much' of it. Many respondents in the BSC survey – particularly women – expressed concerns that television might 'legitimise' early sexual activity for children. However, they also agreed that by the age of 15 young people were able to make up their own minds about what they should watch, a point on which adolescents and many parents also agree (Buckingham 1996; Millwood Hargrave *et al.* 1996). In terms of age differences, this research also suggests that there is likely to be a 'cohort effect' – that is, that attitudes are likely to become more permissive in the future, especially as regards representations of gays and lesbians.

Of course, there are significant limits to the value of such opinion polls. There is evidence that, in the context of interviews, people tend to 'perform' responses that are deemed appropriate for their age and gender: responses given in anonymous questionnaires tend to be more liberal (Barnett and Thomson 1996). Furthermore, there is very little understanding of the relationship between general attitudes (as measured by polls) and the specific decisions that parents (or indeed children) may make about the material they encounter. (This research is discussed more fully in Bragg and Buckingham, 2002.)

Yet despite the limitations of such research, the overall picture is fairly clear. People certainly believe that there is more sex in the media than there used to be; and yet public attitudes towards sex, both in the media and in real life, have also become more permissive over the years. The unanswered question is to do with the relationship between these things. To what extent are more liberal attitudes caused or reflected by the media – or are there other factors that are producing both sets of changes? Is the perceived increase in the presence of sex in the media a result of pressures towards commercialisation, and the search for ratings? Is it a response to changes in sexual behaviour, or simply in attitudes towards that behaviour?

Sorting out the issues

To some extent, this debate reflects an ongoing concern about propriety or decency – about what should or should not be shown or discussed in public. However, it also reflects assumptions about the effects of the media, particularly as regards children. When it comes to sex in the media, children are learning about many things which (we assume) they have not experienced in real life – things about which they may be intensely curious. And for this reason, they are often deemed to be particularly at risk of negative influences.

Yet there is often considerable confusion here about the nature of the material that apparently provokes such concern; and about the kinds of effects that it may produce. Sexual material on mainstream television in Britain, for example, continues to be subject to the restriction of the watershed; although verbal references to sex frequently occur in early evening soap operas and situation comedies, and indeed in daytime talk shows. Yet, as we have seen, talk about sex is more common than visual depictions; and the large majority of visual depictions show precursory activity (flirting and kissing) rather than actual intercourse. We need to make clear distinctions here, both in terms of the verbal and visual 'explicitness' of the material, and in terms of its accessibility to children. What is sexually 'explicit', or indeed how sexually arousing something is, clearly depends on the perspective of the beholder. Indeed, whether or not (or to what degree) something is perceived as 'sexual' in the first place depends on what the viewer already knows or understands – and this may be particularly true with verbal references. As we shall see, children often claim that they know it all already, but there is actually a fair amount that they do not understand – not just about the mechanics of the sexual act, but also about how sex is culturally signified.

Likewise, it is important to distinguish between the different types of effects or responses such material may generate. As in the case of media violence, one can usefully distinguish here between effects on behaviour, effects on emotions and effects on attitudes. Thus, sexual material in the media might be seen to influence sexual behaviour – and particularly in the case of young people, to encourage them to engage in sexual activity before they are deemed to be sufficiently mature. Such material can also generate emotional responses – not just those of arousal, but also of embarrassment, shock and even disgust, especially in instances where the viewer has apparently encountered it without choosing to do so. In addition, such material might be seen to influence attitudes towards sexual activity and personal relationships in general – for example, by encouraging young people to believe that 'promiscuity' is acceptable – or alternatively, by performing an educational function, informing young people about risks or about how to interpret potentially sexual situations.

These kinds of distinctions are frequently blurred in public discussions of the kind we have described. As with the debate about media violence, invoking concerns about children, sex and the media seems to serve as a powerful means of mobilising more general anxieties about social and moral decline. Yet the broad assertion that there is 'too much sex' on TV may conflate a number of quite different issues and concerns: it all depends on what we mean by 'sex', and on what it is about it that makes it 'too much'. If research in this field is to arrive at a more complex understanding of the issues, it will need to move beyond easy generalisations, both about sexual content and about its potential effects.

Previous research

So what does research tell us about these questions? As we have shown, analyses of media content provide some evidence about what is now available to young people. Ultimately, however, they tell us very little about the meaning of that content. Counting references to sexual behaviour on television can involve a considerable amount of interpretation. Innuendo (the form in which most sexual references are couched in comedies) is most obviously problematic in this respect, as is assessing dance movements or gestures in music videos in terms of whether they are 'sexually suggestive'. Attempts to assess the 'messages' or themes carried by sexual content are bound to be even more problematic. For example, researchers have studied the extent to which sex on television takes place in marital or 'committed' relationships; the extent to which such stories mention the risks associated with sexual activity (such as sexually transmitted infections (STIs) or unwanted pregnancy); and, more broadly, whether sex is presented in a 'positive' or 'negative' manner. Perhaps inevitably, the results of this research are somewhat equivocal – and, in some cases, quite contradictory (see Bragg and Buckingham 2002).

Furthermore, such research frequently assumes that analyses of content necessarily tell us how viewers or readers interpret that content. Yet the basis for such assumptions can be quite paradoxical. On the one hand, children are assumed to be able to recognise sexual meanings from passing references, or to infer that sex has taken place between characters even where it has been elided from the narrative. Yet on the other, they are frequently seen as powerless to resist the 'messages' to which they are 'exposed'. They are assumed automatically to believe what they see. Furthermore, this research often reflects a characteristic tension between the world as it is and the world as we might like it to be. On the one hand, the media are condemned for presenting a distorted, unrealistic picture of the world; yet on the other, producers are urged to provide 'positive images' of healthy or responsible behaviour that might offer productive moral lessons to the young.

Research about the effects of this kind of material has been equally problematic. In comparison with the enormous amount of research about the effects of media violence, there has been relatively little previous work in this field. There is a controversial body of research on the effects of pornography, although (for obvious reasons) this has been almost exclusively conducted with adults (see Donnerstein *et al.* 1987; Segal 1993). When it comes to children, and to 'mainstream' media such as television – which are our primary concern here – the research is comparatively limited. Nearly all the research has been conducted in the United States; and much of it has focused on what are seen to be 'negative' effects, such as promiscuity, premature sexual activity and unsafe sexual practices. Most of it seems to be based on the notion of 'role modelling' – that is, the idea that young people identify with 'glamorous' media characters or personalities, and are therefore led to copy their behaviour, or to develop what researchers deem to be 'unrealistic' expectations or attitudes about sexual behaviour in real life.

This research has been somewhat equivocal and inconclusive in its findings. In general, there seems to be little agreement about influences on behaviour – for instance about whether TV-viewing influences the age at which young people first have intercourse, or their propensity to engage in extra-marital sex (Wartella *et al.* 2000). Much of the research on attitudinal influences is correlational: for example, there are studies that purport to show a correlation between heavy TV-viewing and approval of non-marital sex or 'ambivalence towards marriage' – which seem to be implicitly regarded as negative (Bryant and Rockwell 1994;

Signorielli 1991). The possibility that the media might have positive effects in this respect remains largely unexplored.

In all, this work exemplifies several of the familiar problems of American media effects research. It focuses almost entirely on negative effects; it implicitly assumes that correlation is evidence of causality; it relies on simplistic assumptions about the relationships between media use, attitudes and behaviour; it fails to explain why effects arise in some cases and not others; it isolates media use from other social variables, or accounts for those variables in unduly simplistic ways; it does not adequately consider how people relate media to other sources of information; and it tends to oversimplify complex questions to do with the meanings and pleasures people derive from the media.

Furthermore, much of the research is based on quite problematic moral and cultural assumptions. For example, it often seems to equate different kinds of extra-marital sexual activity – adultery and pre-marital sex are effectively treated as equivalent; and it implicitly presumes that these things are fundamentally undesirable, as are (what it defines as) 'premature' or 'promiscuous' – or even 'unnatural' – sexual behaviour. These researchers also generally begin with a clear sense of the kinds of interventions they wish to see. Kunkel *et al.* (2001), for example, state explicitly that 'abstinence or waiting for sex ... constitutes arguably the most effective strategy for reducing one's risk for negative outcomes from sex'; Strasburger (2000) entitles a research article 'Getting teenagers to say NO to sex, drugs and violence in the new millennium'; while Bryant and Rockwell (1994) suggest that the following warning label could be attached to prime-time television shows: 'Teenagers beware. Watching too much television programming featuring premarital, extramarital, or nonmarital sex can be hazardous to your moral health.'

It is worth noting here that several of these studies have been funded, not by media organisations or by the government, but by foundations whose primary concern is with public health and welfare. The fundamental preoccupation here is with sex as a potentially harmful health phenomenon. In this context, content analysis offers a way of making cultural texts available for calculation and regulation. The generation of statistics on the sheer amount of sex viewed (for example, 1,900 to 2,400 incidents a year, depending on the young viewer's orientation (Brown *et al.* 1990; Greenberg *et al.* 1993)) becomes a potential campaigning tool rather than an illuminating statement about media representations.

In these respects, the research seems to reflect the progressively more puritanical moral climate in the United States. Levine (2002) and Landry (2002) describe how sex education and public policy on sexual matters in the US have effectively been monopolised by the moral Right, in alliance with pro-censorship feminists. Public discussion of these issues has been increasingly driven by moral panics about pae-dophiles, crusades against abortion, and the legal pursuit of young people who have engaged in under-age sex. In this climate, it appears that the only kind of sex education that will receive federal govern-ment funding is what is called 'abstinence-based' sex education – despite the fact that there is very little proof of its effectiveness. And this approach also seems to define media education (or media literacy) as a kind of prophylactic: if the media cause premature sexual activity by 'glamorising' sex, teaching children to be critical media users will be the best contraceptive there is.

Starting points

As we have seen, such concerns have been raised in Britain too; but in general, these issues are framed in a rather different way in this country, despite our reputation for being 'uptight' about sexual matters. Similarly, our research also starts from a rather different point from that of the American effects researchers. We can summarise these differences briefly as follows.

First, we begin with different assumptions about media. We argue that media are more diverse and contradictory than simply a collection of 'negative' messages; and that we need to look more broadly at the changing ways in which 'sex' is culturally defined, not least in the context of an increasingly consumer-oriented society. We also begin with different assumptions about learning. We assume that the formation of sexual identity is a complex process – that it is unstable, insecure, always 'under construction'; and we argue that this cannot be explained by mechanistic notions of 'role modelling' or 'sexual socialisa-tion'. We also see this process in social rather than merely psychological terms: we are concerned with how young people use and interpret media in the context of their interpersonal relationships, and how this relates to the ongoing construction of social identities. We also begin, finally, with different assumptions about children and childhood. We start from the view that young people are active users of media, rather than passive victims; and we attempt to pay close attention to the ways in which they interpret and make judgments about what they see.

As this implies, we draw on some diverse theoretical traditions and perspectives. Our approach derives primarily from Cultural Studies – and particularly from the qualitative research on media audiences that has developed over the past 20 years (see Buckingham 2000). However, we also draw on forms of 'social constructionism', deriving primarily from the work of Michel Foucault (e.g. 1984); on forms of discourse analysis developed within social psychology (e.g. Potter and Wetherell 1987); and on psychoanalytically informed theory (e.g. Butler 1990). These diverse – and potentially conflicting – theoretical perspectives surface at various points in the book. We have tried to use them in a heuristic way, in order to explain and interpret our data, rather than attempt to fit the data into a pre-determined theoretical position.

This also leads us to adopt a different methodology from that of effects research. Most of the data in this book is drawn from in-depth interviews with pairs and small groups, as well as personal 'diaries' written by young people. Ultimately, our focus here is not so much on questions of cause and effect as on how young people use and interpret the media, and the kinds of 'identity work' they perform in doing so.

This approach therefore enables us to address some rather different theoretical questions. While we do not share the alarm of the moral conservatives, we do agree that there has been a growing 'sexualisation' of the modern media. Sexual content is now much more prominently displayed, not just in minority media, but in mainstream culture. We do not see this simply as evidence of moral or cultural decline; but neither do we share the view, held by some academic commentators, that it represents a form of 'sexual democratisation'. Brian McNair (2002), for instance, seems to regard the 'mainstreaming' of sexual and pornographic imagery as evidence of a shift away from patriarchal, heterosexist values, and of a growing acceptance of more diverse forms of sexual expression. Far from 'commodifying' sexuality, he argues that contemporary capitalism has offered 'a widening of popular access to sexual discourse' that is broadly progressive in its consequences.

By contrast, we would argue that the sexualisation of the contempor- ary media is symptomatic of more general developments, both in the media and in the relationships between identity and culture in modern societies. Jon Dovey's (2000) analysis of trends in contemporary television, for example, identifies a broader 'subjectivisation' or 'personalisation' of the public sphere, which is apparent in a range of 'first person' genres such as talk shows, docu-soaps and 'reality TV'. Dovey argues that individual subjective experience is now being promoted at the expense of more general truth claims, via a new emphasis on intimacy, confession and reflexivity. Across the range of genres that he considers, it appears that personal subjectivity has become the only point of control in a world that is represented as chaotic, complex and ever-changing.

More broadly, we can see these developments as symptomatic of more general shifts in the ways in which identity is defined and performed. The work of Michel Foucault (1984) provides an extremely influential analysis here of how sex and gender have been constructed within both ancient and modern societies. He proposes that sexuality is not an innate or natural quality that is simply expressed or discovered, but on the contrary that it is produced by institutional and discursive arrangements that 'systematically form the objects of which they speak' (Foucault 1972: 49). Thus, what seem to be our most intimate personal experiences and relationships are in fact intensively socially organised and managed. A prime example of this is the confessional form, for which sex has always been a privileged theme. In modern times, the confession has moved from religious to secular contexts, from an account of sexual acts given to an exterior judge to a more introspective search for the private feelings that surround them – for example, in the context of therapy. Such practices help to determine how we think about and act on ourselves; although they are experienced, not as coercive but as liberating.

Foucault asks us to consider the ways in which particular discourses or forms of knowledge – including those of the human sciences – serve to sustain particular forms of social power. He explores how, as a consequence of what is considered 'true' at particular historical moments, certain people or behaviours come to be seen as problematic, and what kind of interventions thereby become imaginable (medical treatment, censorship, and so on). Thus, the networks of agencies that surround human sexuality (psychologists, doctors, police, social workers, regulatory and welfare bodies) effectively bring new forms of sexuality into being through the act of defining them. The category of the 'homosexual', for instance, was effectively 'invented' in this way in the nineteenth century, and seems to have emerged before the category of the 'heterosexual'. This process also applies to the ways in which sexual imagery is regulated, for example through censorship (Kuhn 1988) and to representations of sexuality, such as pornography. Sexual images are thus not so much representations of sex as 'practices of sexuality', transmitting norms of sexual conduct and installing interests and capacities for actual forms of sexual behaviour (Hunter *et al.* 1993).

Foucault's work therefore challenges the familiar historical narrative which suggests that we have steadily liberated ourselves from the sexual 'repression' of the nineteenth century. The 'explosion of discourses' that characterises modern discussions and representations of sexuality, he suggests, reflects the move towards a new form of social regulation. Social control is now achieved, not through the imposition of power from above, but through invisible strategies of normalisation. Within modern societies, individuals have effectively become self-policing subjects, striving to attain internalised social norms (Rose 1999b; c).

From this perspective, the sexualisation of the modern media and of consumer culture is a profoundly ambiguous phenomenon. On the one hand, as McNair (2002) suggests, contemporary capitalism appears to allow a broader repertoire of ethical behaviours, to the extent that it addresses a wider range of sexual identities, forms and subjects as potential target markets. Examples here might include the growth of pornography for women, TV shows catering for lesbians and gay men, or the invention of the marketing category of the 'tweenager' (8–12-year-olds). It could be argued that this diversification is possible because the market discriminates on the basis of profit rather (or more) than morality. On the other hand, it can be argued that the market simultaneously makes these new identities and desires available for management and regulation by visibly categorising them. This approach also creates new norms, and creates new anxieties, as individuals become 'entrepreneurs of themselves' and subject every area of life (work, leisure, love) to constant self-scrutiny (Rose 1999b). Meanwhile, redefining citizenship as access to consumption excludes those who are economically 'unprofitable'.

Starting from this perspective enables us to move beyond the reductive either/or questions that typically plague media research. The question of whether sex in the media is good or bad for children is one that, in our view, has no absolute or meaningful answer. This is not to suggest that the media do not have 'effects' on children: on the contrary, it is to suggest that their effects are significantly more complex – and perhaps even more pervasive – than most effects researchers have begun to imagine. If we aim to develop a sensible basis for social policy (or indeed for educational practice) in this field, we need to be asking some more sophisticated questions.

We also hope that this approach gets us beyond the stand-off between permissiveness and puritanism, or repression versus liberation (for want of better terms), which tends to characterise discussions of children and sex. The fact is that children are already 'sexual': the media do not make them sexual, and we cannot stop them being sexual. Of course, we believe in honesty and openness; and we believe that it is adults' role to prepare children for life, rather than simply protect them from it. But we would challenge the idea that we can simply teach children to be 'free' or 'natural' – in sexuality, or for that matter in any other area.

The chapters in this book are organised in two main ways. At the centre of the book are three chapters that address children's responses to different aspects of media, or media genres. Chapter 5 looks at responses to the display of bodies in pornography, 'pin-up' or 'glamour' photography, advertising and music videos. Chapter 6 considers a range of 'confessional' genres such as TV talk shows, problem pages in teenage magazines and celebrity gossip in the tabloid press. Chapter 7 looks at television drama series, focusing on soap operas, situation comedies and children's/teen dramas. These chapters are 'framed' by more thematic chapters, that look across a broader range of media issues. Chapter 3 considers how children learn about sex and relationships in real life, for example from parents, peers and teachers. Chapter 4 looks at how children construct and perform gender differences in talking (and writing) about the media. Chapter 8 looks at children's and parents' accounts of family viewing; while Chapter 9 returns to the social policy issue of media regulation. The book is based on a substantial empirical research project. It is to an account of this project, and of the methods we employed, that the following chapter is devoted.

2

Talking Dirty – Research Methods

In this chapter we discuss our research design, in order to help explain both the insights and the limitations of the results we present in subsequent chapters. Research is not a neutral conduit that extracts the 'truth' about a topic or about what participants 'really' feel and think about it. Our findings were shaped by our methods, the contexts in which we worked, the relationships that existed between participants before the research process began, as well as those created during it; and then again by our processes of analysis and interpretation.

This book is based on a project entitled 'Young people, media and personal relationships: a study of young people's responses to media portrayals of love, sex and relationships'. It was funded by a consortium of British broadcasting and regulatory bodies: the Broadcasting Standards Commission, the Independent Television Commission, the British Board of Film Classification, the BBC and the Advertising Standards Authority. During 2001 and 2002, we (David Buckingham and Sara Bragg) conducted 100 interviews with 120 young people aged from 9 to 17 and approximately 70 parents, and surveyed nearly 800 young people. We worked with young people in state schools. In a pilot stage of the study, we talked to 24 students in various locations in the South East: in the main body of the research we interviewed 96 young people, 12 boys and 12 girls from each of school years 5, 7, 9 and 12 (that is, age groups 9–10, 11–12, 13–14 and 16–17), in schools in different locations. One was a commuter belt suburb outside Manchester, surrounded by countryside, in a highly successful and over-subscribed specialised 11–18 secondary school and its primary 'feeder' school nearby. The ethnic intake of the school was predominantly white; only one student out of the 48 who took part in the research was minority ethnic. The other schools were in Essex: their intake, from the surrounding housing estates, was predominantly working class, and six students of the 48 who took part were minority ethnic. Although the secondary school had recently received positive inspection reports and its examination results were improving, its reputation as a 'sink' school seemed to persist and was well known to its students.

In each school, one staff member liaised with year tutors and class teachers who helped to recruit students. This was done mainly through distributing flyers with information about the project and asking for volunteers. Although our offer of cash rewards for participation (between £15 and £25, according to age) was undoubtedly an inducement, in some cases teachers had to encourage particular individuals to make up the numbers. We thus had little control over the sample and, although we specified that we wanted students who would be confident and talkative rather than only academic high achievers, it may be that some teachers encouraged students they perceived as 'more able' to come forward. Each student had to obtain parental consent: only in two cases was this refused, one due to the topic itself, on religious grounds, the other because the parents felt their daughter already had a heavy schedule of schoolwork and extra-curricular activities.

Sara then met as many of the students as possible, talking to them in their year groups (12 students at a time) about the project and what was required from them. This fell into three or four stages:

- Their first task was to keep what we called a 'diary' or 'scrapbook' about images of love, sex and relationships in the media. We supplied a blank, unlined A4 notebook for this purpose. The children were asked to include a page or so about themselves, their families, their access to media, and their tastes and preferences; and then to write either in the form of a daily account of 'anything that they saw in the media' that related to the theme of love, sex and relationships, or to write in general about their views, in both cases including relevant images from magazines or newspapers. The older students (aged 16–17) were also asked to look back on the role the media had played for them in finding out about love, sex and relationships when they were younger. They had two or three weeks in which to complete this task.
- The children nominated a friend with whom they were happy to be interviewed and so talked first in pairs to either Sara or David. In these interviews, we asked them to say more about the content of

their notebooks and talked generally, for instance about 'good story-lines' about love, sex and relationships in the media (particularly soaps), often asking them whether they thought such material contained 'messages' about the theme; we also discussed their family rules about viewing sexual material.

- At the end of these first interviews they were each given a videotape of about two hours' duration to view at home, containing whole programmes and extracts from TV that raised salient issues. It included two clips from talk shows, four music videos and episodes of *The Simpsons* and *Friends*. The two youngest age groups were given an edited storyline about teenage sex from *Grange Hill*, the older ones an episode of *Dawson's Creek*. All of this material was pre-watershed and age-appropriate. The 16–17-year-olds were also given an episode of a Channel 4 British youth drama *As If* and an extract from *So Graham Norton*. They were asked to write briefly about the video, for instance about which extracts they liked or disliked.

- Interviews about the videos took place a fortnight later, in groups of four (hence there were two all-female, two all-male and two mixed groups in each age band). In these, we asked them to talk about the material they had seen, whether they had seen it before, what they thought about the programmes in general, who they thought they were for, their 'messages' and so on. Towards the end of these interviews we showed them a selection of advertisements that had been the subject of complaints to the Advertising Standards Authority (for Lee and Levis Jeans, Opium perfume and French Connection UK clothes). At this point we also asked students to comment specifically on issues around regulation.

- In the final stage of the research, all students in the 11–12 and 13–14 age bands were given sample reading material from tabloid newspapers and girls' magazines and were interviewed about this in the same groups two days after the previous interview. Our funders had encouraged this inclusion primarily in order to get a balanced picture across a range of media, rather than focusing mainly on TV.

Out of the total of 72 interviews in this part of the research, only one student was absent on one occasion. All interviews were in school time, in various locations – offices, seminar and counselling rooms, even a stock cupboard – and lasted about an hour. They were audiotaped, and this material was subsequently transcribed in full and analysed using the computer programme for qualitative data, NVivo. All participants have chosen or been given pseudonyms. We refer to them here by their names, location (in which 'P' indicates the pilot stage in the South East, 'S' the Essex and 'N' the North of England settings) and age (which we have simplified to ages 10, 12, 14 and 17, although some participants may have been a little younger). In addition, unless it is obvious from the context in which it is used, we then refer to the origin of each quotation, as 'D' for the scrapbook or diary, 'P' for the first (pair) interview, 'G' for the group interviews, and 'W' for other writing, such as the notes children made about the videos.

We subsequently conducted interviews with 48 parents, in ten groups of three to seven people. Four of these groups were recruited by writing to parents of young people who had been involved in the research, three were recruited from parents and classroom assistants working in our primary schools, and the remaining three were recruited through personal contacts. Three took place during the day in the primary schools, the rest in the evening at the homes of one of the parents; we supplied snacks and drinks and paid participants £15. Thirteen participants were parents of young people who had also been involved in the research – in one case two brothers aged 11 and 16 and their father all took part. We asked parents first of all to reflect on their own experience of using the media to learn about love, sex and relationships when they were young, and then moved on to talk about what they did about it in their own families – what rules they laid down, what they said to their children about sex, what significant incidents had occurred, and so on. If time allowed, we also showed some short extracts from the videotape that the children had been given and invited comments. This stage of the research is reported mainly in Chapters 8 and 9. These groups are referred to by a number and location ('N' for those in the North and 'S' for those in the South, which included both Essex and other locations in the South East).

In addition to this intensive qualitative research, we conducted a survey in the same schools of the whole intake for each of years 5, 7 and 9 (ages 10, 12 and 14), in the term after our interviews. The questions differed slightly for each age group but all covered issues raised by the interviews – information about themselves, their families, their media access, rules about viewing, the usefulness of various sources of information about sex, their opinions about various statements. Seven hundred and seventy-eight surveys were returned out of a maximum possible of 937 and were coded and analysed using SPSS. The results of the survey will be more fully reported in a separate report.

Fabricating publics, imagined geographies

Ultimately, our decisions about where to site the research had to be made partly on the basis of practicalities, such as our personal contacts and the willingness of schools to support the project. Despite offering a small financial payment – secondary schools received £500, primary £250 – it was not easy to find partner schools, partly because of pressures around assessment that made some reluctant to take students or staff away from the classroom or to impose additional tasks, and partly because of fears about the topic. Nonetheless, our choices of location, and the processes which led to them, are worthy of further comment: they derived from the specific wishes of our funders that the research be based outside London.

The stake of regulatory institutions in investigating young people's perceptions differs from, for example, the public health campaigning bodies in the US discussed in the previous chapter (e.g. Kunkel *et al.* 2001). The latter, we suggested, aimed to use their findings to lobby government from the outside. They might therefore have benefited from emphasising rather than downplaying the prevalence of sex in the media and young people's need for better information about it. By contrast, our funders are mostly within the sphere of government, or mandated by it: they are required to ascertain the degree of match between public perceptions and their policies in order to gain legitimacy for their actions and decisions. One way in which they do this is through public opinion surveys and research. However, public opinion is not a pre-existing entity; it has to be brought into being. As Osborne and Rose suggest (1999), this was achieved in the last century, first through the development of research techniques that made it measurable (such as the Gallup poll) and secondly through the packaging of national or political issues in terms amenable to such polling (as, for example, media issues are often rendered intelligible as 'concerns' about 'sex, violence and bad language'). Being a 'citizen' has been increasingly understood as learning to 'have' and 'express' opinions on such matters (Osborne and Rose 1999). We note below the impact this had on the responses we received.

Further, opinion polls have generally been based on the 'representative sample', with the accompanying claim that the polls can accurately reflect broader trends in the population. In recent years organisations such as the BSC have added in-depth qualitative research to their survey work on public attitudes (e.g. Buckingham 1996). The intensity and small-scale nature of such qualitative work, however, is often held to undermine claims to be representative or generalisable. This caused some concern to our funding bodies. Were our research to be based exclusively in London, it might have been accused of representing only the views of a cosmopolitan (and allegedly more liberal) intelligentsia. In turn, this might have undermined our funders' responsibilities to the wider public to which it is accountable.

Such concerns activate imagined as well as real geographies of sexuality. As Phillips and Watt (2000) suggest, urban, rural or suburban spaces are often defined in different ways in respect of the politics of sexuality. However, in our research we have not assumed that any socially assigned identity, be it gender, race or class, pre-determines responses. Instead, we have looked at how such things became relevant in the process of the research, not least through our interpretive activities as researchers. Nevertheless, our choice of sites did enable us to see how far our participants' conceptions of sexual issues were shaped by a 'sense of place' and an awareness of metropolitan or 'southern' definitions of the suburbs and the North. It also enables us to address fears and fantasies mobilised – often only at an implicit level – around class and other differences.

Defining our subjects

This research is not an in-depth ethnography that would provide 'thick descriptions' about how a few young people use the media in constructing their sexual identities. Inevitably we gained only a brief snapshot of the lives of the many young people with whom we worked. Nonetheless, we hoped to access different voices: schematically, we staged the tasks to invite first a more personal, intimate voice (in their notebooks and pair interviews) and subsequently a more public one (in the group interviews). Much depended on how participants interpreted these tasks, but our diverse methods – writing and speaking, in pairs and in groups, about our choice of media and about theirs, and so on – did produce a range of ways of speaking about (and of constructing oneself in relation to) media representations of love, sex and relationships. (This includes the different accounts given by children and by their parents in cases where both participated in the focus groups.) We aimed at what Laurel Richardson (1998) has described as a 'crystal' structure or a range of viewpoints, none of which is necessarily more transparent or true than any others, but where we can learn from the contradictions and differences between them to develop complex ways of seeing issues.

Furthermore, what individuals say (or write) cannot be taken at face value: it is always contextual. This research is based on 'self-reporting'; and, as such, it is bound to be less reliable than direct observation. However, our analytic approach does not see language as a transparent means of representing reality or experience, but as constructing it and giving it meaning. Ways of talking do not report on pre-existing attitudes or inner states, but are practices or performances that select from culturally available sets of ideas and terms for particular functions: 'people achieve identities, realities, social order and social relationships through talk' (Baker 1997). Moreover, communications are always relational: the tasks we set, and the questions we asked in interview, shaped how young people could speak in response.

In this respect it is worth noting that we defined and positioned our participants in particular and possibly contradictory ways. On the one hand, by asking them to keep diaries or scrapbooks about a topic generally considered to be deeply personal and by interviewing them in relatively intimate contexts, we addressed them as private beings whose 'internal world' and thoughts we desired to know. On the other hand, through our recruitment flyers (with their slogan 'Tell the people who run the media what you think') and our later questions in (especially the group) interviews, we spoke to them as special individuals who had important things to say in the public arena, and whose opinions would be simultaneously 'representative' of their generation. Indeed, opinions are necessarily projected into a public domain, in a context of a whole field of public opinion to which those asked relate their own views (Osborne and Rose 1999). To a certain extent our work reflects how far young people have learnt to become 'researchable subjects' and to 'perform' being a citizen by 'expressing' what they saw as appropriate opinions.

Towards the end of the last interviews, we asked all participants why they thought we were doing the research. There was broad agreement that we were seeking the voices of young people because they 'needed to be heard', and in our northern setting this was further refined as part of rectifying southerners' ignorance of the North. Some thought we would be writing 'a book', others thought it was 'for advertisers', as if to target young audiences more effectively. Some thought we were making a TV programme, a few that our research would help investigate and limit the negative 'effects' of the media. As all this implies, the notion that those who govern, in whatever way, need to know the opinions and attitudes of those who are governed has become part of contemporary 'common sense'. However, it is not clear who exactly might listen and why, as suggested by their references to communications, psychological, market and consumer as well as academic research. In the next sections, we offer some broad ideas about how young people responded to being 'invited to speak' by this nebulous interlocutor.

The diaries and scrapbooks

Diary writing is a genre that has its own specific conventions. Although it was open to a variety of interpretations – Gavin (P, 17) took it to mean a minutely detailed descriptive account of his activities: '7.10 am went running, 7.45 am had breakfast ...' – most young people understood it as concerned with inner emotions: 'I just wrote what I thought' (Courtney, N, 12, P). As well as including reflections on the media, many wrote more generally about 'love, sex and relationships', sometimes dealt with as separate categories. Some adopted a 'dear diary' mode: Leigh (P, 13) signed off each day with her name and a lipstick kiss; Izzie (S, 12) and Alma (S, 10) declared boldly on the cover 'Keep Out!', underlining its private nature. We came across some surprisingly strong expressions of feeling: Emma (N, 10) referred to her family break-up and added: 'I always get this feeling at the back of my head that makes me feel sad. So that's why I'm really stressed and angry at the moment'. Several of the older students referred to their own personal sexual experiences, even though we had not requested this. In general, boys seemed more reluctant to engage with the diary format than girls. Sebastian (N, 14), for example, focused on describing media he had seen, explaining in interview that this was a deliberate strategy because he was not able to write about his 'feelings'.

Even at this stage, however, many students clearly oriented their tasks to a 'public sphere', as when Lysa (S, 10, D), with more than a touch of defiance against an imaginary interlocutor, declared of a problem page 'I want you to know that the page below does not make me feel uncomfortable in any way it's excellent'. Children from the Essex primary school focused especially on images of the *Sun*'s Page 3 models, often with evaluations of their appropriateness. At least one child seemed to have interpreted Sara's comment in the introductory meeting, that it was 'OK' to include such pictures as meaning that they 'had to'; but the task did seem to give children a rare opportunity to air a part of their lives generally ignored in schools. They enjoyed the taboo-breaking nature of it: Clint (S, 10, P) reported gleefully that he had shown his pictures of nude models to classmates who had duly pronounced him 'sick'.

Other students interpreted the task more pragmatically as a 'media studies' project and annotated their cuttings using the vocabulary of media analysis ('stereotyping') and critique ('sex sells'), with less personal comment. Whilst some younger students offered passionate denunciations of the media in a strongly subjective voice (Abigail N, 12, declared many images 'disgusting'), the older students particularly did so within what they construed as more 'critical' terms. In the process, they made claims about their own identities. For example, a comment by Tom (N, 17, D) that Hollywood films 'missed out on gay characters, with strictly stereotypes if shown at all' was as much about establishing his own position as politically progressive and resistant to mainstream media, as it was a reflection of recent trends in the industry. Many older students made sweeping assertions that almost seemed a parody of an 'older generation' position ('romance is dead' ... Britney 'shows poor moral fibre' and is a 'poor role model' wrote Adrian N, 17). Jeff, N, 17, commented that all Craig David's songs were about sex, which 'cheapens the idea of love' and wondered 'Can this really be a good thing to let ten year old children listen to?'. The fact that they then retracted or seemed embarrassed by these comments in interviews suggests that such available discourses have their own momentum and can be drawn on to fill a space where one is 'not sure what to write' (Jeff), rather than revealing deeply felt inner commitments.

Some children insisted that they had not talked about their work with others, because it was 'their' private thoughts. However, for many the process of filling the notebook was dialogic and responsive to what others were doing. For instance, Seth (N, 12, P) claimed that he had included a picture of Britney Spears because his classmate Courtney had told him he should have an equivalent to her images of male stars. Krystal (S, 14) produced a deliberately collective diary, discussed in more detail in Chapter 4, in which she had asked all her friends to write in order to capture 'how we really talk'. Although we had briefed teachers and asked them not to look at the notebooks, some did nonetheless monitor them in the process of collecting them. Some children reported this with chagrin, especially where teachers had told them that their work was 'wrong' or that they had to do more on it – which they rightly felt contradicted our assurances in our guidance notes that the work was private and that 'teachers would be asked not to look at it'. We had to reassure them that what they produced was acceptable and that we would not assess it, but nonetheless it undoubtedly had an aura of 'homework' for some. Parents also contributed, sometimes passing on magazines or encouraging their children to watch particular programmes or films. For example, Wesley (S, 12, P) recounted how his mother had made him watch a Channel Four documentary on the history of sex on the grounds that it might be useful, although he found it 'boring' and irrelevant. Jody (S, 14) included a page of what seemed like much-erased and rewritten pencil explanations of how advertisements worked, which she admitted in interview her mother had helped her 'put into words'. Although Krystal (S, 14) claimed in her diary that her parents would '*die* if they knew half the things kids talk about these days', she also reported in interview that they had survived the experience of reading hers.

Inevitably, the project actively intervened in relationships in other ways. Kurt (P, 13, P) described how his mother had tried to start conversations about sex as a result of his involvement:

> Kurt: Well ... I came home with the diary. And as my mum always does she rummages through my schoolbag when I get home, looking for letters.
>
> David: That's kind of what mums do. Yeah.
>
> Kurt: And then she finds the diary and then she pulls out the letter. And she looks at it. And you like write down what you think, and what you talk about. My mum kept ... My mum kept trying to make me bring up conversations about love, sex and relationships. And I felt really uncomfortable. Because it was really strange, talking about stuff like that to your mum.

Noelle (S, 12, P) described how taking part in the project had made her mother change her mind about allowing her to watch the post-watershed drama *Footballers' Wives*.

> My mum said to me that I couldn't watch *Footballers' Wives* at first, 'cause at first we all sat down and watched it together and then she said 'oh I don't think this is suitable for you'. So I said 'all right then'. ... And then the next like episode of it my mum said 'oh you can watch it if you want 'cause it's alright now'. 'Cause she might not have thought I was mature enough, but then when she found out I was mature enough to do this project she said 'OK then you can watch that' ...

Similarly Bea (N, 10, P) claimed that doing the project had changed not only what she could watch but her mother's viewing tastes: 'I got to watch *EastEnders* and we don't normally watch that and now mum won't let me watch anything else 'cause she wants to watch *EastEnders* all the time'. Lisa (N, 14, P) commented that her mother did not like her reading teenage magazines, but that she had not objected when she had shown her the scrapbook with its many magazine images – perhaps it was acceptable when it was approached as a formal project.

Others described how they themselves had 'thought more' and differently as a result of doing the diary. Nancy (S, 17, D) wrote that she had not been so aware of the 'heterosexism' of the media before. Jon (N, 17, P) said:

> I think the diaries, I just thought, you know, a bit more in depth about the issues. I think when we play [computer] games like that and we read magazines like that *Max Power* and *FHM* we skim, it's just there (...) it's a nothingness really because it's been there all the time and you just read it and it doesn't affect you but if you – I think if I'm sat there and especially writing, I think you get a lot more detail and that's coming out of your head when you write stuff. ... You think more deep of, should it be there, is it right etc etc

Lori (S, 14) presented a meticulous scrapbook, illustrated with extracts, pictures and drawings. She commented disapprovingly on the media messages she identified: 'I didn't and still don't agree with how the media seem to encourage people into being in a relationship and skipping from partner to partner'. She summarised at the end her 'before and after' views on the research themes. It seemed that she was following the conventions of the school project, in which she was obliged to recount how edifying the experience had been.

As these examples suggest, even unbidden, many students responded to the task by reflecting on broadly moral issues and positioning themselves as 'learners'. We should be aware that such responses may be the product of the implicit demands of the research and school context, rather than representing young people's everyday media engagement. However, at times the diaries and scrapbooks did allow a space for different and sometimes more complex voices to emerge. Some used them to express a more straightforward enthusiasm for the media – as shown, representatively, by Tania (S, 10), who wrote on the cover of her notebook 'the media is heavy phat cool wicked fab brill!' In many cases, those who opted for the 'scrapbook' element of the task carried it

Relationships

Before: + After

Well, before this Project,
I had some views on relationships
but wasn't really to bothered
what people get up to, or how
there media portrayed them,
because, I think it is up
to people who they go out
with. and was aware of
alot of media coverage, but
I didnit and still dont agree
with how the media seems to
encourage people into being in a Relationship
and skipping from partner to partner

I have Relised that alot of people in
the media dont seem to be happy being
single, and I dont really understand why.

out lovingly. Girls especially handed in notebooks whose covers they had vibrantly adorned with their names and those of favourite bands and stars in coloured, gold or silver pen, and pictures carefully cut out and glued down on every page. The composition of the pages often conveyed meanings that went beyond what they communicated in writing. For instance, the pictures of products (lipsticks, trainers, clothes, food, music) and stars seemed to testify to the role and significance of the media and consumer culture more generally in their lives, a point to which we will return in subsequent chapters. Lisa (N, 14) cut out a headline 'Lush Lads Ahoy!' with its accompanying collage of attractive young men, and wrote underneath about her own dilemmas over having a boyfriend who was two years older than her. The juxtaposition seemed to offer a poignant contrast between the promise of pleasures held out by the magazine and the more ambivalent feelings she herself was experiencing.

Although we chose a notebook with a black cover that we hoped would seem attractive and gender-neutral, there were some differences in how the scrapbook / diary task was approached, particularly in terms of gender. The girls' notebooks were on average longer at nearly 10 pages whilst the boys' averaged 8.5. These differences would be starker had we calculated the number of words written. This may seem to bear out conventional wisdom about boys and men as emotionally inarticulate and unable to express themselves. However, it would be unwise to assume this too readily; as other research has shown, this is far from simplistically the case (e.g. Frosh *et al.* 2002). To the extent that the realm of feelings and the 'personal' mode of diary writing is coded as feminine, they may have been resistant to adopting it, rather than constitutively incapable of doing so: many of the boys talked fluently and thoughtfully in interviews. Moreover, the length difference was less marked in the youngest participants – amongst the nine and ten year olds, girls' notebooks averaged 7.9 pages, boys 8.1.

The responsibility of being 'representative' proved daunting for some young people. Although Caitlin (N, 12, G) reported that her mother encouraged her to take part 'because I've got a really good opinion on things ... and she thinks I'd be a good representative of what people think' and Krystal (S, 14, P) that her parents liked her being 'out there and opinionated', Reena (N, 14, P) was not the only student who worried that she might say something 'wrong'. Such anxieties may partly have indicated a view of the project as being like homework, all the more concerning because it was to be assessed by standards they did not know. Several others described their confidence draining away

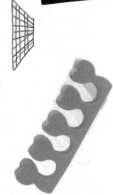

Address :-

Tel :-

Hobbies :- Listening to music,
Shopping, dancing, singing
and partying.

Fave programme :- Bad girls
Fave actor :- Josh Harnett
Fave singer :- Jennifer Lopez
Fave film :- The Fast and the Furious

Your one dream wish :- Is to become
a singer and date Josh Harnett

My opinion of these articles and personal problems are very positive. I agree with the idea of asking people to write in there problems to the magazines because it gives people ways in which they can relieve all there stress and plus it helps to talk 2 someone. I also agree because it helps people who are too shy to reveal there problems and showing viewers and

readers peoples opinions can help them if they are in a difficult situation and need help or advise. So overall I think it is without fail a brilliant idea all round.

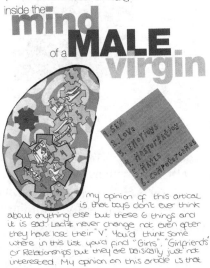

my opinion of this artical is that boys don't ever think about anything else but these 6 things and it is sad. Lad it never change not even after they have lost their "V" you'd think some where in this list you'd find "Girls", "Girlfriends" or Relationships but they are basically just not interested. My opinion on this article is that

Fig. 2.2b and c Many girls, like Lisa and Kelly (N, 14) were enthusiastic about the value of aspects of teenage magazines; while collages of images from consumer culture suggested its importance in their lives

Diary - `love, sex and relationships`

Saturday 23 February 2002
11.45pm – Bad girls replay of the following weeks episode

Sitting in the living room watching bad girls with my mum, little brother and little sister. There are 2 sex scenes involving Tanya. When that comes on, the two siblings look away and start doing something else, one asking me a question involving music and the other playing with his phone.

Thursday 28 February 2002
10.30pm - Club Reps – replay of following week's episode

Clips of nudity. I am watching it with my brother upstairs in my bedroom and he walk in and catches you watching it. He walks in on the part where a girl is half naked and automatically blames you watching porn and teases you for the rest of week as he caught you watching something that involved nudity. I blame my brother Nik and when dad tells the two little siblings that he caught Nik watching porn, they tease him and I join in.

Fig.2.3   Glenn (S, 17) offered vivid cameos of 'family viewing' (a,b) while Seth (N, 12), like many other boys, wrote less extensively (b)

I Like films with sex and relationships in iall so like Action films with guns and things Like that. I Like games on the P.C because you can put passwords in and see naked women and on this game you can ~~talk~~ talk on the phone to a girl and ~~to~~ press a button and it shows her having sex the game is called Duke Muckem.

IN my room I have lots of media equipment souch as t.v, computer, hi-fi , mobile phone. in my house we have 4 teles, 3 computers, 3 mobile phomes, 2 hi-fis, 2 DVD players.

as they contemplated the task, such as Izzie (S, 12, P): 'I didn't know as much as I thought I would know, about the media. I thought I'd know much more, but I don't .... I thought I'd be able to write loads but then some bits I couldn't'.

Similarly, Rollo (S, 12, P) noted that 'Sometimes I can have it in my mind and I wanna write it down but I don't know how to set it out 'cause ... I write in rubbish and it doesn't make sense'. Rollo in fact wrote nothing at all in her diary, claiming also that she hadn't been able to find anything 'about' the topic in the media – although she was then able to speak forthrightly and articulately about a range of media in the interview. It may have been that she panicked when confronted with blank pages on which to construct herself as a 'knowing subject' with 'something to say' and doubted that her everyday life could really provide relevant material. This aspect was particularly marked in the Essex secondary school; in general their diaries were shorter than those of the young people in the North. However, we should not read this as a lack of literacy skills or motivation. As sociological work has shown, the school as an institution does not grant legitimacy to the knowledge and competences of working-class young people and as a result they may not be as able to make cultural capital of their experience as are middle-class students (Bourdieu and Passeron 1977; Richards 1998). Moreover they are rarely given the message that their views are significant, and they may simply have been unsure of how to deal with this new responsibility and identity. Following Osborne and Rose (1999), we might argue that they have had less chance to be disciplined into the current requirement for citizenship, of 'being opinionated'.

Interviews

Whilst participants had much to say about 'love, sex and relationships', they did not necessarily wish to construct themselves as 'sexual selves'. However, some of our questions in interview, and the framing of the project, may seem to have invited them to do so. For instance, Sean (N, 12) wrote at length in his diary about his strong and loving relationship with his mother's woman partner, and may even have welcomed the diary as an opportunity to discuss this aspect of his life. In the pair interview his co-participant and childhood friend Damian spoke movingly about his experience of family breakdown. Yet they gently refused David's questions about how they 'felt about' sexual pictures in magazines or on the Internet, explaining that they didn't 'really think of stuff like that' and that they preferred building dens or playing on their rope swing. We can only speculate about whether some young people decided against participating in the project because they did not want to position themselves as 'sexual' in this way.

The interviews trod a delicate balance between being shaped by the school context and by the topic. Hence on the one hand, as we have seen, the project was like school work. It became increasingly so when we asked them to give opinions on the videos and articles we showed them – particularly since it turned out that one year group had previously watched and discussed *The Simpsons* in both English and Religious Education. Noelle (S, 12, G) acknowledged this when she exclaimed at a chaotic point in a group interview 'get on with the lesson!'. We were inevitably positioned as middle-class, teacherly figures. Many students worried or joked about 'speaking posh' in front of us, some using formal terms or euphemisms like 'sexual intercourse' or 'making love', others drawing on a technical vocabulary learnt from Media Studies ('connotations'). It is worth noting that several of the sixth form students we spoke to were taking Media Studies A-Level, although most of the secondary school students would undoubtedly also have encountered formal study of the media as part of their English classes.

We also repeatedly questioned them about media 'messages' or what they 'learned' about love, sex and relationships from the media. Whilst such questions do echo how the media are approached in public debate, they may seem reductive. Some participants relished the opportunity to send up both the questions and the interviewer, as in these examples:

Sara: So what do you learn about love, sex and relationships from things like page 3 girls, or *Confessions of a Window Cleaner* or whatever?
Dale (S, 14, P): Most of the women want it.
Pierre (14): Most of the women want it.
Dale: And most of the windows don't get cleaned!

David: do you think this programme (*Friends*) has messages? Are they giving you messages? Are they ... teaching you things about relationships and so on (....)?.
Rachel (N, 10, G): It's like don't get drunk [laughs]. Don't get drunk or you'll get married to Ross!

However, the majority tried to answer our questions seriously, in accordance with what they thought we must want. For instance, Kelly's (N, 14, W) notes on the video assessed each one in terms of its didactic content in earnest terms that seemed almost out of place in relation to a cartoon: 'Watching *The Simpsons* made me think what "love" is really about and what it really does mean. (...) I think this helps people to try and be faithful to their partners and how to tell a partner the truth about past cheatings etc'. As with the scrapbooks, then, our research often provoked a moral discourse that Phil (N, 12, P) identified bluntly as 'a mum thing'.

We need to be wary here of what Joke Hermes, in her study of the readers of women's magazines, calls the 'fallacy of meaningfulness' – that is, the notion that the media are always necessarily invested with meaning (Hermes 1995:16). Unlike many audience researchers (e.g. Ang 1985; Radway 1987), we were not seeking the responses of devoted 'fans' but general views across a range of media. Few of our interviewees were committed aficionados of particular texts, although genres such as teenage magazines proved an important interest for some. For much of the time, we were asking young people about media texts that they may not have read or watched with sustained attention and concentration, that for them were often ephemeral, picked up and just as easily discarded. Indeed, as Hermes remarks, media are often pleasurable precisely because they do not have to be learnt from, memorised or even remembered.

Sometimes interviewees may have expressed contradictory views simply because they did not hugely care either way; their arguments may therefore reflect not what they actually do with texts, but what they wish to do, or what serves to present themselves in a particular way. In this respect, for instance, many young people adopted 'critical' personas that defined them as discriminating and rational media consumers. Certain terms recurred in the vocabularies of taste on which they drew – material evaluated negatively was repeatedly said to be 'boring' 'pathetic', 'immature' and so on; that deemed praiseworthy was said to be 'realistic', to 'make you think' or 'allow you to make up your own mind'. Such evaluations, prioritising the pleasures of the mind over the body, may have been specific to both the research and the school situation, as they echo the evaluative hierarchies so often promulgated there.

In other instances, we were struck by how widely young people's responses varied according to context. For instance, Lori – whose scrapbook work was mentioned above – when interviewed with her close friend Jessica (S, 14), described their relationship as pleasurably and intensely bound up with communicating through and about the media. For instance, they had developed their own code so that they could write and talk about things that mattered to them without others knowing:

> Gareth Gates is called Charmin ... because we couldn't think of a name for him. So we said, 'right the next advert that comes on the telly, we'll call him that'. It was the Charmin, like, Ultra Toilet Paper advert [both laugh]. And so that's what we called him [laugh] ... So we say 'oh it's Charmin coming on telly tonight!'.

When we talked to them in a group, however, they were distant and guarded, producing polite but stunted responses that made us both feel like English teachers unsuccessfully trying to generate 'a debate'; their passionate involvement with media seemed to have been leached away by the group interview context. In our analysis, therefore, we have tried to acknowledge the ambivalences and varied meanings of young people's media usage, rather than seeing any one account as 'truer' than others.

On the other hand, the interviews were a break in school routine. Students missed a lesson to attend the interview, predictably requesting that it be 'double maths'. As interviewers, we tried to set them at ease – supplying large quantities of biscuits and chocolates to help do so – and to reassure them that we could maintain confidentiality and were unshockable. Some were delighted by our informality: Ethan and Seth (N, 12, G), amongst others, reported to Sara that David had said 'fuck' when considering the French Connection UK advertisements and repeated amidst much hilarity his casual joke in the context of a discussion of local sex workers that you 'probably couldn't get much for a fiver'. Perhaps we had a certain exoticism attached to us simply as outsiders: after their first interview with Sara, two 14-year-old girls rushed off to try to catch a glimpse of David, and we doubt that this was because they had been impressed by his professorial status or international academic reputation. They put together a sense of who we might be from a mixture of observation and fantasy. At best they had only personally met Sara before starting the work, although even at that stage more than one group were curious to know if she and David were a married couple. They closely scrutinised us, remarking on David's designer glasses, the brand of Sara's shoes, and asking if we had been 'on telly'.

The topic of love, sex and relationships was also decidedly un-school like and offered some rich opportunities for subverting the cultural hierarchies and values of the school, both inside and outside the inter-views – as when Ethan and Seth, again, informed their classmates that we had given them a 'porn video' to watch. They were working out what kind of a context the interviews were and what would be appro-priate. They were often aware of participating in a larger research project. Hence a group of primary school girls, in the middle of a chaotic interview in which they couldn't stop laughing, asked David whether theirs was 'the funniest interview you've done'. Kelly (N, 14, P) was keen that Sara should pass on what the boys in her year had said, particularly anything about her. Dale (S, 14) persistently asked to hear more about the northern students' ideas – although he admitted his interest was also due to a desire to miss more lessons.

Even so, the interviews were not quite a licence to 'talk dirty', since they provoked a degree of anxiety in participants – possibly focused around the display of 'feeling' that the project might seem to demand. We explore the kinds of performance they induced in later chapters, but here one indicative example will suffice. In the introductory meeting, Sebastian (N, 14) made several jokes about how he would print out porn images from the Internet and write about porn films on cable TV in his diary. However, he did not do so and in his pair inter-view with Sara subsequently was reluctant to talk about whether he had seen any porn. Indeed, he claimed he spent too much time playing football to watch much television at all. As this implies, talk about the media is a form of social action, a way of defining ourselves and negotiating relationships with others. The purposes that talk about porn served Sebastian in a group context were no longer achieved in a more intimate setting with a woman interviewer.

The role of the researchers

Feminist and postmodern researchers stress the importance of reflexivity – that is, the role of researchers in interpreting, representing and producing knowledge from the voices of research subjects. We have already suggested how the research process itself shaped the data we report. Further, Walkerdine, Lucey and Melody (2001) have explored how unconscious, emotional and intersubjective processes also intervene in the research context: interviewers are not just ra-tional, conscious professionals. In the course of the research, we tried to understand how our own defences, fantasies and desires impacted on the process. We did this by noting and recording our feelings and responses to interviews, comparing these to the impression given by the tape recordings of the interviews (which were often very different), and returning to memorable moments. We came to acknowledge that the power relations of the interviews were certainly not clear-cut or hierarchical in one direction only. Sometimes interviewees reminded us of our own adolescent pasts in ways we would wish to remember – or, equally likely, to forget. Researching the topic involved us in a certain vulnerability, an awareness that we might be scrutinised for our own possibly voyeuristic motivations and sexuality, and a concern about how to present ourselves. For instance we did not want to seem too old or out of touch, whilst acknowledging that as middle class and in our late thirties and forties this was probably inevitable. David would occasionally identify himself as a heterosexual father by talking about his two teenage sons and family life. Sara referred neither to her present heterosexual or previous lesbian relationships. She perhaps hoped to present herself more ambiguously, although as a consequence simply felt insecure instead. Our own sense of awkwardness did at least enable us to understand why (as we discuss in Chapter 4) none of our interviewees were prepared to discuss their own non-normative sexual feelings.

One key finding that emerged derived from a decision we had made to divide the pair interviews so that we each talked predominantly to pairs of the same gender as ourselves. We assumed that girls would prefer to talk to a woman and boys to a man. However, whilst this might have been true for the young people, it was not necessarily the case that we found it easier ourselves. Sara sometimes seemed more relaxed with male participants and David established positive relationships with many of the girls, not least since he was able to reassure them that 'it's all right, I'm not a boy any more'. Although most of the interviews were constructive, we thought it important to learn from interviews that felt as if they had 'failed', because these could be particularly revealing. For instance, Sara conducted an interview with Suzanne and Izzie (S, 12, P), which seemed quite tense for all concerned. They admitted they were talking 'posh' for the purposes of the interview, and Suzanne that she had bought magazines such as *Elle* specifically for the research rather than using ones she usually read. Izzie seemed occasionally embarrassed by Suzanne, correcting her in a furious whisper when she mispronounced *Elle* as 'Eggy'. At one point the conversation wandered on to the designer label clothes they owned, perhaps in an effort to demonstrate to Sara how 'proper' they were. Although aware of their discomfort, Sara initially found it hard to set them at their ease, and even seemed to block the conversation when it could have developed in more interesting directions – for instance, when Suzanne mentioned *Elle*'s 'sexy men' supplement, Sara changed the subject rather than asking Suzanne more about it. Later, however, they relaxed and spent some time discussing the sexual mores of the school, with Suzanne confidently instructing Sara in the meaning of various sexual slang terms. Suzanne may have represented something anxiety-provoking for Sara: a girl whose main power lay in her sexuality and who had little future in conventional middle-class terms. Sara, whose route through life had been through educational qualifications with its accompanying denial of the body and permanent fear of failure (cf. Walkerdine *et al.* 2001), seemed ill at ease with what Suzanne might have to say.

Similarly David returned from one interview declaring that it was 'the worst' he had done and angrily blaming Grant (S, 17) for being so unwilling to talk that he had blocked the other two boys from joining in. His reaction to Grant was so strong that Sara was surprised when she met him and found him affable and prepared to participate. Nor did the tape of David's interview reveal any overt hostility from Grant. The interview seemed to have deteriorated partly because David had posed abstract 'why' questions that required explanations, which the interviewees may have found hard to answer. Although we tended to construct the interviews with sixth formers more as a formal 'Media Studies lesson' anyway, entering into a hyper-rational, intellectualising mode seemed to provide a defence against David's own difficulties in dealing with working-class boys.

By contrast, our interviews with the middle-class students were often much more comfortable. Whereas on one occasion in Essex Sara aggressively challenged an older student (aged 17) about his negative views on gay sexuality, she conducted the interviews with the older middle-class northern students in a more approving tone. This was partly because for these groups (as we explain in Chapter 4) demonstrating their anti-homophobic credentials was important and Sara felt at home with their liberal views. However she realised subsequently that she had failed even to notice (much less to challenge) their derogatory references to the implicitly working-class viewers of talk shows. We felt familiar with their sexual identities (or with what we imagined them to be), whilst those of our working-class participants remained somewhat 'other'.

Social class, then, was highly relevant not just at the level of who participated, but at the level of the fantasies that were activated in the research process. However, we would argue that these fantasies are not individual, but socially produced. Our projections and defences reveal a long history in which working-class sexuality has been constructed as problematic – as excessive, pathological and out of control (Mort 2000). Such images extend also to fantasies of television watching, since over-consumption of media images is also often attributed to working class families. In a world in which social class will not go away, we should bear in mind the persistence of such constructions and their resonance for issues of sexuality.

Conclusion

In this chapter, we have drawn attention to some of the ways in which our methods (and our own identities as researchers) shaped the data we were able to obtain. While this is a common concern for qualitative researchers, it clearly applies to all research; and readers should be wary of the extent to which *all* methods necessarily constrain what research is able to show or to prove. However, we also feel that the methods we used have several advantages over alternative approaches. Without being naïve or sentimental, we believe that our methods *do* give us access to children's voices and perspectives in ways that other methods do not; and that they provide insights into how children use and inter-pret the media that are frequently ignored or oversimplified in other research. We would strongly contest the idea that qualitative research is automatically more 'subjective' than quantitative research, or more subject to interpretation. The methods we have used enable us to be systematic and rigorous, both in ensuring the representativeness of the data we present and analyse, and in comparing material gathered through different methods and in different contexts.

Ultimately, what perhaps most deserves attention here is what passed unremarked in our research project – its intelligibility. During its course, we approached hundreds of children and their parents and demanded that they tell us their 'views' and their 'opinions', what they 'thought' and 'felt' about 'love, sex and relationships'. Our request could be refused, objected to, parodied and mocked as well as acceded to: but no one found it incomprehensible. When in interviews we asked a question such as 'how did you find out about it?' everyone involved acted as if they knew what the 'it' was – although of course we were all constructing this imaginary referent in the process of talking about it. The fact that children already have ways of talking about 'love, sex and relationships' could be seen as evidence that we are indeed a 'sexual storytelling society' (Plummer 1995). As we have seen in Chapter 1, a new 'culture of the self' may be taking shape in contemporary society, in which the public discussion of sexual matters now forms part of the texture of everyday experience, not so much to express inner guilt but to bear witness, or to offer opportunities for 'personal growth' (Rose 1999b). In the chapters that follow, we will debate and explore the relevance of this argument to the young people we encountered.

3
Living and Learning

Courtney (N, 12, P): My mum doesn't say anything about it [sex on television], because she knows I know everything about sex and relationships.

Courtney's claim to 'know everything' about sex and relationships was one that was repeatedly echoed by children throughout our research. As we shall see, a few of the youngest children asserted that there were things they did not *want* to know, or that they did not feel ready for; while some of the older children, looking back, were inclined to date their acquisition of such knowledge somewhat later:

Harvey (N, 17, P): Like, I'd heard of it or something when I was about ten. But then probably by the time I was about 14 I knew everything I needed to know.

Nevertheless, from the age of 11, most children claimed to enjoy a state of absolute knowledge. According to them, sex education in schools taught them nothing new; while parents' efforts in this respect were generally quite misplaced:

Kelly (N, 14, P): My mum has spoken to me about bits, but it's embarrassing. And we kind of know it all already, don't we?

Indeed, for some, much of the embarrassment here seemed to derive from having to pretend that they did *not* know about such things, in order to keep their parents happy. While some, like Courtney, believed that their parents were content for them to 'know it all', others felt that parents might be disturbed to discover the full extent of their knowledge. In our survey, 69 per cent of children responded positively to the statement 'I know more about sex than my parents think I do'. (In fact, one 14-year-old who piloted the survey suggested that the statement should read 'I know more about sex than my parents'.)

Of course, it would be easy to mock the idea that 11-year-olds (or even 14-year-olds) could possibly know 'everything' about sex and relationships. Whether or not we can claim to 'know it all' partly depends upon what we mean by 'it' – and, as we suggested at the end of the previous chapter, the nature of 'it' was defined in various ways here. 'Knowing it all' implies a position untroubled by uncertainty or contradiction. Yet, as we shall show in this and subsequent chapters, there are all sorts of paradoxes here. You may believe that you know everything, but it may simply be that you are not aware of the existence of what you do *not* know. Like Harvey (above), you may feel you know all you 'need' to know; but this depends upon being completely confident about the extent of your needs. You may believe you know more than your parents think you know, but it may be that this is precisely what they would like you to think. For Courtney's mother, assuring her daughter that she already knows everything might be a good way of avoiding some of the embarrassment of discussing such matters; and Courtney herself might well choose to go along with this for the same reason. Learning 'the facts of life' is thus a rather more complex and uneven process than these easy assurances might seem to imply.

In this chapter, we consider the various ways in which children learn about love, sex and relationships. Our main concern is not so much with *what* they learn, but with how and where they learn it. Our focus here is primarily on the younger children in our sample – those aged between ten and 14 – although we also draw on the older children's recollections of this period. We focus, firstly, on what children learn from observing and interpreting the world around them; and secondly, on their responses to various more or less explicit forms of instruction, on the part of parents, school and the media. We conclude by briefly considering some general implications of this in terms of how children come to define or construct their own sexual identities.

Tales out of school

We did not set out in this research to gather systematic information about children's sexual experiences, or to assess their levels of sexual knowledge. However, we did learn a good deal about how they defined and perceived the 'sexual worlds' in which they lived. In many cases, these worlds appeared quite ambivalent and contradictory. They combined realism and fantasy, the romantic and the sordid, sentiment and sexuality, in sometimes uneasy combinations. In this respect, they were perhaps not too different from the sexual worlds of the majority of adults.

School obviously provided significant opportunities for sexual learning – and not just through the explicit instruction provided in sex education lessons. On one level, schools operate to 'police' sexuality, preventing it from manifesting itself in certain ways (Wolpe, 1988) – although, as we shall see, this might in itself have the effect of inciting it. On the other hand, schools also actively organise masculine and feminine identities (Connell 2000; Mac an Ghaill 1994); and, as some have argued, they may seek to enforce a form of 'compulsory heterosexuality' (Epstein and Johnson 1998) – although here again, the effectiveness of this may be far from guaranteed. School can therefore prove to be a highly ambiguous site for sexual learning.

For many of the children in our sample, romantic relationships – if that is indeed the correct description – appeared to have begun at quite a young age. Several of the ten-year-olds claimed to be 'going out with' children of the opposite sex; and some, like Rory and Skye (N, 10), who specifically asked to be interviewed together, claimed to have been doing so since the age of five. In many cases, 'going out together' did not appear to involve very much actual 'going out'; and in some instances, children who were 'going out together' did not even seem to spend much time in each other's company. Nevertheless, the pressure of playground gossip appeared to be quite intense. Children described how they would be 'called' (that is, teased) for 'fancying' people – particularly if those people were deemed to be 'ugly'; or alternatively (in the case of girls) condemned for being 'frigid' if they had not kissed anyone yet. Some of the girls felt rather excluded because they did not yet have 'boyfriends', although few of the boys appeared to take the matter quite so seriously, and some claimed to find the whole issue rather embarrassing. Emma and Rebecca (N, 10, P) complained at some length about how stories about 'who fancies who' were circulated among their peers; while Rory and Skye provided an elaborate account of the 'dumping' and 'two-timing' (and even 'three-timing') that had been going on among their classmates. Apparently Skye had even forbidden other girls to be friendly with Rory, on the grounds that he was *her* boyfriend.

Not all relationships were quite as intense as Rory and Skye's, however. For example, Alicia (N, 10) wrote in her diary that she had sent a 'love letter' to Neil, despite the fact that he was 'not hot whatsoever'; although in our interview, she explained that she only really needed him for his ability at maths. She went on to claim that she had three other 'boyfriends'; although one turned out to be a character from *Buffy the Vampire Slayer*. Alicia and her friend Melanie recounted elaborate fantasies, based primarily on American teen shows like *Buffy*, *Clueless* and *Saved by the Bell*, which they acted out in the playground. They described how in a future life they would have boyfriends who 'went to the mall', and how they would go to 'rock parties' wearing 'mascara and blue lipstick' in order to 'kiss behind a curtain'. Neil himself might play a part here – perhaps as Spike from *Buffy* – but of course they wouldn't be 'getting really romantic' yet – not least because the teachers would give them 'a three' (a severe punishment) for kissing in the playground. Alicia's story displays a mixture of aspirational fantasy and reality that was characteristic of several of youngest children.

Phoebe, Naomi, Chantel and Reena (N, 14, G) looked back on this period with a kind of ironic nostalgia. In a scenario that would certainly reinforce criticisms of the 'compulsory heterosexuality' of schooling (Epstein and Johnson 1998), they recalled how they had 'got married' in primary school, with the collusion of their teacher, who had involved the whole class in making paper flowers and confetti. Phoebe claimed to have had two bridesmaids, along with a vicar and a best man for her groom – although it subsequently emerged that this was the second of two marriages, the first having taken place at the age of five. Although this marriage had lasted only one month, Phoebe had been 'going out' with the boy for five months – 'better than normal marriages last', she remarked.

Even without the benefit of hindsight, the younger children were clearly aware of the difference between these playground relationships and 'serious' ones. In general, it seemed to be agreed that such relationships were just 'something you giggle about with your friends', as Izzie (S, 12, P) put it. According to Wesley (S, 12, G), 'going out' with girls was mostly a matter of 'hanging around with them', with the occasional 'kissing' (or 'snogging' or 'getting hold of'); although Izzie (S, 12, P) asserted that even kissing was something for girls a couple of years older than herself. Indeed, some of the girls accused the boys of being too crudely 'sexy' in their approach, while others seemed rather dismissive of the boys' attempts to impress them by applying copious amounts of hair gel.

The overtly sexual dimensions of these relationships were much more apparent among the 14-year-olds. By this stage, it seemed that school itself had become quite a sexually-charged place (cf. Wolpe 1988). There were plentiful stories in our diaries and interviews of children gossiping and bragging, not just about who was 'going out' with whom, but also about their sexual exploits. According to the girls, it was the boys who were particularly inclined to engage in this kind of sex talk, not least as a form of harassment. Thus, boys had been overheard discussing the details of masturbation in their technology lesson – 'ooh, we didn't need to know that', said Lara (S, 14, P) – while others were accused of putting pin-up pictures on their school folders (or drawing penises on them), and of passing round porn magazines in class. In some instances, this was more than just talk: there were several accounts of boys 'groping' or 'fingering' girls, either in school or on the way to school. In some instances, the girls fought back by teasing boys about their lack of sexual knowledge: 'sometimes the girls say stuff and then the boys go "what does that mean?" and we go "oh, we'll tell you when you're older"'(Izzie, S, 12, P).

On some occasions, teachers were also implicated in these accounts. There were several stories about children 'fancying' their teachers; while Dale and Pierre (S, 14, P) teased each other about which of their teachers they would most like to 'bang'. This issue was addressed more specifically in one of our interviews, where we had asked the children to read a newspaper story about the case of the Canadian teacher Amy Gehring, who had been accused (and acquitted) of having sex with some of her under-age students. Gehring herself was generally dismissed as 'sick' or as a 'pervert', and the story was accused of feeding a more general distrust of teachers. Nevertheless, a few of the boys seemed to believe it might be acceptable to have sex with your teacher, although (as Pierre (S, 14, G) put it), it would depend on how 'fit' she was. (In fact, the boys seemed rather more shocked by a detail in the story about how Gehring and one of the boys had had their belly buttons pierced, a practice they perceived as unambiguously 'gay'.) Several of the children were able to describe similar encounters from their own experience, including the case of a male teacher at their school who had been dismissed after being found having sex in a cupboard with a sixth former, as well as other teachers who would keep girls behind after lessons or leer at them 'under the table'.

Despite these latter incidents, sex manifested itself in school mainly through talk. Rumours were rehearsed in our interviews about the 'quiet' girl in Year 9 who had got pregnant, or the girl in Year 7 who was always bragging about how often she had sex. Sharmaine (S, 12, P) described how she herself had been accused of snogging a boy in Year

10 and 'putting my hand down his pants', although she vehemently denied this. According to Olivia (S, 17, P), 'gossip goes round this school like wildfire. You can tell someone something in the morning and by the afternoon the whole year, the year above and the year below, would know it, what was going on.' These kinds of rumours obviously contributed to the building of individuals' reputations, but they were also a means whereby sexual knowledge and assumptions about sexuality were circulated and reinforced. Gossip therefore provided a means for the children to police each other's behaviour; but it also served as a pleasurable subversion of the monotony of lessons. Certain individuals appeared to be seen as authorities on the matter: Izzie and Suzanne (S, 12, P), for example, spoke in admiration of their friend Dion, whose mum was 'really, really cool' – 'like, Dion knows everything, and that's how I knew at quite a young age, 'cause she used to tell everyone, and the boys like said it as well, everyone talked about it'. In this context, displays of ignorance and uncertainty were clearly to be avoided, for fear of being 'called' or publicly shamed.

As we shall see in more detail in Chapter 4, these accounts were also infused with discourses about appropriate gender roles. These were most explicit in the girls' accounts. Thus, girls repeatedly argued that boys were just interested in sex, whereas *they* were interested in a boy for his 'personality'. Boys of their own age, they asserted, were emotionally immature and inarticulate. On the other hand, boys were accused of dividing girls into two categories, 'slags' and 'frigid' (cf. Lees 1986); whereas, the girls argued, boys who were promiscuous would see themselves as 'studs'. As we shall see, the girls were often keen to refute these 'double standards', but assumptions about 'natural' sexual behaviour seemed to persist as a form of taken-for-granted commonsense wisdom.

The family and other romances

Like the school, the family is obviously another major source of such 'observational' learning: children will learn from observing parents' behaviour, irrespective of what parents might overtly attempt to teach them. In many instances, the children's experience of family life was one of break-up and separation. Not all the children included information about this in the personal profiles they wrote at the beginning of their diaries, but many had parents who lived separately (as do approximately one third of British children). Several did not see their fathers at all, or only did so rarely; while others saw them on a couple of days each week. Even where fathers were present, they seemed to be more likely to be working than involved in child care. Others reported that they could regularly hear their parents arguing. Whether from their direct experience, or from friends, many children knew the distress this could cause:

> Rebecca (N, 10, P): If they start arguing, I think that they should try and get back together. But if they don't, then they'll have to break up because it's harder to just ... on the children to just keep arguing. 'Cos it would just upset them. If my ... Anita my friend, her mum and dad used to always argue and she was in bed one time and her mum and dad were arguing in the kitchen. And she went ... Her grandmother only lives down the road. So she went to her grandmother's in her nightie.

As such, there was little evidence here of parents providing positive 'role models' of romantic relationships. The influence parents have in this respect – which is obviously profound – must be largely implicit. While older siblings, and even aunts and uncles, can be seen as sexual beings – and several of the children made quite satirical observations of this – there is a widespread resistance to seeing parents in this way. Several children expressed revulsion at their parents kissing, let alone the idea of them actually having sex. Few, perhaps, would be as accommodating as Sharmaine (S, 12, G), who recounted the following incident amid much teasing and embarrassment:

> Sharmaine: Once I walked into my mum and dad's room [laughter] ... Because I thought no one was in there and they've got these big mirrored doors that are like from the ceiling to the floor and I wanted to see how I looked in my suit 'cos I was going to a party and ... And I walked in and ... it was about the middle of the day though. Can't they even do it at night when I'm in bed? And I just go 'I'll leave you to it!' and closed the door.

If children sometimes appear unwilling to acknowledge their parents' sexuality, the feeling is clearly mutual. Several girls described how their parents – particularly their fathers – would try to prevent them from wearing 'revealing' clothes on a night out; while others complained that they were 'not allowed' to go out with boys. As we shall see, this was part of a general view that, in this area at least, parents were inclined to be 'too protective', particularly of girls.

Yet if the family does not generally appear to encourage much optimism about romantic relationships, other experiences the children have may positively undermine this. For example, even the 12-year-olds in our sample were well aware of the operation of the sex industry in their area – and this was particularly the case for the children in the more middle-class northern suburb. Several children described to us in detail how they had seen 'prostitutes' working in the centre of town, while others described a sex shop they had seen in another part of town. For these children, this kind of sordid sexual activity was part of the 'otherness' of the mainly working-class areas in which it occurred. Several pointed us towards housing estates where, we were assured, prostitution and rape were commonplace, and the streets were littered with discarded condoms.

For the working-class girls (although not exclusively for them), this sense of sexual danger was closer to home. Several spoke of the threat of 'shady men' and 'paedophiles' in their area, and in some cases in their own street, or near their school. Many said that their mothers would not allow them to go out on their own, or to the local park, even with friends, for this reason. They did not seem to regard this as a restriction on their freedom: as Noelle (S, 12, P) argued, 'I think [my mum's] right. I wouldn't let my child go over the park even if I lived one door away from it.' Others described how they would always carry a mobile phone in case they were attacked.

This anxiety was reinforced by media reporting, particularly of cases such as the abduction and murder of Sarah Payne (in 2000); and while few of the girls wanted to read about such things, they nevertheless argued that it was necessary for them to know, and to be warned. Yet the stories they recounted did not only refer to the threat of abduction by strangers: several girls quoted examples of press reports about 'normal' husbands and fathers (or indeed teachers) suddenly turning into rapists and serial killers. In some cases, the girls' parents positively reinforced the lessons of these stories: Tina and Lysa (S, 10, P), for example, described how their mothers had explained to them about the dangers of 'rapers and paedophiles', and indeed about the threat of domestic violence. Such stories appeared to feed a powerful sense of dread:

> Kim (N, 12, P, G): I find it really scary. Because it is all over. Every day there is something bad happening like rapes and that. And it is really frightening how the world is more corrupt with people like that. Scary.

Yet the source of this threat was very clearly from *men*, whether they were anonymous paedophiles or sexual partners. And for Chantel (N, 14, P), as for many of the other girls, the lesson was very clear: 'don't trust boys'.

Nevertheless, romance continued to exercise a certain pull. Coincidentally, Valentine's Day fell during the period when one group of children completed their diaries. On the one hand, they saw Valentine's Day as a fundamentally commercial phenomenon – 'it's all right for the card companies', as Caitlin (N, 12, P) put it. Yet on the other hand, they clearly wanted to have a space for romance: Courtney (N, 12, P) even confessed to buying her boyfriend a box of chocolates, as it was their 'two month anniversary' – although we had to question the seriousness of their relationship when we discovered that, two weeks later, she had still not yet seen him to hand them over. Even those who were not in a relationship, like Phoebe and Naomi (N, 14, P), said they were 'depressed' at feeling left out. Needless to say perhaps, such emotions were not expressed by any of the boys, even if they may have felt them.

Taken together, these experiences form a complex picture. On the one hand, sex was associated with prostitutes and paedophiles; with used condoms and sex shops; and with the experience of parents arguing and breaking up. Yet on the other, it meant 'going out' and even 'getting married' in a way that might be described as merely playful. Even the 14-year-olds seemed to be able to sustain romantic aspirations despite the crudity of school gossip and the sexual dangers that they saw surrounding them.

Needing (and not needing) to know

Most of the children in our sample claimed to have learnt about sex for the first time at around the age of nine or ten. It seemed to be at around this time (in school year 6) that formal sex education began, although most claimed to have known a good deal before this. As such, some of the nine-year-olds in our research were still at a point of transition. As we shall see in the following chapters, some of them failed to understand some of the sexual content in the media we discussed – particularly where this was merely suggested, or in the form of innuendo. Elsewhere in our interviews, some striking gaps in their knowledge were revealed: Bea (N, 10, P), for example, assured us that lesbians could not really have sex because 'to be able to have sex ... a man's penis has to go into the lady's belly button to send the sperm in'. In other instances, we were probed for more specialised information, as when Sara was asked to explain to Sharmaine and Noelle (S, 12, G) why anybody would need to use flavoured condoms.

For some, the media played an important role here, sometimes against the judgment of parents:

> Rachel (N, 10, P): I know it sounds weird – but you sort of like want to watch it to learn about it. But like you're scared ... you're sort of like embarrassed in watching it in front of your mums because they sort of say like 'turn away' and if you like say 'no', and they sort of like go 'well it's a bit rude and I think you should like go to bed'. And I say like, 'but we've got to learn about it', but she doesn't know that I sort of know about it yet ... but I do and I want to learn about it, but she doesn't know that I want to learn about it.

Interestingly, Rachel seemed to have learnt most from a sex education programme she had seen on TV one day when she had been off sick from school. Yet despite her almost desperate insistence on wanting to learn, it would be false to suggest that the children were necessarily possessed of an insatiable curiosity about such matters. Indeed, several of the younger children argued quite strongly that they were not yet ready to learn about sex, or that they did not need to know. Tania and Lucy (S, 10, P), for example, argued that they did not really need the advice about snogging they had found in *Mizz*, a teenage girls' magazine, because 'we're not the age to do that yet'. Likewise, Kim (N, 12, P) argued that 'in this age group', she did not want to watch all the 'picturing' of sex in programmes like *Coronation Street*; and she even resisted her mother's attempts to teach her about sex on similar grounds:

> Kim (N, 12): Like when she's telling me what's going on, like, and explaining that when you're a teenager, like ... when you're a teenager, do you know [about] your hormones? right. She's doing that and I'm going 'oh, I don't need to know this right now'.

Even among the 14-year-olds, there were those who argued that there were things they did not 'need' to know – although there was also a kind of shy excitement about these responses, which was accentuated by the difficulty the girls seemed to encounter in discussing sexual pleasure. Lara and Jody (S, 14, P), for example, claimed not to enjoy reading stories about 'positions' in their magazines, or seeing sexually explicit content in documentaries: as Jody said, 'I don't watch it because I don't feel that I need to know about that yet. Because it's not something I'm planning to do until later.'

One of the most interesting expressions of this view came from Will (S, 10), who wrote in his diary in response to a 'sexy' advertisement for beer, 'I think I should know about it, but not right now, because I think I am too young to understand'. He could not really understand, he said, why beer adverts should feature 'girls in bikinis':

> Will (S, 10, P): I shouldn't know about them right now. When I know a bit more about them [I'll be ready] ... Well, when I get a little bit older and I've learnt about the body a bit more and I know what happens. And about people who want to do this and why they want to do it.

When we asked whether he would expect to find out about all this from school or from his parents, Will replied:

> Neither. I think I've got to work it out myself ... By doing research and then eventually when I get older I'll find out.

As these observations imply, children appear to locate themselves within developmental narratives, in which particular kinds of knowledge are 'needed' at particular ages. They calibrate themselves in terms of what is seen as appropriate or necessary to know. Will's curiously academic notion of 'research' also seems to encapsulate something of the gradual, even haphazard, nature of sexual learning. Despite the assurances of children who claimed to 'know it all already', it was clear that their knowledge was much less than absolute. 'finding out' was not a once-and-for-all event, but an ongoing process, a matter of 'piecing it together' from a variety of sources. And finally, Will's insistence on 'working it out himself' was also typical of the independent approach many of the children adopted, or sought to adopt. As we shall see below and in Chapters 6 and 8, they were generally quite resistant to explicit attempts to teach them, whether these came from school, from parents or from the media.

Sex lessons

All the older children in our sample had experienced some kind of formal sex education in school. Many agreed that, at least in principle, it

Probably the sexiest advert in the world

LOVELY head, fantastic body — and the beer's not bad, either. But Helena Christensen, 35, is so sexy in this new advert for Carlsberg Export that the lager ends up as second-greatest Dane. Not probably, but definitely.

I think I should know about it but not right now because I think I am to young to understand

Fig. 3.1   Will (S, 10) diary extract

was necessary – not least because, as Angela and Chloe (N, 17, P) argued, 'not everybody does know about it ... and not everybody can talk to their parents'. Nevertheless, the children's responses to sex education lessons were almost uniformly negative. There were many hilarious recollections of videotapes about 'spots and armpit hair' that – it was alleged – they had been obliged to watch several years running. Others exchanged (perhaps apocryphal) stories about boys who had allegedly fainted during films of women giving birth. Sex education, it appeared, was widely seen as ridiculous, and as an opportunity to 'muck about'.

Perhaps predictably, the most familiar complaint here was that sex education taught you what you already knew. Several children – particularly (though by no means only) boys – claimed that 'they didn't teach us nothing' or that there was 'nothing new'. Of course, there is bound to be an element of self-presentation here. As we have implied, many children had a good deal invested in the claim that they already knew it all – although, according to Nancy (S, 17, P), this nonchalance was sometimes punctured in sex education lessons:

> When sex education came round, I learned a lot about people. Like people in my year, because you get ones that go round saying 'yeah, I've done this with this person, I've done that with that person'. Like they know everything ... And then it gets to the sex education, they're like 'what?? woah, what is this???'

Others – like Jessica and Lori (S, 14, P) – found this 'know it all' stance rather tiresome and 'immature'. Although they too claimed to 'know it anyway', they were annoyed that other people in the class would laugh at them for trying to listen to the teacher.

There was clearly a gendered dimension to this: several of the girls argued that boys were embarrassed or disgusted by the information about periods and childbirth, and tried to disguise this by laughing about it or fooling around with the condoms or tampons that were supplied. However, this was accentuated by the perception that – as several children maintained – sex education was mainly aimed at girls. According to the girls, this effectively permitted the boys to 'take the mickey' and embarrass them; and in some cases to harass them, for example with references to menstruation. They also argued that sex education seemed to place the responsibility – for example, for contraception – all on them. These criticisms are broadly reinforced by the findings of research on sex education (e.g. Lees 1994; Measor *et al.* 2000; Wolpe 1988).

Some children were prepared to admit that sex education might have taught them something; yet even here, there was a sense that the focus was much too narrowly 'medical' or 'scientific'. They might have learnt about 'the insides and all that' (as Glenn (S, 17, P) put it), or about different forms of sexually transmitted disease, but they argued that the 'really useful knowledge' they actually needed had to be obtained elsewhere. As Adrian (N, 17, P) argued, sex education might give you information about methods of contraception, 'but it doesn't tell you how to do it' – or even 'how you feel, when you first do it'. Only in rare cases, it seemed, were the children able to ask direct questions, and in some instances, the teachers appeared to have been too embarrassed to answer them. However, Noelle (S, 12, P) described how her class had been invited to place written questions anonymously in a box for the nurse to answer:

> So right, this boy goes 'well, what's a blow job mean? Please answer this question 'cause I really wanna know and I bet somebody else in the classroom will want to know as well'. So he folded it over, he put it in the box, yeah. Nobody else knew that it was him but they said it's a boy. So ... then the nurse come back the next day. She opened the box out, she took the question out and ... she explained what it meant ... And then everybody's like, 'now I get it'. And so we all got it.

Unlike in the United States, where so-called 'abstinence-based' sex education is now the order of the day (Levine 2002; Weis and Carbonell-Medina 2000), the official approach to sex education in the UK purports to avoid moral judgments. Nevertheless, the more open approach adopted by Noelle's teacher seemed quite rare. Several young people perceived there to be a moral agenda in sex education which was fundamentally about 'just saying no': as Phoebe (N, 14, P) argued, 'schools are serious. "Oh, you don't want to get pregnant." "Oh, you don't want to have sex."'. Eve (N, 17, P) described one young teacher who had actually acknowledged that sex was pleasurable, but argued that this was the exception: 'a lot of teachers say "no, no, sex is bad, sex is very very bad ... never ever do it!'. Pleasure and fun, they argued, was not mentioned here: as Chantel (N, 14, P) asserted, 'school puts like a downer on things, 'cause they just make it sound so serious and like ... it should be something that you like!' As these girls suggested, this kind of approach was almost bound to prove counter-productive: as Eve said, 'you always do the opposite of what people tell you, don't you?'. Furthermore, as Ceri (N, 17, P) argued, the actual experience of sex might reinforce this:

> You know if you're saying 'it's bad, it's bad, it's bad', then they're gonna think 'well, why is it bad? I'm gonna try it anyway'. Then when they find out that it can be quite enjoyable, it's like you're just gonna go 'well, why should I believe anything else you say?'

'It's really embarrassing when they give you talks' (Chantel, N, 14, P)

It may be that each generation has its own narratives of progress and enlightenment when it comes to sex education. Many of the parents in our focus groups (see Chapters 8 and 9) claimed that talking about sex with *their* parents had been difficult; and they tended to assert that they were doing much better with their own children. In some instances, stories of the repressive practices of the past were held up as evidence of how much more enlightened we have now become. Most parents we spoke to gave illustrative examples of television viewing, where sexual material was immediately censored: Imogen even recounted how as a child visiting her Catholic grandparents, 'if something [sexual] came on you actually had to kneel down and say a decade of the rosary, if you'd seen anything' (FG3N). Their own approach, they implied, was much more open-minded.

Yet the children did not paint such a positive picture. If school was not very positively rated as a source of sex education, neither were parents. A few did express a positive preference for finding out about sex from their parents: Rollo (S, 12, P), for example, claimed 'I can talk freely with my mum about sex. Some parents get shy [but] my mum's not, 'cause she knows that sex is part of life, I'll find out about it'. Nevertheless, this matter-of-fact approach appeared to be rare. As we shall see in much more detail in Chapter 8, family discussions of sexual matters – at least in relation to the media – were frequently characterised by a great deal of mutual embarrassment. Indeed, several children claimed that our interviews were much less embarrassing than talking with their parents: as Lara (S, 14, P) told us, 'I don't talk about anything that I'm talking about now to my parents – because I just don't want to talk about it.' Many children described how they had attempted to avoid the moment where their mother or (less frequently) their father had tried to offer them advice or information: 'my mum just came downstairs one day and said "here's a book, do you want me to go through it with you?" and I just said "no, it's all right"', said Chloe (N, 17, P). (Indeed, the parents' purchase of a 'sex book' appeared to be a common strategy, which was described by several children.) On the other hand, parents themselves could be equally evasive, as Emma (N, 10, P) described:

> I'm talking to her about something [to do with sex] and she goes 'what did you want for your tea?' or something, an excuse. And I say 'mum, stop changing the subject, I'm asking you a question'. And she has to tell me then.

Like shame, embarrassment is partly a response to social or moral norms – in this case, to beliefs about what children should or should not know, or about what should be acknowledged in a public context (see Chapter 8). As we have noted above, several children claimed that their parents were too 'protective', and that this made it difficult for them to discuss such issues together. As Melanie (N, 10, P) put it, 'they want to keep me a child for ever'; or as Eve (N, 17, P) argued, 'they think you are six until you are 26, don't they?' As we have seen, some children felt they had to pretend not to know about certain things in order to conform to their parents' image of them as 'innocent': as Danielle (N, 10, P) put it, 'you feel embarrassed about asking your mum because your mum might not know that you know about [these things], and you might feel embarrassed about asking her'. However, this embarrassment clearly worked both ways, as Heather (N, 12, P) implied: '[it's embarrassing] because you know your mum's been there, you know your mum's done that and you don't really want to think about it, do you? She's your mum!'

In some situations, children felt that parents were likely to 'hold back' from a full explanation, or be unduly formal. Seamus (N, 14, P), for example, said that '[my mum] wouldn't tell me everything. She just says like "protection" and stuff like that.' Like teachers, parents were sometimes accused of trying to teach children things they already knew. Kelly (N, 14, P), for example, expressed exasperation at her mother's constant warnings to her when she went out with her boyfriend – 'they just underestimate us!'. Some children argued that parents tended to leave 'the chat' – that is, the discussion of sex – until it was too late, well after children had already seen such things on television. Perhaps more frequently, parents and children appeared to agree that children 'knew it all already', on the grounds that this would make it unnecessary to raise the matter, and hence spare the embarrassment.

In general, fathers were seen as particularly difficult to talk to. While girls were inclined to approach their mothers, boys appeared to do the same, if indeed they looked to their parents at all. Fathers were seen as more inclined to tease their children about such matters; but they were also frequently accused of being unduly protective of their daughters. Kim (N, 12, P), for example, described her father's reaction as follows: 'my dad's just like, he doesn't talk to me about anything like that. The word 'boys' just sends him jumping, like flying! Honestly, he just won't talk about it. And if I do mention it and he's there, he's just like, he kind of walks out the room.' As Abigail (N, 12, P) and other girls suggested, some fathers appeared to operate a double standard here: '[he says] "you're too young for boys, too young for boys!" He doesn't mind my brother, though, and he's 14, like going out with girls'. (We will be examining parents' perspectives on some of these issues in Chapter 8.)

By contrast, children with older siblings – particularly same-sex siblings – frequently claimed that they were better off in terms of learning about sex and relationships. Rebecca (N, 10, P), for example, described how her older sister had told her about sex, even though her parents did not know that she had done so: 'she thought I needed to know'. One interesting aspect of this was to do with the use of language. Several children described how they would have been embarrassed to use everyday words to describe sexual matters with their parents, but did not feel so inhibited with their older brothers or sisters. Joshua (N, 14, P) and Rhiannon (N, 17, P) both described how they would ask their older siblings about the meanings of particular 'slang words'; while Matthew (N, 14, P) suggested 'I don't think mum and dad know all the words'.

Learning from media

We will be discussing how children learn from the media in much more detail in later chapters, but it is worth noting a few general observations at this stage. Many children clearly saw the media as a key source of information and ideas about love, sex and relationships. Soap operas and (for the girls at least) teenage magazines were frequently mentioned in this respect; although it was accepted that, like parents, the media could be evasive and that (as Neville (N, 14, P) put it) 'they don't always show you that much'. In general, the children were keen to reject any suggestion that there was 'too much sex' in the media – even if they did express concern about its possible impact on children younger than themselves. While some of the older children accused the media of 'glamourising' sex, others argued that they also showed 'the negatives' – and that the media were just as inclined to warn children about the dangers of sex as to encourage them to engage in it 'prematurely'.

In general, the media were seen to possess several advantages over other potential sources of information. They addressed topics directly that many children found embarrassing to discuss with their parents or teachers, or that parents might feel they were not 'ready' for. In some cases, this included information about physical development: for example, Bea (N, 10, P) described how she had been 'helped' by reading a four-page feature 'all about boobs' in the girls' magazine *Shout*. For the older children, the media also offered information on sexual 'techniques' which was harder to obtain elsewhere: as Chloe (N, 17, P) pointed out, sex education in schools did not tell you '*how* to have sex', whereas magazines would tell you 'anything you wanna know'. A couple of the younger children, however, had clearly found this kind of material disconcerting, and had stopped reading the magazines for this reason (see Chapter 6).

While the media were seen by many as a valuable source of information about matters such as contraception and sexual health, it was also argued that they should avoid the tendency to 'preach'. As we shall see in Chapter 7, this was particularly an issue in TV drama programmes, where the incorporation of (for example) 'safe sex' messages was sometimes seen to compromise the integrity or plausibility of the narrative. In our final interviews, we asked the children to look briefly at an ad from a teenage girls' magazine encouraging the use of condoms. This ad was generally praised for taking a humorous approach, and for avoiding the preacherly tone that was often seen to characterise sex education in school; although here again, there was some concern among the girls that the ad seemed to place the responsibility on them, and that there did not appear to be equivalent advertising aimed at boys. This informative but not unduly 'serious' approach was seen as a positive quality of teenage magazines more broadly, and to some extent of soap operas as well: as Phoebe (N, 14, P) argued, the magazines didn't 'tell you what to do … they just put it in and see what you think about it'.

The media also seemed to offer the benefit of anonymity, particularly if they were consumed privately. As Rachel (N, 12) put it, when you are reading a magazine, 'it's as if someone's having a conversation with you but they don't know who you are and you don't know who they are. So you're just finding it out but no one knows about it. No one has to find out …' Unlike school, media did not have the element of compulsion: as Reena (N, 14, P) put it, 'it's there if you want to read about it', but 'they don't go on about it so much'. And, as Lara (S, 14, P) pointed out, reading a magazine privately meant that you could avoid the 'mickey-taking' that occurred during sex education classes in school.

Nevertheless, it was clear that this was not just an either/or choice. The children described various ways in which these different sources could be combined, or might complement each other. As we have noted, some parents positively used the media as a kind of 'teaching aid', in some cases (for example by offering their children 'sex books' to read) in order to avoid mutual embarrassment. As we shall see in more detail in Chapters 8 and 9, television in particular was seen by both parents and children to offer valuable opportunities to discuss topics that might otherwise prove awkward to raise. Some children described how they would read about certain topics in magazines or watch things on television and then ask their parents about them: as Skye (N, 10, P) pointed out, 'you can't ask the TV questions – your mum can tell you about it in more detail'.

Learning about sex and relationships thus appeared to be seen as a form of *bricolage*, a matter of 'piecing it together' from a range of potential sources. It was also often a collective process, conducted among the peer group. Chantel (N, 14, P), for example, described how she and a friend had bought a book called a *A Girl's Guide to Sex*, and would talk about such matters at sleepovers. In general, girls appeared to find this process easier than boys: many boys agreed that they were less likely to discuss such things with their friends, for fear of more 'mickey-taking' – particularly if they were to do with their own relationships. In general, however, children appeared to use several sources in combination, talking things through with friends or older siblings (and sometimes parents) if they were in doubt. Ultimately, like Will (S, 10) conducting his 'research' (quoted above), they attempted to work it out for themselves. As this implies – and as we argued in Chapter 1 – the media do not have 'effects' in isolation from the social contexts in which they are used, and the social relationships that surround them.

Learning identities

In learning about sex and relationships, and in constructing their own 'sexual worlds', children are necessarily also coming to define their own sexual identities. While there may be 'unconscious' dimensions to this process, it has not been our intention here to psychoanalyse our subjects. What our research does allow us to identify is the conscious – and indeed self-conscious – aspects of this process. As we argued in Chapter 2, accounts given in the context of research interviews (or indeed in the apparently more 'private' form of our diaries) should not be taken at face value, as straightforward evidence of what happens in 'real life'. Yet we would argue that the data we have gathered do tell us a great deal about how children construct – and indeed actively work on – their sexual identities. Much of this is achieved by virtue of how they position and locate themselves in relation to 'others' of various kinds.

Age is certainly one dimension of this process. This is apparent, for example, in the accounts children offered us of their family histories, and of the ways in which they had been shaped or influenced by their upbringing (cf. Plummer 1995). It is also evident from their accounts of their younger selves, and of the process of growing up; and indeed in their fantasies or projections of their own future lives. As we have noted, the children frequently sought to calibrate themselves in terms of age, and in relation to assumptions about what children of different ages *should* know about or be able to do. While some of the ten-year-olds claimed they were happy to remain children, most looked forward to the freedom they imagined would come a few years hence. The pressure to 'grow up fast' was certainly a powerful one – although what 'growing up' *meant* was defined in some quite diverse ways.

As we shall see in more detail in Chapter 9, children of all ages expressed concern about the potential influence of the media in this respect, but only on children younger than themselves; and indeed, this expression of concern appeared to serve in itself as a manifestation of their own maturity. Several of the older children also rehearsed a familiar narrative, according to which 'children today' were learning about sex at a much younger age than they had themselves; although their responses to this ranged from anxieties about social decline to welcoming what they perceived as a greater openness and liberalisation. As this implies, arguments and assumptions about the effects of the media, particularly in relation to children, also necessarily entail claims about our own identities.

There are also broader social dimensions to this process. As we have noted, class was certainly a factor here: some of the middle-class children in particular were keen to present themselves as more sophisticated and more liberal on sexual matters (for example, on gay and lesbian relationships) as compared with what they imagined were the views of their working-class counterparts. Likewise, there were some self-evident differences here in terms of how boys and girls defined their own – and each other's – gender identities. As we have seen in this chapter, children of both sexes routinely rehearsed arguments about the innate differences between the sexes, for example to do with 'personality' or sexual behaviour; and while some of these amounted to an indisputable commonsense wisdom, others appeared more open to challenge and debate. Sexuality was also a crucial dimension of this process. For most children, and particularly for boys, the claiming of a secure heterosexual identity seemed to involve distancing themselves from images of gays and lesbians, and in some cases expressing vehement disgust and disapproval.

These issues will be addressed in various ways in the chapters that follow. Chapter 4 is directly concerned with gender and sexuality; while Chapter 9 particularly addresses the issue of age. These issues, together with that of class, also arise at several points in Chapters 5, 6 and 7, which deal more directly with the children's responses to specific media forms or genres. We should emphasise, however, that our approach to these issues is not that of a social survey. It is not our intention to generalise about the differences between boys and girls, or middle-class children and working-class children, or ten-year-olds and 14-year-olds. There is far too much variation and diversity in our data to permit us to do this. Ultimately, we do not see identities as given or fixed, but as flexible and diverse – as always inevitably 'under construction'. We are interested in the *processes* through which children construct their own identities, not least by drawing on the 'symbolic resources' that are available to them. For example, how do boys define what it means to be a boy? How do middle-class children define what it means to be middle class? And indeed, how do children define what it means to be a child, or a child of a certain age?

Conclusion

Learning about love, sex and relationships is not, we would argue, a matter of some inexorable form of 'socialisation'. It is an uneven and uncertain process, which is often fragmented and contradictory. Above all, it is a social phenomenon, which happens in the context of inter-personal relationships, and involves the ongoing construction of a social identity. Yet for children, this is largely a vicarious process. Despite the apparently complex romantic lives of the ten-year-olds, and the more serious relationships emerging among some of the 14-year-olds, most of the younger children in our sample were merely observers of 'adult' sexual worlds, rather than participants. And, as some of the oldest children pointed out, there was a limited amount that you could learn about this simply from being taught:

> Eve (N, 17, P): Like, drugs and sex, you have to do it either yourself or someone you know ... I don't think media can on its own, or teachers or anyone, is gonna like teach you on their own.

> Glenn (S, 17, P): You learn it from your friends and you learn more from the world around you than actually being told something by your teacher or a television programme.

If the media are indeed a powerful source of information about sexual matters, it is clear that their power is not exercised in isolation. However implicitly, the media may indeed attempt to teach; but how and what children actually learn from them is a rather more complex matter.

4
Boy Meets Boy Meets Girl Meets Girl – Gender, Sexuality and Performance

One of the most immediately striking (and perhaps predictable) differences across our sample was between the boys and the girls. As we noted in Chapter 2, girls tended to write in greater detail in their diaries, and drew more willingly on the conventions of the confessional diary form. In interviews, they often seemed more forthcoming, or at least competent at 'talk and chat', than the boys. However, factors such as age, class, interpretation of the nature of the task (as being 'like homework', for instance) and the school context, relationship with the interviewer and other interviewees, also clearly affected how boys and girls engaged in the project. We therefore tried to be circumspect about attributing such differences to the inexorable determination of biology.

However, our interviewees did not seem to share our misgivings. They spoke volubly on the subject of what boys and girls were like and how different they were. In the interview context, at least, they offered familiar and even traditional images of men as less civilised, more subject to urges, more uncontrollable and less responsible than women (cf. Moore and Rosenthal 1993). We were frequently told that boys were 'sex mad', 'just after one thing', with 'sex on the brain'. Apparently boys 'have sex then bog off': they just want to 'have their way' and 'treat women like slaves', or would if they could. Whilst such statements were made particularly by girls, Joseph (S, 12, P) too observed that men like to 'beat up women (...) then rape 'em, really' and Pierre (S, 14, P) assured us that although 'girls are all worried about having it', boys 'just like shagging' and are always 'up for it'. Moreover, men like looking at naked bodies (but of women and never of men) and set more store by a woman's looks than her personality. They have 'big egos' (Reena, N, 14, P), are 'all cocky' (Izzie, S, 12, P), and think they 'know it all': which is why they don't take advice, don't read instructions and won't ask for directions (a view put forward by both genders, in some cases as a result of discussions in psychology classes). They aren't interested in other people's problems; they can't admit that they have problems of their own, but in any case 'don't have such big problems as girls' (Seamus, N, 14, P). They don't talk at all, or not 'seriously', or only about football, or differently (in a more explicit way) about sex. They swear and fight, but don't cry; still less do they get their navel pierced. Perhaps it is fortunate that their main function is just to 'fertilise the egg' anyway (Krystal, S, 14, P). Girls, by contrast, were repeatedly described in terms such as 'helpful', 'open minded', 'comfortable with naked women', as more 'emotional', 'sensible', 'serious', 'mature', 'cuddly and kissy' or 'lovey dovey', more interested in personalities than looks; they 'stick together with their friends' and 'help each other', although Blake (S, 12, P) claimed they 'can't be understood'.

Some of these descriptions, self-servingly, were more or less flattering according to the gender of the speaker. Some boys described women's lives as devoted to what they saw as trivial – 'women always go round the shops and chat and go out and buy clothes and handbags' (Wayne, S, 12, P) – and contrasted their own ability to 'just take it as it comes' to women's 'dreaming of weddings' (Russell, S, 14, P). Girls meanwhile depicted themselves as having 'self-control' and being able to 'distinguish reality from make believe' (Krystal, S, 14, P). However, there was also a remarkable degree of concurrence between both genders, particularly about female virtues (for more on boys' idealisation of the feminine, see Frosh *et al.* 2002; Way 1997). Boys frequently stated that girls were 'easier to talk to' and could be more reliable sources of information on matters such as sex and relationships, although sometimes they 'hit you with rulers' for asking (Pierre, S 14, P). At times, some boys sounded almost wistful in describing female solidarity and physical ease with each other (exemplified, Seamus and Neville (N, 14, P) argued, by their habit of going to the toilet together, an option permanently denied to males). Girls, for their part, did concede that boys 'could be funny' (Kim, N, 12, P), and that for many girls, 'the sole topic of conversation is always the lads or the boyfriends, or the lads they like or the lads they split up with' (Flora, N 17, P). Perhaps such reaching out across the gender barricades consoled them for the fact that most of them – as we have seen in the previous chapter – assumed that their destinies would ultimately be entwined. If (as we will discuss later) they were prepared to admit the possibility of lesbian and gay relationships, most seemingly assumed their own lives would involve heterosexual relationships, often in the context of marriage, and procreation.

Young people's attempts to explain the causes and origins of such differences drew on a form of popular science, particularly relating to genetics and evolution. From this perspective, gender differences were designed to 'fit perpetuation of the species' (Jon, N, 17, P). Male activity and female passivity, so we were told, were hardwired into the brain: Phil (N, 12, P) explained that men had been 'programmed to do more' and Henry (N, 12, P) that 'in the wild ... the females had to like give off a scent or something and then sit there and wait for the male to come, to attract them so (...) the females attract the males and the males aren't actually designed to attract the females'. We were assured that it had 'actually been on the news' that girls evolve to become 'naturally more sensible' (Ethan, N, 12, G). Trevor (N, 17, P) argued that 'men and women like neurologically are more or less completely different and (their) brains work in different ways'. Jeff (N, 17, P) suggested that 'going down to a molecular level they're made up from chromosomes... They're two different things aren't they? Which is the base for what we're created on'. Caitlin (N, 12, P) related how she had quizzed her art teacher about why they studied so few male nudes, only to be told that women were inherently 'more elegant and beautiful or something like that'. Women's greater maturity and sense of responsibility was held to derive from their 'maternal instinct' that inevitably meant that the consequences for a woman if she got pregnant were more serious than for a man. More generally, many accounted for their own actions as teenagers in terms of 'developmental stages' and 'hormonal changes' that held them in their grip. These made women prey to moodiness and unpredictability; while men were driven to the male machismo that Trevor (N, 17, P) held was 'more of a hormonal and neurological thing than anything else'.

Such deterministic accounts – omitting any reference to socially structured distributions of power, for example – would seem conservative and pessimistic about the possibilities of change. Yet, unsurprisingly, the stories they told of their everyday lives suggested a more confused or fractured picture. In the first place, they identified inconsistencies and often exempted themselves or their friends from the gendered polarities they otherwise claimed to be true. Trevor (N, 17, P) distanced himself from hegemonic masculinity, declaring 'I don't consider myself a man', while Krystal and Holly (S, 14, P) praised one of their male friends for being the almost unimaginable, 'a straight version of Graham Norton'. Girls described boys who would read their teenage magazines and Jay indicated that Richard (S, 17, P) had talked to him about his relationship almost to the point of tedium. Caitlin (N, 12, P) argued that 'some boys are just like, feel the same way as girls' and pondered whether she was perhaps herself 'a boy really' because she wrestled with her brother and played his computer games. As this implies, there was a plurality of femininities and masculinities on display amongst our sample.

Secondly, much of what they said supported Judith Butler's argument that gendered and sexual identities are 'performative', about *doing* rather than *being*. That is, that they are brought into being and consolidated through repeated acts, rather than already-existing identities that can be simply 'reported on' (Butler 1990; 1991). Consider, for example, this description given by Courtney (N, 12, P) of the rituals in which girls might engage in the morning before leaving for school:

> We're all trying to make their image look as best as they can. Like in a morning when you get up, you brush your hair, you make sure your face looks nice and you put your skirt on and you straighten yourself up so you've not got any dirty marks down your jumper. You don't come to school with your hair like a rats' nest and like your face is all pale and you've got your skirt on the wrong way and you've got a big dirty great big mark down your jumper and – you don't wanna come to school looking like that – and a big ladder in your tights do you. (...) You wanna come as best as you can, don't you. So you don't want to make yourself look as ugly as you can, do you. (...) Even people who haven't got a boyfriend, they're always trying to impress the lads as much as they can aren't they. I mean I admit to doing that but I don't really go up to a lad acting all goofy and sad and everything ...

Courtney's first sentence suggests that acquiring the collective identity of a girl – becoming a 'we' – requires learning to see oneself as a 'they', from the outside, as an object of potential desire and scrutiny. It is also produced through a bodily performance and discipline that requires sustained attention to myriad details of dress, acts, behaviours and gestures. Eventually it is inscribed on the body; in how one holds oneself – how you 'straighten yourself up' – how one addresses others, particularly the opposite sex, and so on. The 'personal is political' here, in that power permeates even the most intimate relationship, the one a woman has with her body. Even so, there is a delicate balancing act between doing it well and getting it wrong, being 'goofy and sad'. Courtney's insistent repetition of 'you don't want to' and 'you want to' conveys that gender is articulated through desires that come to seem natural – girls really want to be girls, to do what girls do. Yet it contains within it a command or threat, the echoes of other voices (parental admonitions and the like), that enforce such identities coercively. It creates both fear and desire for what is disallowed – as Courtney, in her third and final interview, played distractedly with the ladders on her tights until they were shredded, as if drawn to precisely what she had earlier denounced.

Similarly, when Caitlin (N, 12, P), cited above, expressed doubts about her gender, her friend Heather supportively searched for evidence of Caitlin's true 'girlness' not in the 'facts' of biology but in acts and desires, by claiming 'but you still like to go out in your nice clothes. You still like to do things like that, don't you?'. She may barely have been reassured, however, by Caitlin's response that 'I hate my nice clothes'.

In the last chapter, we saw how gender and (hetero)sexual identities were explicitly enforced by institutions such as the school and family. In conversation, vocabularies too were used to establish sexual hierarchies and police behaviour. Interviewees explained how girls who were into football or computer games were 'weirdoes' or 'tomboys' (a term generally used with a negative valency, although older girls were able to reclaim it). Those who had vowed to remain 'virgins' (which in their terms, meant choosing not to kiss boys) were picked on in the playground. Non-normative forms of sexuality were termed 'sick' or 'perverted' – although as we discuss below, this term did not apply, as it might have done in the past, simply to lesbian and gay sexualities per se.

In later chapters, we will see how the younger boys in particular anxiously and repeatedly asserted heterosexual desire and exhibited what Sedgwick terms 'homosexual panic' (Sedgwick 1990). They insisted on their interest only 'in the girls not the boy' when looking at sexual scenes on television, prefaced statements about male images by insisting 'I'm not gay or anything' and even expressed concern that merely looking at images of men might make them 'turn gay'. Ultimately such declarations served to suggest the fragility of heterosexuality, that it might be so easily overturned by the simple act of 'looking'. But homophobia may be seen as part of the regulation of the homosocial (all-male) bonds that structure public, heterosexual culture. Thus on the one hand, it was clear that many of the children we spoke to led largely gender-segregated lives, even within their co-educational schools. Whilst misogyny ensured that boys were frequently dismissive of women's or 'girlie' culture, particularly in all-male discussion groups, homophobia served to police all boys with the threat of violence and shame if they engaged in any behaviours or expressed feelings that might be thought 'gay'.

Nonetheless, it is important to note that our interviewees' performances of gender were shaped by the context of our research. Pierre (S, 14), for example, elaborated in all three interviews and alongside his friend Dale, a particular version of 'hegemonic masculinity' (Connell 2000) defined primarily by a willingness to objectify and 'shag' women. Most of his contributions were aimed at underscoring his hot-blooded heterosexuality, for instance declaring which female celebrities were 'minging' or 'fit', fantasising circumstances in which he might 'bone' a teacher, proclaiming the pleasures of watching characters 'getting laid' in *Sex And The City* and reporting how he would disrupt lessons by posing questions about girls one would 'bang'. He was evasive about his emotions, parodying the interviewers and himself, often challenging the 'moral' tone to our questions. However, he also presented a more vulnerable self-image than he may have consciously intended. Transcripts of his interviews reveal repeated fantasies of pain and humiliation. A discussion of navel piercing led him to speculate about penis piercing ('a nail going through your jap. Ohh!'); talk about buying condoms provoked comments on being embarrassed by female shop assistants: 'you see a girl at in the counter, you give her it, she will look at it or start smiling or just laugh – you would be like "Oh my god" and you think "bitch, slag"'. In the context of a pair interview with Dale and Sara, he came across as less certain and tough. In a long discussion about how boys might resolve any problems they might have, he provided the example of 'having a problem with your todger ... can't get it up,' as if only mechanical failures of masculinity could be imagined. He and Dale explained how boys would have to 'get pissed' to share a problem with a male friend, would laugh heartily if they were the recipients of such confidences, and would direct friends to talk to their girlfriend or to go to the doctor rather than giving them advice themselves. They painted in all a picture of isolated boys with few resources or places of safety to call on. Whilst for Sedgwick and other analysts homophobia and hegemonic masculinity allow access to the privileges of homosociality, it was hard to see at this stage precisely what gains this offered for some boys.

The media's role

In many mainstream discussions of gender construction, the media figure primarily as sources of negative stereotypes and limiting images of masculinity and femininity imposed on young people (e.g. Moore and Rosenthal 1993). By contrast we see them as resources, on which young people draw in an ongoing, active construction of gendered identities. As Ien Ang argues, 'it is in and through the very practices of media consumption – and the positionings and identifications they solicit – that gender identities are recursively shaped, while those practices themselves undergo a process of gendering along the way' (Ang 1996). The media act as resources in various ways. In one straightforward sense, media texts provided evidence for interviewees' assertions about the biological or genetic determination of gender difference of the kind described above. Documentaries and the news were cited here, as well as an article that had appeared in *Sugar* magazine at the time of our interviews, entitled 'Inside the mind of a male virgin', which claimed that teenage boys' thoughts are dominated by sex. But they also provided evidence to contest such claims – such as a storyline in *Hollyoaks* where a father's 'maternal instinct' to care for his baby proved stronger than the mother's.

More broadly, the media provide (some) young people with categories of self-definition around which to mobilise and negotiate, to claim as their own or disrupt. They allow them to play with identity and to learn to 'do' boy or girl. When Caitlin, above, argues that she is a 'really a boy' because she prefers media that are gendered masculine, she indicates that choices of media do not simply express pre-existing gender identities, although for many it may have seemed that way. In the research, young people were able to constitute themselves as certain types of people through the attitudes they expressed towards particular stars, genres and programmes. A sense of gender-appropriateness ran through many discussions. Thus, Izzie (S, 12, G) argued that boys could not buy girls' magazines or they would 'look like poofs'. Like many others, Ethan and Seth (N, 12, P) argued that 'watching stuff about love and sex is more of a woman thing' and that 'women like romance, men like action and shooting'. (Such arguments persisted despite the fact that the boys were talking to a male interviewer who had seen most of the 'chick flicks' they mentioned and a female one who hadn't.)

Young people also learn to engage with or interpret media in gender-specific ways. Assertions that boys would watch particular pop videos with their 'tongues hanging out' or would 'laugh' at girls' magazines where girls would be 'serious', did not just reflect what actually happened. They also acted as injunctions about what *should* be the case – an issue to which we return in Chapter 8, when we consider how such 'reading formations' (Bennett 1983) are developed within the family.

Our young participants also policed their tastes in the context of the particular groups in which they were interviewed. For instance, when Richard (S, 17, G) referred disdainfully to *As If*, a Channel 4 drama centring on the tangled sex lives of a group of young people including two gay men, as 'that gay thing', Jay subsequently specified that he liked it but 'not the gay characters, all the rest of it', disavowing any suggestion that its gay content could be a source of appeal. Some interviewees criticised the dissembling of media tastes that they identified in their peer groups:

Eve (N, 17, P): But the critics assume that guys aren't gonna like [romantic comedies].

Ceri: And they do, cause like we go watching these films with big groups and I'll sit there with a lad next to me and he will just laugh all the way through it but then they'll say 'oh yeah I didn't like that.' You know. 'Yeah you did. I saw you. You're lying!'

David: Right. So there's what people enjoy and then there's what they say about what they enjoy.

Eve: Yeah, I mean, if you get to know people well then they'll eventually say 'oh yeah'. You know that they like stuff even when they're hiding it. So it's just funny. So – don't go hiding it, we know you liked it!

Eve's last comment suggests a public–private divide in terms of what preferences can be admitted, urging an audience beyond the interview to be more 'true' to themselves. Yet, as Hermes remarks, it is perfectly possible for any of us (including critics) to take pleasure in material of which we may elsewhere be equally genuinely critical – without either version being less 'authentic' (Hermes 1995).

A place to speak from?

Within the context of the project, some media acted as resources that gave participants a 'place to speak from' about gender, with confidence and pleasure. The lengthy diary-cum-scrapbook – 'my personal and complete views on the situation' – produced by Krystal (S, 14), for instance, deserves closer analysis. It drew on some of the conventions of the diary form, such as daily entries, address to a reader, claims to transparency ('honesty is what this book and project is about') and self-revelation ('my favourite 2 films have to be (ready 4 this) *The Little Mermaid* and *Cruel Intentions*. I'm such a baby! Ryan Philippe rules oh yeah'). But it also owed a lot to the conventions of teenage magazines in its layout – short 'soundbites' interspersed with icons of hearts and flowers and doodles, the use of colour to highlight key statements, a conversational style and immediacy of voice ('Newsflash 3, watching *Neighbours* the *ugliest* baby has just been born'). On one page ('My beliefs') she set out a variety of questions, opinions and statements, as if in response to an imaginary interview: 'why is love always so perfect or totally shame ridden on television?', 'I believe that stars should have a right to tell the press to BACK OFF their business (but I want to be a reporter so don't get the right too quick!)', 'Why are girls mainly the softer sex?'. The advantage of this 'youth magazine' style may have been that it enabled her to explore a range of contradictory feelings and views without enforcing closure. On other pages, she invited her friends to contribute, in order (as she put it) to 'give you an idea of things we talk about and the influence I'm under every day'. This produced the effect of a series of 'vox pop' views on men and the media, along with requests for Gareth Gates to 'call me' and for Josh Hartnett to 'die'. This was not the voice of passive 'romance' as identified in earlier girls' magazines (McRobbie 1991), but an active, self-conscious, reflective one, playing delightedly both with identity and with the literacies acquired from immersion in teenage girls' culture ('most things we talk about have to do with the coolest boy on TV, the hottest guy in the magazine, coolest song on the radio and the hot, hot, hot film and pop starz'). Some analysts see youth audiences as passively acquiescing in gender identities pre-packaged for them by the media. By contrast, Krystal's familiarity with media conventions gives her a place to speak from, to develop a confident, collective speaking voice that is able to articulate forms of desire or 'girl power'.

However, it is also worth noting that the media do not serve all equally in this respect. Pierre's diary, for example, ran to little over a

Fig. 4.1   Extract from Krystal's (S, 14) diary

page in which he noted that he lived with his mother, that his father had died when he was young, and that he loved football. It then petered out, as if refusing the practices of self-revelation and individuation that the diary format required. Similarly, Lee (N, 12) was – on her teachers' accounts – extremely keen to be involved in the project, and her written work showed considerable effort and serious attention to the task. We were therefore struck by how hard she seemed to find it to be forthcoming in her diary. At one point, taking up our invitation to write about 'what you like', she wrote 'Now, I'm not writing about Media, I am writing about just today, Pancake Day. I am writing about what I like and well I just love pancakes'. She was also extremely quiet in the interviews. Her interest in participating in the research may have indicated that love, sex and relationships were pertinent issues for her. However, as a girl who was passionate about football, uninterested in 'girlie' culture and described herself as 'not a romantic type', her dilemma may have been that the dominant discourses available to her did not give her a position from which to speak as they may have done for Krystal, for example.

Images of the self

Our arguments so far suggest that young people fashion different 'styles' of femininity and masculinity through their investments in media texts, and through their presentation of these choices and readings in their diaries and interviews. For instance, there were marked disparities in responses to 'chick flicks' such as *Bridget Jones's Diary*, *Shallow Hal*, *The Wedding Singer*, *Runaway Bride*, *What Women Want* and women-oriented programmes such as *Ally McBeal*. Many younger boys had seen some of these films on video, perhaps reflecting their lack of power to determine media choices within the family, or the fact that such films may have been considered 'safe' material for family viewing. However, Rory's (N, 10, P) account of *The Wedding Singer* focused on a fight scene rather than the romantic ending. Leo and Clint (S, 10, P), who were self-consciously developing a style of masculinity defined in opposition to femininity, confined their recollection of *Bridget Jones's Diary* to a scene in which she had worn a 'transparent top'. Offering such a reading distanced them from 'feminine' interpretations focused on romance and reclaimed the text for an objectifying male gaze. Older boys had seen such films on collective, mixed outings to the cinema, but also expressed distaste for them. Trevor (N, 17, P) claimed not to have been 'paying much attention' to

Bridget Jones's Diary, but (in a typical move within 'critical' discourses) claimed to identify its potential negative effects: 'I can understand how the film sympathises with the way a lot of people feel about that sort of thing, but as a role model I think she's like ... She's being sympathetic to people failing but she's also in a way encouraging it saying "Oh it's all right if you're gonna get into loads of failing, pathetic relationships, 'cause I did and they made a film about me!"'. Similarly, for Adrian (N, 17, P), *Sex and the City*'s focus on shopping and consumerism were deemed sufficient grounds to dismiss it altogether. Fans of the programme were equally aware of this but claimed to find other pleasures within it.

Awareness of male contempt for such texts may have only reinforced their usefulness for some girls in maintaining their gender identity. Their accounts suggested that they found them useful in addressing fears and offering imaginary solutions, in ways that both confirmed existing beliefs about gender relations and consoled them. For instance, *Shallow Hal*, where a man is put under a spell that means he sees only 'inner beauty' and not his girlfriend's actual obesity, appeared to confirm Krystal and Holly's (S, 14, P) pessimistic view that men are 'as shallow as a puddle' and simultaneously to hold out a comforting 'message' about 'personality not looks' – 'It actually shows a man realising that it's not just about their body, it's about what they're like underneath' (Krystal S 14, P). Likewise, *Ally McBeal* showed, according to Flora (N, 17, P), that 'there is somebody out there for somebody' and held a message about 'waiting for the right person' although she added (switching again into critical mode) that 'that's not a good thing to teach, is it, because ... you could be waiting forever if you wait for that one person'.

Girls often presented their relationship with preferred texts in terms of identification with a character. Flora (N, 17, P) remarked of *Ally McBeal* that she was like Ally in being 'a bit gone in the head'. Krystal (S, 14, P) claimed an identification at the level of both professional career and fantasy life:

> I always wanted to be a lawyer or a journalist when I grow up and she makes it so fun and the way she's hallucinating things like most people do, it's like, you wouldn't think about it, but, you always, say, have an argument with someone, you imagine punching in their face but you'd never really do it. (...) She does that all the time and she imagines dancing babies and all that and I do all the time.

Similarly, Lisa and Kelly (N, 14, P) claimed that *Bridget Jones's Diary* was a transparent reflection of themselves as women:

> Lisa: She tells the truth on everything really. (...) it's like how we actually act in life and it like shows like, like a thong and like, some like massive knickers (...) she's like trying to keep her bum in and things like that.
> Kelly: It's like she resembles all women and you know it shows what all women are like (...) 'Cause they are all ... Mostly, like, self-conscious and everything
> Lisa: (...) you see how we react to things, don't you, and you see how women actually think of life, and it is quite good to watch.
> Kelly: It makes you feel that you're not the only one who's conscious about the way you are or it makes you think that other people are feeling the same way as well.

Such claims to wholesale identification and absorption into the world of a text might seem to endorse Trevor's warning, above, about the dangers of inappropriate role models. However, the girls discussed their relationships with these texts with laughter. In the case of Lisa and Kelly, this was addressed both to each other and to Sara as interviewer. They suggest that such texts are not to be taken so seriously; that they feed fantasies, not actions in the real world (cf. Hermes 1995). They offer a chance to 'try on' other identities in fantasy (Friedberg 1993), as a rehearsal for what being an adolescent girl or an adult woman involves. As Hermes (op. cit.) suggests of women's magazines, in the process, they also help one to feel connected to others, clarify feelings (of self-consciousness or vengefulness, for example), give meaning to problems and experiences that may have been felt to be an individual burden or not named at all. As a result, the media might be seen to proliferate rather than curtail identities.

Moreover, audiences identify with partial objects not with the whole; or, as Phoebe (N, 14, P) does in her description of her 'favourite bit' in *Bridget Jones's Diary*, disperse themselves across a scene of fantasy (cf. Cowie 1990):

> When they're on the river ... And he [Colin Firth] is thinking like, he's with this boring person going on about Law and all this lot when she's over there with the other guy, just laughing her head off. And he wants that but he's with this other miserable woman. She just thinks work, work, work.

Without claiming an unduly intimate knowledge of Phoebe, one might speculate that this scene – including the male characters as well as the female – dramatises different aspects of Phoebe herself. As many participants reminded us, their lives as students involved conflicts between their duties or commitment to 'work, work, work', and their desire for fun and relaxation; in learning about sex, as we saw in the previous chapter, they were caught between injunctions to be responsible and to maximise sexual enjoyment. The scene Phoebe describes dramatises and resolves such conflicts, associating women temporarily with a disruptive principle of laughter and pleasure.

Of course, not all girls shared these positive responses to such films – Phoebe's friend Naomi condemned *Bridget Jones's Diary* (2001) as 'pathetic' in much the same terms as boys. Some texts, meanwhile, appeared to offer reading positions to both male and female audiences. *American Pie* (1999) was one example here. For Chantel (N, 14, P), it gave insights into what she saw as 'other worlds' and she described watching it to learn about boys: 'what they talk about when girls aren't around and stuff! So, it's really funny to hear that sort of thing. And then like what they feel like and like how nervous they are and stuff! [laughing]'. In this respect, such films seem to have something in common with the problem pages discussed in Chapter 6. Jacob's (N, 14) account of watching *American Pie* on a Friday night after his birthday bears comparison to Phoebe's investment in the *BJD* scene. In his diary he wrote 'it's lots of scenes of sex, nudity and partying, and it's the same as what teenagers do and it's really great'. The issue is not how closely it resembled Jacob's actual life but the media's powerful capacity to offer modes of feeling and utopian impulses in the scenes they portray. *Sex and the City* was another example that was popular with both (older) boys as well as girls and was readily construed by both as a means to learn about the opposite sex and about specific issues (testicular cancer was mentioned by both Jon (N, 17, P) and Jay (S, 17, P)). The enthusiastic descriptions of dilemmas portrayed and the learning offered by such texts contrasted vividly with what many interviewees perceived as the one-dimensional moralism of sex education lessons at school – or even in more mainstream media such as soap operas (see Chapters 3 and 7).

Further, a text like *Sex and the City* gave the girls, particularly, ways of thinking about themselves; discussions were often dominated by debates about which of them were like which character from the programme. When, for example, Nancy and Olivia (S, 17, P) agreed on the former's similarity to Samantha, they drew on the kinds of psychological concepts and language popularised within the show's self-help style:

> Olivia: It's very hard to break her [Nancy's] barrier ...
> Nancy: (...) Definitely. I think I'm sort of, scared of commitment in a way.

In another interview, Luisa and Leigh (P, 13, P) described their friends as if they were all characters from an imaginary teen drama:

> Luisa: Cause I know this is a bit stupid (...) there's like a whole crew of us –
> Leigh: – Yeah like we're all the best friends.
> Luisa: (...) I think we've all got different things which we're all –
> Leigh: Care for each other.
> Luisa: So I mean there's Avril, you can talk to her whenever you want, and there's Kay she's a laugh you know.
> Leigh: And then there's Tatum who's nice and she'll like understand, (...) and then there's Laura who's –
> Luisa: She's just ... fun and she's really nice.
> Leigh: Yeah. And then there's me.
> Sara: So you've all got your different kind of roles in the group.
> Leigh: And I can keep a secret and Luisa is just a good friend to talk to.
> Luisa: And I'm – If anyone wants anything told I'm the person to come and see!

Spectacular masculinities?

Inevitably, we had a particular agenda of texts we saw as relevant to the issue of love, sex and relationships, such as soap operas. Perhaps because these are often seen as 'feminine', some boys claimed to be uninterested or not knowledgeable about many of the programmes we tried to discuss. As a result, we may have overlooked other texts or forms that were salient for boys in particular and which do raise issues of love, sex and relationships. An interesting example here is wrestling (another might be the more recent genre of 'men behaving dangerously' as in *Jackass*, a programme described by Jeff (N, 17, D) as 'the finest art ever made'). Few boys discussed wrestling in relation to the theme, although for Sebastian (N, 14, P), it was the only genre about which he became animated in his first interview. Since those who did assured us that it was very popular with their peers, we might assume that watching World Wrestling Federation (now World Wrestling Experience or WWE) was more common for boys in our sample than our findings suggested. Wrestling is a neglected mass form in cultural analysis, generally held to be tasteless or unredeemable. It is therefore not surprising that we ourselves marginalised it to some extent in our project.

Nonetheless, it would seem to have much to say about sexuality and gender relations, particularly given its increasing emphasis on narrative and relationships in the 'behind the scenes' sequences that are interspersed with the actual bouts. Kurt (P, 13, G) commented that it 'kind of like turns into a soap opera more every day'. Joseph (S, 12, P) described it as 'wrestling with drama', in which, despite the emphasis on spectacle, narrative discontinuity could be irritating ('They were meant to get divorced. They went away for a couple of months and they came back and they seemed as happy as ever. They didn't explain what happened'). The narratives lack closure, since the roles of hero and bad guy are interchangeable over time. Wesley's (S, 12, P) account emphasised its knockabout, comic humour and preposterous violence: 'the men are in the ring and the other person gets chucked out the ring and his girlfriend's out there trying to beat him up. And she gets hurt and he kind of ends up beating up the other man'. Joseph (S, 12) described in his diary how 'the character Triple H was meant to renew his marriage vows to his pregnant wife Stephanie, but his mother in law sent a video showing that she was not pregnant. Triple H then went out and smashed everything in sight, including his father-in-law. He also knocked his wife to the ground and then knocked her out.' In the interview, he explained that Stephanie had not been punched, but rather 'shoved' and that 'because it's wrestling she stays down'. The conventions of wrestling, that is, meant that its violence was clearly to be distinguished from the 'realistic' domestic violence shown for example in *EastEnders*. Instead, he insisted that it was really 'mind games'.

According to their accounts, wrestling offered an antagonistic and instrumental view of personal relationships: 'You marry the wrong people and sometimes – sometimes it's just marry for money really' (Joseph). Females figured as tricksters and as powerful agents within these stories. For instance, ex-wives would get vengeance by teaming up with opponent wrestlers. Wrestling puts the male body (and male anger) on display and makes a spectacle of masculine pain and humiliation. It savages codes of decorum and middle-class ideas about sexuality, albeit within a framework of iconoclastic humour that renders moral schemas irrelevant. Constance Penley suggests that like other 'white trash' forms such as porn, it may express and form changing ideas and anxieties about sexuality and sexual roles, and even act as a resource for countercultural ideas about them (Penley 1997). We would suggest that – like some other 'masculine' genres – it is deserving of closer study in this context. In Chapter 6, we also note parallels that critics have drawn between wrestling and 'new wave' talk shows.

'Living the life': consumption and gender identities

According to Nikolas Rose, the neo-liberal 'consumer cultures' that have emerged in industrialised societies over the past few decades offer new understandings of the self (Rose 1999b; c). Rose discusses the rise of ideas of 'active citizenship' and how the celebration of values of choice, autonomy and self-realisation in contemporary western society have produced individuals who are 'capable of bearing the burdens of liberty' in advanced democracies (Rose 1999b). Yet he argues that such notions also generate the 'commitment of selves to the values and forms of life supported by authorities', particularly those of consumption. 'It is through the promotion of 'lifestyle' by the mass media, by advertising and by experts, through the obligation to shape a life through choices in a world of self-referenced objects and images, that the modern subject is governed' (Rose 1999b: 261). This analysis is particularly pertinent in considering how the media invite young viewers to imagine or construct themselves as particular kinds of selves or sexual beings.

The notion of self-creation through consumption was evident in the pictures of products (food and drink as well as make up, shoes and clothes) and media stars that featured prominently in several of the diaries and scrapbooks. It was also apparent in some interviews. For instance, Lisa and Kelly (N, 14) testified to the importance of shopping ('I don't think I could live without shopping'): they argued that 'the topic [of love, sex and relationships] also has a lot to do with clothes' and explained the relative merits of 'trackie lads', 'smoothies' or 'rough types', each defined by their dress style. Whilst youth culture may have placed an importance on consumption since its postwar 'invention', this may have been intensified in recent times and extended its hold on men as consumers (Nixon 1996). As we will see particularly in Chapter 5, both boys and girls referred to masculine physical ideals (particularly the 'six pack') as well as feminine ones. The worked-on muscular body appeared to symbolise other ideals that are arguably typical of recent consumer culture, such as willpower, self-discipline and self-control (cf. Jagger 1998; 2001).

One participant, Ed (P, 17), exemplified the new kinds of relations to the self that analysts have argued are encouraged by trends towards consumerism (see Gauntlett 2002) – although he was one of the few who did so overtly. In his diary, he offered a witty portrait of untrammelled adolescent desires, drawing on a range of styles and genres (such as text-messaging):

> By ten mins b4 I'm supos 2 B round me m8s house im nt redy. This new txtn is making me go crazy (....) I go to the library and read a magazine and see a pair of amazing puma trainers, 30 minutes later I have been to town and bought them (....) another advertisement is seen, this is of smoking and I have a craving for my pack of Marlboro lights. I have one as I get off the train (....) Stay round my friend's house I have known her for a few weeks through working @ H&M. So one thing led to another and I didn't get much sleep. Stayed up all night went straight to work (....) I see a man holding a well nice mobile phone which is smaller than the 8210 which I have I want it

In his interviews he offered lively justifications of his interest in men's style magazines such as *FHM*, along with overviews of their differentiated target audiences (as he did also for porn magazines). Moreover, his self-stylisation involved some interesting departures from traditional masculinity – such as an interest in fashion, or an ability to comment on the desirability of male figures such as Robbie Williams, whom he described as 'sweet'. His self-ironising but highly developed 'art of living' (or in his terms, 'living the life') through consumption depends, of course, on a relatively high level of disposable income.

In turn, this might suggest that those who lack access to such material resources will find it harder to survive in such consumer-oriented times. Redefining citizenship as access to consumption excludes those who are economically 'unprofitable'; arguably, however, it also requires a reconstruction of masculinity. Here, some boys' affective investment in traditional forms of masculinity (termed by Pfeil (1995) a 'warrior' or 'heroic' masculinity) that aggressively insist on invulnerability, individualism and 'knowing it all' do not serve them well. In discussing a 'guide to kissing' in a girls' magazine, for example, Wesley, (S, 12, G) insisted that such teaching should not be necessary for boys. 'It's a boy!' he exclaimed, 'He should already know how to turn a girl on, and nibble and all!'. Such ideals of masculinity may be self-limiting in a world that defines the self as always incomplete and requiring continuous work.

'Shall I pretend to be gay?' – the cultural chic and contemporary meanings of 'being gay'

As we argued in Chapter 1, consumer culture legitimises a wider range of sexual identities, forms and subjects, other than heterosexual, as potential target markets. In the process, gay and lesbian people become objects of consumer curiosity and knowledge claims. Yet we should be wary of assuming that this necessarily marks a new stage of sexual liberation that opens up new possibilities in terms· of gendered and sexual identities.

It was noteworthy that all our interviewees demonstrated a familiarity and confidence with the categories of lesbian and gay – whether as sexual populations represented in the media or as putative audiences for particular texts. This extended throughout the age range – for instance, Alma (S, 10, P) recounted how her six-year-old sister had chanted 'Gypsy is lezzie, Gypsy is gay' after seeing a lesbian storyline on *Home and Away*, and that she 'knew what a lesbian is'. Rory (N, 10, P) discussed how, in *2000 Acres of Sky*, a character had responded to the revelation that his father was gay. All claimed to have 'got' jokes about lesbianism and gayness in the episodes of *Friends* we gave them. As we shall see in Chapter 8, taking a position on gay issues proved an important aspect of many parents' self-definitions of themselves as parents.

Participants tended to hold what Sedgwick (1990) terms a 'minoritizing' view, in which sexuality is a matter of inborn essential identity, and sexual desire is fixed in terms of an either/or choice (that is, either for same-sex or for opposite-sex partners). For instance, Eve (N, 17, P) argued 'you can't encourage gay people to be straight. They never – even if they had a wife and three kids, they still wouldn't actually be straight would they? They'd still be gay.' Sedgwick contrasts such views with the 'universalising' one that would see sexual desire as a continuum, or as configured differently in different cultural contexts. Nonetheless homosexuality (and sometimes bisexuality) was nameable, at least as seen as a distinct category of person, defined by same-sex desire. It may have been peripheral, but it was symbolically central to imaginings of the self and identity (cf. Stallybrass and White 1986).

I just believe that the media put much enthasis on deciate, infidelity and break ups. This leaves us with the feeling of no hope.

^ ^ ^ ^ ^ ^ ^ ^ ^ ^ ^ ^

I bought 2 top teenage magazines, including Bliss and Sugar. I found this particular headline made me think about the pressure on teenage girls to be attracted to teenage boys. I never noticed until a friend of mine confided in me and told me that she believed she was gay, how much enthusiasm is put on the idyllic boy girl relationship. She told me about how hard it was for her with all the media expectations. I guess for me it was a social norm girls fancy boys and vice versa, even though a close friend of the family is gay and I have had a very open up bringing.
I've found that the media projects a certain amount of insecurity due to the high-pitched story lines of betrayal, deceit and so on.

"I use girls"

"I'm single and happy with it"

I think these two women who are lovers are ok to be in newspaper because they are happy together and if their happy their happy. ✓ ☺

Fig.4.2 a and b Many young people reflected on lesbian and gay images (or their absence) in the media, such as (a) Nancy (S, 17) and (b) Tina (S, 10)

We do not have evidence in our research about how self-identified lesbian or gay teenagers related to media depictions of love, sex and relationships. No young person in the project was prepared explicitly to name themselves as lesbian or gay. However, given the numbers who participated, it is likely that several were already, or would come out later in their lives, and that many more would have same-sex sexual experience of some kind. Moreover, some older lesbians in a parent focus group reminisced about the importance of media figures – such as Kate Jackson ('the dark one' in *Charlie's Angels*) or Madonna – with whom they had identified in building a nascent lesbian identity as teenagers. They indicated that the media may provide resources for building alternative sexual identities that are not otherwise available, as other critics have argued (Dyer 1993; Whatling 1997).

However, we can comment on the varied meaning of lesbian and gay sexualities. As we have already observed, and explore further in other chapters, younger children, boys in particular, exhibited 'homosexual panic' in discussion of media images and more general issues. 'Gay' seemed to serve here as a catch-all term denoting something to be feared, that was used to police their own and others' behaviours and statements.

By contrast, asserting support for gay rights and gay identities was a distinctive feature of interviews with the older teenagers, particularly the middle-class students, in the North and in the South East interviewed during the pilot stage of the project. (In Chapter 9 we will also see its importance for some of the mothers who took part in the focus groups). It is worth exploring what role these young people's declared attitudes to gay issues might play them in thinking about themselves and others.

In their diaries, several were critical of what they saw as a lack of gay representations in the media, or discussed those they had seen (such as *Ellen* or *Queer as Folk*), in generally approving terms. In interview, Chloe (N, 17, P) argued that 'if you show gay and lesbians and mixed marriages and all that kind of thing, I think they should show a bit more of that so people are aware that it happens'. They criticised 'compulsory heterosexuality' – Ceri (N, 17, P) remarked that in teenage magazines 'If you are unsure of your sexuality, then there is a lot of pressure to be heterosexual you know because like, oh you must go after boys (...) You never really see any, "No this is the alternative"'. They supported gay stars' right to come out – for instance, Eve (N, 17, P) defended George Michael – 'people are horrified that he was gay and it's just like, why? What is he doing to offend you at all? (...) I think that's really bad'. She went on:

> Eve: I think they should have the right to be gay and they should have stuff in the media that tells them that.
> Ceri: Yeah that it's ok to be gay. That you don't have to feel pressured or you don't have to feel like it's a secret. You know that you can be gay and everyone – and people will accept you. Obviously you're gonna catch some flak for it 'cause there are still intolerant people.

None of these participants discussed gay identity in terms of whether it was 'right' or 'wrong' according to predetermined traditional moralities. It seemed on these accounts to have become a question of ethics (of work on the self) – a matter of being 'honest' about yourself and accepting of your own gay identity in order to achieve fulfilment and happiness.

During one of the introductory talks about the diary, Trevor (N, 17) asked 'shall I pretend to be gay?' when writing it and whether if so he could be given more money to purchase the video of *Metrosexuality* (a Channel 4 fantasy-soap about the lives of a group of people of various sexualities and races). Combined with his remark in interview that he didn't think of himself 'as a man', one might identify the emergence here of new, anti-homophobic masculinities and femininities amongst these young people. Trevor's comments indicate a certain positive valency to gay identities – assuming as they do that such perspectives would be welcomed, politically desirable, perhaps even more valuable than those of straights. Perhaps in declaring them publicly, he sought to challenge normalising assumptions that might be made not only by us as interviewers, but also by his peer group. Yet at the same time, his question 'shall I pretend ... ' implies that same-sex desire is not present or readable unless a distinct, separate identity is adopted. It disavows Trevor's own 'gayness', in that if 'being gay' is the pretend identity, then his heterosexuality must be real; although of course, this could be a double bluff. It might erase the achievement that lesbian and gay identities represent, implying they are easy and optional, that one can 'be whoever one wants to be', without struggle – a view which existing research into lesbian and gay teenage experiences denies.

On our video, we gave the older teenagers an episode of *As If*, a Channel 4 drama revolving around a gay main character, presented in a 'youth' style. Their responses are discussed in more detail in

Chapter 7. Inevitably this produced further reflection amongst participants about their attitudes to gay and lesbian relationships in general, with many keen to convey their anti-homophobic stance.

> Harvey (N, 17, G): Well, I kind of know some gay people (…) and I know people who I don't know if they are straight or they are gay but you know it's only people who are outside that circle of friends who won't accept it. And I think if you have a group of friends where some of them are gay some of them aren't gay it's very unlikely that someone in that group of friends is gonna start a fight with them or something because they're gay. (…)
>
> Tom: (…) It's just like, I've got a friend who's Asian and he – I know it's not the same thing and it's about sex and that – but he's Asian and we all accept it and we can make jokes – not like racist jokes or anything but have a laugh – and he has a laugh with us.

Most of their talk was of how they accepted or supported homosexuality in others rather than finding it within themselves. Harvey's remarks suggest that discussion of sexuality – making decisions about what one 'is', taking a stance – is an important part of youth culture, openly debated within particular friendship groupings. For others, however, *As If* was also utopian – Lois (P, 17, G) argued that it showed life as she would like it to be rather than as it was, in the sense that its sexual tolerance and liberation was not as close to her daily experience as she would wish. As suggested above in discussing women's genres, media use can work at the level of fantasy rather than (or as much as) everyday experience. We might say that watching *As If* and other gay-themed shows helped these teenagers to feel part of a tolerant, inclusive community and provided opportunities to rehearse liberal versions of the self. Nevertheless, Tom's comparison with race issues reminds us that we do not have any evidence from within this project about how self-identified lesbian and gay teenagers experience this, just as we cannot know how amused Tom's Asian friend really is by the jokes made about his ethnicity.

However, these expressions of liberal tolerance had other social functions too. In the context of comparisons between *As If* and *Dawsons' Creek*, the style and stylishness of the former contributed to a view of Britishness as relatively sophisticated, ironic and so on (see Chapter 7). The depictions of non-normative sexualities and the supposed values of programmes like *As If*, *Metrosexuality* or *Queer as Folk* were also identified with a metropolitan vanguardism – a point we touched on in

Chapter 2. Jon (N, 17, G) remarked of *As If* in connection to a debate about how 'realistic' it was that 'I think in places like – that's set in London isn't it, like Soho or whatever – that sort of things like that are like that but I guess up here it's slow... It's slower and we just copy them'. Tom, in the same group, ironically compared the characters to 'us country folk!'. Thus the conversations turned to what sort of a place they lived in, and how it related to others. Recall that these interviews took place in a commuter suburb rather than an urban area; participants' points of comparison were both the more rural and the truly urban, although both were imaginary as much as 'real' landscapes. For instance, Eve compared the relative enlightenment of their suburb to villages 'in the middle of nowhere' with 'like three houses in it. And they just wouldn't... if someone were gay it would be like "Oh my god". And they just don't like it (...) They'd try and like herd them out the village or summat'. Trevor related how some young people he had met 'down south' near Oxford had been shocked that he had 'gay friends', and praised *Metrosexuality* for being 'quite, you know, metropolitan, the ideas, it wasn't a sort of classic get married and all that lot... It was a lot of cheating involved in it and it didn't necessarily portray it in a terrible way'. Geographical space, that is, is not a backdrop, but – in both its real and imaginary forms – shapes notions of sexual identity and is part of the spectacle, performance and regulation of sexuality (cf. Mort 2000). Here, the city signified as a set of radical, polysexual and cross-racial values. Approving of the programmes enabled these young people to invest in a 'metropolitan ideology' of sexual egalitarianism that erases differences of gender, sexuality and race, in favour of an ideology of harmony and assimilation (Sinfield 2000). 'Gay' here signifies as a set of consumption choices and a lifestyle category (Valocchi 1999), perhaps helped by the fact that the male lovers in *As If* were not marked as gay in any of the conventional ways (such as campness).

However, difference and hierarchies do not disappear altogether in these formulations; there was some evidence that they were instead displaced onto class identities. The students here agreed that their liberalism was enabled partly by their relatively privileged position of being in the sixth form. As Eve remarked: 'by the time you get to sixth form, all the stupid idiots have all left who are prejudiced so we can actually be open minded with things'. Prejudice here is seen as inhering in particular inadequate ('immature') individuals and is implicitly seen as characteristic of the working-class. When discussing talk shows, as will be seen in Chapter 6, this submerged class hostility became more overt and was encoded in venomous descriptions of the audiences and guests on talk shows (as 'inbreds' and the like). Where in the past it might have been the Victorians who figured as the foil for contemporary sexual progressivism (Mort 2000), here it is the working classes. Arguably, poor (white) trash is necessary as something against which 'civilised' whites can measure themselves (Newitz 1997).

Amongst our older teenage interviewees in Essex, by contrast, such anti-homophobic identities had less purchase. Although they were equally (and perhaps more) likely to state that they had gay work colleagues or gay relatives who were an established part of their family networks, fewer stated that they knew gay people in their friendship circles. Even older interviewees were less than politically correct in their language – referring to 'poofters' or 'queers', for example. Richard (S, 17, G) became quite angry in discussing *As If* (although perhaps goaded by the interviewer), claiming that it made him 'feel sick'.

There was a marked contrast between boys and girls, with girls noticeably more liberal on such issues – Nancy wrote at length in her diary about the absence of lesbian and gay relationships from teenage magazines, for instance. Girls themselves argued that homophobia was gendered. Della (S, 17, P) (whose 'boyfriend' in question is Richard) mused:

> I don't think a boy … I know my boyfriend wouldn't, he's really funny about it, he would never get changed in a changing room if he knew there was a gay boy in there. He just wouldn't do it for the fact that he'd have this feeling he was gonna rape him or something. He's really funny about it. Whereas if I was in a room or if Melissa turned round and said to me 'I'm a lesbian' I wouldn't not sit next to her. Like it wouldn't bother me to still sit next to her because I wouldn't think 'oh she's gonna like try to kiss me'. Boys seem to get really funny about it.

Melissa added that homophobia was an issue 'especially around here'. That is, she suggests it is not about individual psychology or prejudice, but an issue of culture. However, our findings too easily suggest an image of more prejudiced, less enlightened working-class young men. As with the middle-class young people above, it is worth exploring what gay identities signify and what uses homophobia serves in these contexts. In Chapter 2, we suggested that the differentials of power between interviewer and interviewee were starker in the Essex schools. It may have been that the programmes we gave them to view, and ourselves as interviewers, became identified with middle-class, professionalising, London-based or metropolitan values ('promoting homosexual awareness' as Richard (S, 17, G) put it). Whilst the northern young people embraced these, seeing in both the programmes and the values an intimation of what their future might hold, some of the male interviewees in Essex may have resented these values as (another) imposition of power from the centre. Perhaps 'homosexual awareness' became elided with other agents of professional control and expertise, imposed against their culture and values, and homophobia became a channel for resentment and a sense of class injuries (cf. Pfeil 1995). Their homophobia may thus express a grasp of – and a misdirected anger about – the fact that, despite an apparent extension of social tolerance, there had been no real shift in power relations in their own life experience.

Conclusion

Our evidence here suggests that the media, far from imposing unitary gendered identities on hapless audiences, are actively used to fashion a sense of self by the young people to whom we spoke. In many cases, they provide positive resources for developing understandings of themselves and of gender relations in contemporary society. The media do not put forward singular ideologies of gender and sexuality. In some cases, they appear to enable young people to challenge traditional norms of gender identity, such as female passivity or male disinterest in fashion; although we have noted the limits of this for particular groups or individuals. Moreover, it is clear from interviewees' varied readings of similar material that the media are only meaningful within practices of use and interpretation, which vary according to the cultural, social and economic circumstances in which young people live.

5
Bodies on Display – Pin-ups, Porn and Pop Stars

The public display of images of naked human bodies cannot be seen merely as a manifestation of our allegedly 'sexualised' modern culture. On the contrary, it has a very long history. Some of the earliest visual representations yet discovered feature images of the naked human form, clearly designed for the contemplative erotic gaze. The Victorian moral campaigners who covered over – and in some cases, defaced or damaged – such images evidently recognised as much.

Yet the display of bodies in painting and sculpture – and within the specialised domain of museums and galleries – is generally mediated by its presentation as 'art'. The notion of 'art' invokes a philosophical discourse that justifies bodily display, for example in terms of arguments about beauty, nature and purity. Art somehow transcends the baser, carnal instincts; and to label an image as art rescues it from the possibility that it might produce a merely physical response. By contrast, the display of the body in advertising images or newspapers or music videos is rarely defined as art – despite the protestations of some of their producers. Here, the display of the body is often seen as mere 'titillation' – or, in more directly critical terms, as a form of 'exploitation' or 'objectification'. Unlike 'art', which is seen to invite distanced contemplation, the degraded forms of the popular media are often seen to function on a much more directly physical level – of arousal, sensation and visceral thrills.

Thus, a distinction is frequently drawn between 'pornography' and 'erotica'. To some extent, this distinction appears to be a matter of taste or cultural value; although, according to many commentators, such distinctions have become much harder to sustain in our 'postmodern' times, as artists increasingly draw on the resources of popular culture, and vice-versa (Collins 1990). For media regulators, this distinction is partly perceived as a matter of authorial intention. The defining characteristic of pornography is generally seen to be its intention to produce sexual arousal: whereas erotica may deal with similar content, it is seen to do so in ways that are more diffuse and subtle – and, perhaps above all, less *physical*. However, there are self-evident problems in identifying the intention of a work, or in assuming that responses necessarily correspond to intentions: people can obviously be aroused by a whole range of material that does not necessarily 'intend' to arouse (Hunter *et al.* 1993). Ultimately, what lies behind such judgments are assumptions about the *effects* of such material on audiences. Indeed, the ultimate consideration for regulators appears to be whether such material is 'acceptable' for the potential target audience. Particular images or sequences can thus be justified for inclusion on the grounds that they would not cause offence to their audience; and so material might be deemed acceptable for some audiences but not for others. Yet how valid are such assumptions?

As we have implied, distinctions of this kind are becoming more and more difficult to sustain. The proliferation and increasing accessibility of media images; the blurring of boundaries between 'art' and popular culture; changing assumptions about audiences, particularly younger audiences; and the more general liberalisation of attitudes towards sexual representation sketched in Chapter 1 – all these have contributed to a growing uncertainty here. As the pornography industry continues to expand at a phenomenal rate, porn itself has become a popular topic for talk shows, documentaries and movies, and many visual artists now use pornographic imagery in their work (McNair 2002). Meanwhile, a greater frankness about sexual matters is increasingly deemed necessary, not just for the psychological health of individuals but also for the prevention of disease (most obviously in the wake of AIDS). Male bodies are now increasingly displayed in sexually-charged ways in the mainstream media, alongside female ones. Gay men and lesbians have been recognised as significant (and lucrative) 'niche' audiences, and gay and lesbian 'chic' has been seen to be marketable to mainstream consumers. As a result of these and other developments, it is now much more difficult to find an agreed basis for judgment about what is 'acceptable' and what is not – not least because different criteria seem to be applied in different contexts.

In this chapter, we explore the children's responses to these kinds of images, in advertising, in newspapers and magazines and on television. We look firstly at their attitudes towards 'pin-up' images, ranging from the 'Page 3' models in daily newspapers through to pornography itself. We then consider their responses to a series of advertisements featuring naked or semi-naked bodies; and finally we look at their readings of sexual images in music videos. Some of this was material that we introduced, but none of it was especially unfamiliar to them. Indeed, several children chose to write about this kind of material in their diaries (and in some cases, to paste in copious quantities of it).

Three broad themes or discourses can be traced across these accounts. First, there are questions of *propriety* – that is, moral debates about what is 'decent' to display, particularly in public settings (for example, on advertising billboards). This discourse frequently entails judgments about psychological 'normality': those who violate accepted standards of propriety are often described as 'sick' – that is, psychologically warped or perverse. This discourse can also invoke popular theories of media effects. 'Indecent' images are seen to have psychologically damaging consequences for those who are deemed to be particularly vulnerable or impressionable. Like adults, the children whom we interviewed frequently expressed concern about the role of such material in the premature sexualisation of 'little children' – or alternatively, expressed the view that its primary appeal was to 'dirty old men'. In this respect, judgments about propriety often entail a 'performance of age': they represent claims about one's own maturity, generally in relation to others who are deemed to be less mature. However, as we shall see, there were also significant differences between younger and older children in terms of what they perceived as 'sexual' in the first place.

Secondly, there are questions of *ideology*. Here, we can identify arguments about what these images 'say' – or what messages they convey – about men's and women's roles (in personal relationships, or in society more broadly), and about how they should behave towards each other. This discourse can entail a critique of sexism, and of the 'objectification' of the female body in the media, that was particularly prevalent among some feminists in the 1970s and 1980s – although it should be noted that this kind of criticism was often prompted by us, and was only rarely taken up by the children with any great enthusiasm. This discourse also entails a form of 'media literacy' – that is, an awareness of how the media are produced and circulated, that is often manifested in the view that the media are simply 'selling sex'. Clearly, this discourse also invokes assumptions about media effects; although the concern here is not so much with the moral consequences of these images, as with the attitudes or values they might be seen to promote.

Thirdly, there are questions of *spectatorship* – that is, questions about what happens when males and females look at these images. Within this discourse, certain forms of looking are deemed acceptable, while others appear problematic. In several of our interviews, both boys and girls strongly asserted a 'logic' of heterosexual spectatorship, in which it was acceptable for men to look at images of women, but unacceptable (and even, for some, positively dangerous) for them to look at images of men – although this kind of 'homosexual panic' did not appear to apply with such force to female spectators. These arguments also invoked a popular theory of media effects, in which the media are seen to have the power to 'cultivate' our desires: several of the boys positively feared to look at particular images on the grounds that they might 'turn gay'. Both this and the previous theme are clearly connected to the social performance of gender discussed in Chapter 4.

These discourses inevitably overlap, and they recur with different degrees of salience and force across the various media genres we will be considering here. Broadly speaking, the children were keen to present themselves as competent, self-regulating consumers: even if these images might hold dangerous consequences for others, they themselves professed to be relatively unconcerned about what they had seen. The media were seen as part of a process of sexual learning, but their veracity and authority were frequently challenged; and – despite the fears of some conservative critics – they did not seem to have produced a widespread abandonment of 'moral standards' among the young.

Pin-up girls (and boys)

Despite decades of feminist condemnation, images of semi-naked women remain a regular feature of many of Britain's most popular newspapers (see Holland, 1983). The *Sun*'s notorious page 3 continues to offer topless female models with accompanying 'saucy' captions, as do several of the Sunday tabloids; and they have been joined by even more downmarket rivals like the *Sport* and the *Star*, whose content is dominated by soft-core images and features. At the time of writing (September 2002), it is 'Bum Week' in the *Sun*, although (predictably) the bums on display on the front page are exclusively female.

While some might perceive these images as a prehistoric relic of patriarchy, many of the children whom we interviewed saw them as little more than a banal fact of life. Unsurprisingly, given the more working-class readership of these newspapers, the Essex children were more familiar with this kind of material; and in some of the comments of the older Northern children, there was a suggestion that these images lacked 'class' – as Harvey (N, 17, P) put it, 'they're all glamour models, but there's nothing glamorous about it, is there?' Inevitably, the most enthusiastic advocates of Page 3 were the boys, particularly the younger ones such as Clint (S, 10, P), who had thoughtfully visited the *Sun*'s website and downloaded several pages of such images for his diary. They were 'wicked', he proclaimed, and much better than those in the *Mirror*, which had recently abandoned its topless policy in an attempt at product differentiation. Among some of the older boys, there was a little embarrassment and mutual teasing around this topic; although, according to Jessica and Lori (S, 14, P), the consumption of Page 3 was often a collective activity:

> Lori: I saw them go to the shop in the morning and buy the *Sun*, just for the picture. (...) They take the page three out and they throw the newspaper [away] ... They'll just sit there and stare at it. [laughs] They just sit round in a big group and they're just looking at it. They're just sitting there for ages, just staring. [laughs]

Like several other girls, Jessica and Lori appeared to base their argument on the figure of the pathological male reader, a person who was so 'sad' (that is, pathetic) that he would buy the newspaper solely for the pin-ups. Yet while mocking and condemning such behaviour, Jessica also suggested that there was an element of performance here: 'sometimes they just do it because they like their mates looking at it'.

For understandable reasons, there was little evidence of this in our interviews, but there was certainly a sense that some of the more macho older boys were 'getting the message'. When asked what they might be learning from this material, Pierre and Dale (S, 14, P, G) confidently asserted 'most of the women want it (...) they're just gagging for it'. And the discussion continued:

> Sara: Well, how does that make you feel?
> Pierre: I'm gonna get in there! Know what I mean! Get in there with the Page 3 models!

In fact, however, very few of the children expressed much concern about the *ideological* dimensions of this material: there were very few complaints about 'sexism' or women being shown as 'sex objects', although we would be surprised if the children had not encountered these arguments in their social education classes (if not elsewhere). The key issue was rather one of *propriety* – that is, of precisely how much flesh was on display. Some of the girls said there was little difference in their view between Page 3 and pornography; while others described how they would accuse the boys who read it of being 'perverts'. Some of the younger boys, however, argued that this kind of material was acceptable, both because it did not show 'too much' and because it was not pornographic. As Francis (S, 10, P) put it, 'it's showing that they're sexy, it's not showing anything rude'; while Theo (S, 12, P) distin-guished it from some 'really sick' material he had seen, which he defined as follows – 'two girls or something, or men doing it, men and a woman doing it, on a thing where kids read'. Even for Pierre and Dale, lines had to be drawn: Page 3 was acceptable because it was 'low key', but the model Jordan giving birth on the internet was 'just wrong' – not least, perhaps, because the latter was not so obviously designed for male pleasure (for more on this story, see Chapter 6).

As in Theo's comment above, several expressed concern about the potential influence of such material on 'little children'. Blake (S, 10, G) suggested there should be an 'age limit' on these newspapers, although Will (S, 10, G) argued that parents would not allow their small children to see them – unlike advertising billboards, which were 'there for everyone to see'. Nevertheless, the 'little children' concerned were invariably younger than those who expressed anxieties on their behalf:

> Lucy (S, 10, P): If I had children, like two boys, and like opened the page, they opened the page and they saw her in there, I'd be a bit embarrassed.
>
> Tania: Men would, like they would probably look at it all the time, but I don't think little boys should.
>
> David: Right. So what do you mean by little boys? I mean, how old?
>
> Tania: Like 10 and down. [...] Like going on to 12 they're like going into teenager, so like you would expect it.

As Tania's final comment implies, there was a sense of inevitability here: for older boys to enjoy these images was only to be expected. Yet it often seemed hard for the children to identify the exact nature of the influence such material might have, even where they appeared quite strongly criti-cal of it. When pressed, she suggested that little children might 'laugh about it' and 'be silly'; while Blake (S, 12, P) suggested that 'they might say it all in the school', implying a concern with 'bad' language rather than images. In such cases, it was hard to avoid the conclusion that the children were offering what they believed to be an approved response – and this was reinforced by several stories about boys who had been in trouble with teachers for bringing such newspapers into school.

Nevertheless, few children mounted any sustained criticism of this kind of material – even when we attempted to encourage this by adopting a contrary position. While some of the older middle-class children complained about the trivialisation of news – Tom (N, 17, P) suggested that the papers should be prosecuted under the Trades Descriptions Act – most refused to accept that this material was a matter of concern. As in Tania's comment above, it seemed to be regarded as an unavoidable fact of life, or at least of adult life: as Lysa (S, 10, P) put it, 'it's nothing like you won't see when you're older'. Even the older girls professed not to be 'bothered' by such material; as Melissa (S, 17, P) argued, 'it's the women's choice to do it, isn't it? I mean, it's not as if they're being forced to go and pose naked or whatever.' Not surprisingly, this was an argument echoed by several of the boys.

Some of the more interesting debates around this issue arose when the possibility of male nudes was raised (frequently, but by no means exclusively, by us). Izzie and Suzanne (S, 12, G), for example, asserted that Page 3 'should be stopped' although (amid some mutual teasing) they then argued that there should be equal opportunities in this respect. As Izzie put it, 'it's sexist! Why don't they have pictures of men? It's not fair!' Likewise, Holly (S, 14, G) exclaimed that it was 'really out of order' that the papers did not feature 'Page 3 men' as well as women; and even Theo (S, 12, G) carefully suggested that a more egalitarian approach might be reasonable: 'I'm not gay or anything, but why is it women, why not men that ... Why don't men be in the back [of the newspaper] and girls in the front?'

However, several girls suggested that in fact women were less likely to be interested in such images – or at least that they were themselves. Eve (N, 17, P), for example, proclaimed a personal preference for 'men in little boxers', but argued that in general topless men were 'less attractive' than women. In the course of our interviews, several of the girls expressed an interest in the 'fit' (that is, attractive) bodies of male stars – Joey in *Friends*, Gareth Gates or the members of various 'boy bands' – but these were always people whom they felt they knew, rather than anonymous models.

This view coincided with a commonsense wisdom among some of the girls that boys were only interested in women for their bodies, rather than their personalities:

Lara (S, 14, P): If we took away from boys like all pictures of women with their tits out, I think there'd be like ... literally like panic or whatever. [laughs]

Jody: If they had just pictures of just faces like we do, I think they'd be like "she's not very interesting, is she?"

Lara: Exactly. They might just as well have a headless woman with their tits out ... [laughs]

Jody: Because they go on about how big someone's boobs are and stuff like that. But us girls go "Oh he's got a nice face and a nice chest" and stuff and that's about all, because that's all girls get to see in the magazines, that's all they can talk about.

Jody's final comment leaves open the possibility that girls might be equally inclined to 'objectify' men if they were given the opportunity. As the girls pointed out, the 'chest or the six-pack' featured in their teenage magazines was not equivalent to the topless models in the newspapers. As Lara suggested: 'if there was a man in the newspaper with his, like, dick out, like maybe there would be a lot of complaints. But if there is a woman with just her tits out, there wouldn't be.'

However, Theo's qualification above ('I'm not gay or anything, but ...') reflects a more general difficulty faced by the boys here. As Melissa and Della (S, 17, P) suggested, men would be unlikely to buy a newspaper that featured male pin-ups – 'the boys would be going "I'm not gay, no way"' – whereas (according to them) the equivalent anxiety did not affect girls. These issues of spectatorship will be explored in more detail later in this chapter, but they were partly put to the test when we gave the children an image from a teenage girls' magazine featuring a male pin-up (of sorts). Here, girl readers had been encouraged to 'rate' a boy primarily on the basis of his (shirtless) image: a low rating would merit a 'peck on the cheek', whereas a top rating would result in a 'full-on snog'. In this instance, unlike some of the others we will consider below, the boys appeared to be relatively relaxed. They argued that the use of such images by girls was really 'up to them': as Neville (N, 14, G) put it, 'it doesn't really matter – because they can do what they want, just as we can'. The image in question was, they argued, equivalent to Page 3 or the images in young men's magazines, and as such, they could hardly complain. Here too, we see an early indication of the heterosexual 'logic' that informed all the discussions of this issue:

Joseph (S, 14, G): But the thing about it is that we like looking at the girls with their tops [off] ... well, naked. And the girls [who] wanna look at the girls as well, they're lesbian. But [most girls], they wanna look at men.

However, several of the boys professed not to know how girls might respond: Pierre (S, 14, G), replaying his earlier analysis of Page 3, suggested that girls might look at the picture and 'think "yeah, he looks all right, I'll shag him"', but Jacob (N, 14, G) was much less certain – 'we don't really know about girls, how they think, we're not like that'.

In fact, most of the girls in our interviews were far from interested in this particular image, beyond dismissing the boy as 'ugly'. However, several argued that the image and the 'rating' exercise did to some extent reflect how girls regarded boys in real life. As Courtney (N, 12, G) put it, 'I think it just shows that it's something that does happen. Girls do look at lads and then think "fwooorh, he's nice", "no, he's ugly". They don't just say "hello you, my friend".' Likewise, Sharmaine and Noelle (S, 12, G) asserted that 'boys look at girls the same way girls look at boys ... The boys, right, they need to have nice bums, nice legs and they can't be too fat. And they must have nice eyes.' This almost technical inventory of body parts might seem to have much in common with men's assessments of women, although some girls asserted that there were important differences here. For girls, looking at such images was apparently 'just a laugh', whereas for boys it was 'serious', despite how they might wish to appear to their friends.

At various points in these interviews, our own efforts to encourage a critique of this whole process fell on stony ground. Replaying the kinds of criticisms of the effects of these images made by feminists in the 1970s cut no ice whatsoever:

> David: One thing that people have said about these magazines is that they're all encouraging girls to think about boys all time. How do you feel about that?
>
> Jody (S, 14, P): Girls *do* think about boys all the time, though!

Likewise, our references to arguments about sexual 'objectification' seemed quite outdated:

> Sara: Some people would say they encourage girls to look at boys as objects and they don't allow –

Phil (S, 14, G): They are. Objects that move and breathe... And work and have decent jobs and incomes.

Sex, the children, seemed to be saying, is all about objectification; and so long as we can have equal opportunity objectification, where's the harm?

Men only?

As we have seen, the majority of children made a distinction between the Page 3 images and pornography, although there was certainly some debate about where this line was to be drawn. A similar debate recurred in their discussions of young men's magazines. While there was a lingering sense of shame or embarrassment surrounding these magazines, the boys firmly distinguished them from 'real' pornography.

Thus, several of the younger boys discussed *Max Power*, a car and motorbike magazine which routinely includes pin-up images. However, they claimed that their interest here was primarily in the cars rather than the women; and at least some of the sexual appeal appeared to be quite lost on them – as Blake (S, 12, P) revealed when he spoke with some puzzlement about the prevalence of 'lesbians' in the magazine. Certainly, these boys' other reading material seemed to focus mostly on computers and sport (particularly wrestling). Nevertheless, some were aware of their mothers' disapproval of these magazines – Phil (N, 12, P), for example, claimed that his mother had taken them away from him, but that he still had a 'hidden stock'.

When it came to young men's magazines of the *Loaded*, *FHM* and *Maxim* variety, there was a stronger sense of parental (or at least maternal) disapproval. Joshua (N, 14, P) described how his mother had questioned him about including some images from *FHM* in his diary, and suggested that 'the older generation don't seem to like them kind of pictures'. Likewise, Pierre (S, 14, P) described how his mother would tease him about reading these magazines – 'she'll give me like a dodgy smile' – implying a recognition of his interest in girls that he clearly did not want her to display. Others claimed not to buy these magazines, while nevertheless managing to have read them. In general, however, the boys seemed to shrug off any potential embarrassment. These magazines, they argued, were 'just to entertain', and they couldn't really see why people should be offended by them. (For contrasting analyses of these magazines, see Gauntlett 2002; Jackson *et al.* 2001).

The magazines were distinguished from pornography on several grounds. Most obviously, this was to do with the degree of bodily display. As Joshua (N, 14, P) asserted, 'in porno, they have everything off'; while Blake (S, 12, P) argued that the models in these magazines were not 'properly naked'. Jared (S, 14, P) also noted that, while *FHM* did include sex articles with women 'actually in positions', the illustrations were only in the form of drawings; and, according to Seamus (N, 14, P), these magazines did not 'show you all the dirty actions and what people do'. By contrast, pornography was frequently described as 'dirty' and 'rude', as were the people who used it. As we shall see, the readers of pornography were defined as distinctly 'other', whether this was seen in terms of pathology (a matter of being 'sick' or 'sad') or alternatively in terms of age – for example, in Harvey's (N, 17, P) distinction between the 'lad culture' of the *Loaded*-style magazines and the 'old men's stuff' that was porn.

Several boys also pointed out that these magazines contained material other than sexy pictures; although some of the older boys sought to distinguish between more 'classy' titles like *GQ* and the 'cheap reading' represented by *Loaded* and others. Several also asserted that the magazines were simply 'selling sex' in order to entice readers. As Neville (N, 14, P) argued in relation to *Max Power*, 'they're just trying to make more people read it by putting women on the bonnet [of the car]' – an argument which Sebastian (N, 14, P) extended to the scheduling strategies of the cable channel *Men and Motors*. Here again, the boys appeared to need to distinguish themselves from a pathological (or at least degraded) reader who would – in the words of Warren (S, 14, P) – 'just buy it for the girls'.

Some of the older boys extended this to a critique of the ideological effects of these magazines. Trevor (N, 17, P) argued that they cultivate 'this macho image', and that the men featured in them were 'fake', not least physically: 'if you're gonna take a realistic cross section of male society then not everybody's gonna have six-packs and huge biceps and all this kind of stuff'. Jay (S, 17, P) argued that they might also encourage boys to make superficial judgments of girls on the basis of their looks: 'you wanna go and pick up the most prettiest one who hopefully looks like one of the girls who hopefully could be in those magazines, you know' – although whether he himself was prone to such illusions was left unclear.

Not surprisingly, these criticisms were much more prevalent among the girls. There was a widespread belief that the articles in the magazines were simply a respectable pretext for the sexy pictures. For some,

these kinds of images were seen as superfluous: as Chloe (N, 17, P) asserted, 'I don't like looking at car magazines and all the women with no clothes on, bending over the car. What is the need for it?' Meanwhile, Chantel (N, 14, P) argued that such images were off-putting for potential female readers: 'they think it's just boys that are interested in cars, so they put naked women in car magazines – and what if a girl wants to look at car magazines, [and] there's naked women in there? You just don't wanna look at it.' Others were even more forthright: Eve (N, 17, P) dismissed these magazines as 'completely sex-oriented'; while Phoebe and Naomi (N, 14, P) asserted that the images were 'offensive'. Melissa and Della (S, 17, P) accused the features in the magazines of encouraging men to be 'really macho': '"get your girl screaming in bed ... and if you're dumped don't be hurt, and tell your mates that *you* dumped *her*"'.

Significantly, few of the girls had much hesitation in describing magazines like *FHM* as 'porn', or in expressing their disapproval:

> Kelly (N, 14, P): Boys' magazines are all about cars and porn. Like that magazine called Maximus [sic]. That, it has got porn on the front cover. first page, second page, third page, all the way through the book it has – you can't have a page without a picture of a naked woman on and they just – urgh, I'd hate to read one. I just wouldn't like to sit there staring at the naked women.

The disgust expressed by Kelly and by Chantel above seems to conform to the heterosexual logic of spectatorship identified earlier in relation to boys and male pin-ups: their reaction is not simply one of moral outrage, but an almost physical disgust – not so much at the image itself, but at the *act* of looking or 'staring' at an image of somebody of the same sex. The act of sexual looking ('leering', perhaps) seemed to be regarded as the domain of boys: as Della (S, 17, P) put it, 'I wouldn't really get a thrill out of it ... Whereas boys are like "cor, look at her". And "cor, she'd get it". Whereas girls don't really talk like that.'

'A bit of an education'

The difference between the girls' and the boys' definitions of pornography partly reflects their different positions. For most people, 'porn' is a stigmatised or debased category of representations – as indeed are those who are believed to use it. For girls, labelling particular images as 'porn' served as a powerful index of disapproval – even if boys may have

attempted to exempt some of the same images from this category. However, our research suggests that boys (and some older girls) are also more likely to have seen hard-core pornography, and hence to be in a position to make finer distinctions. Indeed, despite the apparently principled rejection of porn that was apparent above, it was clear that some of these boys were using porn, or at least were quite familiar with its conventions; yet the only way they had of discussing this was through a form of disavowal.

In our interviews, many boys said that they had seen material that they regarded as pornography – although they claimed that this was more often 'by accident' than design. Even in the youngest age group, boys described how pornographic images had appeared on their computers without being requested. Clint (S, 10, P) attributed a touching human failing to his web browser in this respect: 'I asked Jeeves where I could find PC cheats [for games] and I don't think he understood and it come up with a page of naked women and all things like that'. Others described how they had been sent unsolicited images in e-mail attachments, or via chat rooms; while others had come across magazines discarded in the street, in their older brother's bedrooms or in the newsagent's shop.

However, some of the older boys did describe how they had actively looked for porn, often with their friends. Ed (P, 17, G), claimed to have found a batch of porn in some woods and to have made 'loads of money' selling it on to his friends. He offered us an overview of the porn market and what made particular magazines 'class' or 'trashy' ('the innocent ones [models] are always the best ... '). Adrian (N, 17, P) described how he would visit porn sites while downloading music, describing it as 'a bit of an education, if you haven't seen stuff like that before'. Richard (S, 17, P) said he had looked for porn on the internet 'for a laugh', but expressed frustration at the way it was sometimes impossible to escape: 'you just can't get rid of them and you close it down and more things come up'. However, these boys still wished to distance themselves from the 'sad old perverts' whom they perceived as regular users of porn: their own use, as they described it, was motivated by curiosity and occasional desperation – as Jay (S, 17, P) put it, 'desperate times can need desperate measures, you know'.

In some instances, however, this amounted to more than occasional use. Phil and Henry (N, 14, P), for example, had got into considerable trouble with their parents for running up a large telephone bill visiting porn sites on the Web; Theo's (S, 12, P) older brother had apparently been involved in trading pornographic videos and magazines; and Jay

(S, 17, P) described how a friend had an illegal 'black box' that enabled him to access porn channels on his TV. (And, as we shall see in Chapter 8, some fathers implicitly condoned the use of such material.) While there may have been grounds for exaggeration here, the children's descriptions certainly suggest that some of the material in question was hard-core. There were several expressions of disgust and incomprehension at images of 'disgusting big holes', 'girls licking their own pee', 'girls doing animals', 'men's parts peeing into girls' mouths' and so forth. As we have seen, the boys drew very clear distinctions between pornography and more mainstream sexual images: this kind of material was very firmly rejected as 'sick' or 'minging' – as were the people who used it – 'sick men who's got a boring life', as Damian (S, 12, P) put it.

In some cases, porn viewing was described as a group activity: this was seen by Richard (S, 17, P) as 'more of a laugh', although he acknowledged that the laughter was partly a response to feeling 'uncomfortable'. According to Glenn (S, 17, P), '[people] try and joke about it to hide the fact that they have taken it seriously'. Indeed, there were some indications that porn disturbed the 'logic' of heterosexual spectatorship we have described above. Kelly (N, 14, P) described one such incident as follows:

> Kelly: In Year 8 we went to a lad's house and they had porno. And like if you looked at the TV [and] see like what they were watching, they'd go 'ooh look at her, look at that girl'. I mean, they're also looking at a *man*!

Nevertheless, Dale (S, 14, P) took some comfort in the fact that, as he put it, 'you see more of a woman than you do of a man, so I'm all right with that.'

The use of porn was not confined to the home. Kim and Abigail (N, 12, P) described how boys would circulate porn images in their classroom, and in some instances use them to harass girls and to disrupt lessons: according to Kim, 'sometimes it'll get really serious, like they'll start putting like dirty pictures, messages on the phone and screen savers and everything, oh it's disgusting'. For them, boys' use of porn simply confirmed their own degraded status, as summarised by Abigail: 'I think boys are more like into it than girls are, because boys are like really disgusting'. However, other boys saw this kind of activity as a symptom of immaturity: Seamus and Neville (N, 14, P), for example, described how they had been impressed by the kind of material that

was circulated in the playground at junior school, not least because it was so obviously forbidden by teachers and parents, but claimed that they now saw this as 'pointless' and 'immature'. In general, the boys were keen to distance themselves from the 'others' who were users of pornography. In several cases, porn was defined as the domain of much older men – such as the 'ninety year olds', who according to Dale (S, 14, G) would use it as a cheap alternative to Viagra in order to give their wife 'the best time of her life'. The users of porn were consistently stigmatised as 'obsessed', 'sick', 'weird' and 'sad perverts'; or alternatively as just inadequate – in Theo's (S, 12, P) words, 'girls just don't like 'em, so they just look at girls [on the internet]'.

However, many stopped short of total condemnation. As we have noted, pornography was seen to satisfy aspects of boys' curiosity – as Jay (S, 17, P) acknowledged in referring to it as 'a bit of an education'. Likewise, Phil and Henry (N, 14, P), of the enormous telephone bill, had described their motivations to their parents in similar terms: 'I said "well, I'm sort of curious and wanting to know a bit more"'. However, other boys appeared to recognise that, for better or worse, real life was not like pornography – as Jay (S, 17, P) said, 'I wouldn't expect women to be that slutty'. Nancy and Olivia (S, 17, P), who had seen porn at a male friend's house, mocked the idea that it would offer a realistic view of the world – 'like that would happen!'. They argued that boys enjoyed it precisely because it was 'fantasy', and clearly saw this as a symptom of their immaturity:

Olivia: Whereas with probably boys of our age and maybe a bit younger, say 15, 16, would sort of say if they watched a porn video, say 'my girlfriend's gotta be like that'. Or 'I want my girlfriend to look like that'. But there's not a hope in hell, 'cause not everyone's plastic.

Nancy went on to describe how she had intervened in similar terms when she discovered her younger brother and a friend reading porn magazines:

Nancy: I just laughed a bit and then I went ... I said 'oh I'll leave you to it, shall I? Don't want to get in the way of, like, your learning process!' I say to him, I say 'look, you know, it don't happen like that in real life. Trust me!'

However, it was a boy, Theo (S, 12, P), who was most overtly critical of the 'sexism' of pornography – 'I used to read [porn magazines] and I thought that's an insult to girls really'. However, as we saw above, he also followed the logic of 'equal opportunities' by arguing that equivalent material should be available for women too. In general – as with the other material we have considered so far in this chapter – it was argued that the availability of such material did not in itself constitute a significant problem. Even those who condemned pornography as 'sick', or claimed not to like it themselves, were inclined to regard it as a fact of life. As Trevor (N, 17, P) put it, 'it's to entertain people, people get kicks with it. People enjoy looking at flesh, yeah. There's nothing wrong with that – I just don't really think it's that important.' Here, as in several other areas considered in this book, the children were inclined to represent their own generation as more 'relaxed' and open than their parents'. Melissa and Della (S, 17, P), for example, argued that the 'older generation' might class magazines like *FHM* as porn, but that they would not do so themselves. They argued that whereas their fathers would only have had 'proper porn magazines', they had a wider range of material to choose from – and even if they themselves did not like such material, they agreed that this was an improvement.

Taking offence

Several of the issues we have been considering thus far were addressed more directly when it came to looking at advertisements. We asked the children to look at a series of ads that had been the subject of recent adjudications by the industry regulator, the Advertising Standards Authority (ASA). We will consider three of these here, in addition to a further advertisement that was included in the material we had gathered from the tabloid press (the latter was distributed only to the 12 and 14-year-old children. All featured male or female bodies in various states of undress.

The first – and perhaps most widely known – of these featured the model Sophie Dahl in an ad for the Yves Saint Laurent perfume 'Opium'. The ad shows a woman, completely naked apart from jewellery and high-heeled shoes, set against a dark blue background consisting of some kind of silk or velvet material. She is lying on her back with her knees raised, her head reclined and her lips parted. Her left hand is touching her left breast, and her right breast is exposed. The skin tone is very pale, almost ivory in colour.

There were predictable differences here between the boys' and the girls' responses to this image – and, perhaps more interestingly, between the older children and the younger ones. The ten-year-olds in particular professed to be quite disgusted and shocked by it; although they also appeared rather more confused, both about the sexual connotations of the image and about the advertisers' strategy. By contrast, some of the older children were inclined to dismiss it as 'just an advertisement'. Yet for all age groups, the issue of the public display of such images – and the possibility that they might be witnessed by 'little children' – was a key concern.

Criticisms of the ad were principally concerned with propriety. There were several exclamations of disgust among the younger girls – 'urgh, it shows her boobs!' 'you can see her nipples!' – and in one instance, Rachel (N, 10, G) even expressed revulsion at handling the photocopied image – 'uuurgh, I'm touching it!' Some of the boys were clearly more interested than disgusted, but even here there was a general sense that, as Sharmaine (S, 12, G) put it, the ad was 'too revealing' or 'over the top'. Theo (S, 12, G) even claimed that the ad was 'insulting women', although this apparently principled stance was rather undermined by the fact that he then attempted to take it away with him at the end of the interview.

On one level, the issue here was simply to do with *how much* was shown: Bea (N, 10, G) was one of several who argued that it was acceptable to show the 'top half', but not to be 'totally naked'. However, these arguments were also informed by assertions about the possibility of 'little kids' seeing such images. Henry's (N, 12, G) comment was representative of many: 'my parents would probably think it was bad because it's sort of on public display with all like the toddlers and the children in like prams and that'. Here, as in many similar comments, the concern was to some extent displaced onto parents, and expressed in relation to very young children. (However, it should be noted that the parents in question were generally mothers: according to Dale (S, 14, G), 'parents [would] be like 'oh, don't look' – no, that's your mum, like your dad would be like 'Go on, son!'). The typical scenario was one in which, as Joseph (S, 12, G) put it, children would ask their parents 'uncomfortable questions'. This was seen to be particularly an issue given that the ad might be displayed on a billboard in a public place: some argued that it would be acceptable in a magazine, where it would only be seen by older readers (such as them), but not where 'more kids will see it'.

This issue was clearly reflected in the Advertising Standards Authority's adjudications on this ad. In the form of a billboard poster, the public complaints (almost 1,000 in total) were upheld, and the advertisers were told to withdraw the ad immediately. The ASA rejected the advertisers' claim that the image was 'sensual and aesthetic', arguing rather that it was 'sexually suggestive and likely to cause serious or widespread offence'. However, complaints about the appearance of the same ad in the national press were not upheld, presumably because the press is not regarded as such a 'public' medium.

Despite all this, the children did not wish to be identified with the complainants. As in other instances where we introduced the issue (see Chapter 9), those who complained about such material were condemned as 'opinionated middle-aged women' who 'take things too seriously' and 'just like a good nag' (Richard and Jay, S, 17, P). (Significantly, complainants were frequently assumed to be female – which may reflect assumptions about the different positions of mothers and fathers on such issues: see Chapters 8 and 9.) Only Gareth (S, 14, G) suggested that the attempt to annoy such 'goody-two-shoe righteous people' might be a deliberate attempt on the part of the advertisers to make it 'go on more' – that is, to attract more publicity.

However, there was some confusion when it came to identifying the potential *effects* of this image on the 'little kids' who might see it. Most of the suggestions here were quite facetious. Jason (N, 14, G) said that children might 'run around naked' as a result of seeing the ad; Harvey (N, 17, G) ironically suggested that they might 'lose their innocence'; while Dale (S, 14, G) predictably asserted 'they'll think "nice tits!"' Others in fact suggested that the most dangerous effects would be on adults: Will (S, 10, G), for example, argued that 'men will probably think that that's more beautiful than their wife ... and the wife won't like it'. In fact, it was fairly clear from our interviews that the younger children did not fully recognise the 'sexually suggestive' aspects of the ad – and specifically, the implication of masturbation. When gently pushed, some of the older children indicated that 'she looks like she's having an orgasm' (Louisa, S, 17, G) or – a little more coyly – that she was 'enjoying herself' (Jeff, N, 17, G). Some of the 12-year-olds identified a sexual atmosphere in the ad – 'it means, the more perfume you put on, the more sex you get', as Darren (S, 12, G) put it – but this was not quite so specific; and some of the ten-year-olds puzzled over the image at length – 'uurgh, weird, what's she doing?' 'she's clutching her tit' (Rachel and Bea, N, 10, G). For the younger children, the 'problem' with this image was primarily that it was a naked body, rather than that it had any overtly sexual connotations.

When asked, the children also expressed some confusion about the advertisers' strategy here. Several complained that there seemed to be no association between the image and the product – as Phoebe (S, 14,

G) put it, 'I don't see what that has got to do with women's perfume' – while others expressed confusion about the 'message' – 'I mean, what's it meant to say? I mean, you don't see any perfume. You might just think 'What's that all about?' (Caitlin, N, 12, G). The older children were predictably more fluent in this criticism of advertising, suggesting that the ad was appealing to women's 'aspiration' and recognising the advertiser's intention to employ a more 'artistic' visual style. Louisa (S, 17, G) suggested that the advertisers might be able to 'get away with it' on the grounds that 'it's got, like, 100 times more class than page 3 girls'; and there was some evidence that this approach has been effective, at least as far as Izzie (S, 12, G) was concerned – 'a painting is not like the best thing in the world of a naked woman, but it is better than a photo'.

As with several of the other ads, there was considerable debate about whether the image was aimed at women or men. Men, it was argued, would certainly be attracted by the ad (as indeed were some of the boys we interviewed); but women would not want to look at it – unless, according to Kim (N, 12, G), 'they are gay'. This led on to some criticism of the advertisers' strategy:

> Chantel (N, 14, G): I mean, women aren't gonna look at it and go 'oh, that's nice perfume, let's go and buy it', are they? They're just gonna go 'that's sick!'.
>
> Phoebe: They're just gonna think the picture's horrible.

Here again, there appeared to be a strict heterosexual 'logic', which was enforced even within our interviews. Men could look at pictures of women: that was perfectly normal. Women could also look at pictures of men: it was only fair that they should have the same opportunities. In both cases, the only possible problem was one of 'going too far', by displaying an undue interest in images deemed to be too 'rude' or 'dirty' (or pornographic). However – as we shall see in more detail below – men definitely could not look at pictures of men, unless they were gay; and indeed, if they did so, they would run the risk of *becoming* gay. There was no real evidence in our interviews – even with the older boys – that boys might gain pleasure from looking at images of men, nor of much interest in 'gay chic' of the kind that some have seen as characteristic of contemporary young men's consumer culture (Mort 1996; Nixon 1996). By contrast, there appeared to be less danger for women in looking at pictures of women: while this might, as in

Kim's comment, serve as evidence of them being lesbians, in general it seemed to be regarded as something that women 'didn't mind'. Women, we were repeatedly told, might find other women attractive, without them necessarily being lesbian; but there was simply no way that men would feel the same way about other men, unless they were gay. This inexorable logic was firmly and consistently proclaimed by both boys and girls in our interviews, and was never overtly contested.

We will return to this issue of spectatorship in our discussion of the final two advertisements below. Before doing so, however, we would like to focus briefly on another ad that raised further questions to do with propriety. This was a poster ad for Lee 'boot-cut' jeans. It featured a picture of a woman's leg, clad in jeans and a stiletto-heeled boot, with the toe resting on the buttocks of a prostrate, naked man. The headline read 'put the boot in'. This ad had been the subject of protests to the Advertising Standards Authority on the grounds of 'offensiveness' and 'condoning violence', although these had not been upheld.

As with the Opium ad, the question of 'offence' (or indeed of harm) must to some extent depend upon the viewer's understanding. In this case, it was only the 17-year-olds who immediately recognised the sexually-charged 'dominatrix' aspect of the image – or, more precisely, recognised that there were elements of the image that were *culturally defined* or coded as 'sexual'. Trevor (N, 17, G), for example, said that the ad showed a woman being 'sexually dominant' – although he argued that if the positions were reversed, it would be perceived as more problematic. Nevertheless, he argued that such images were acceptable: 'it's what floats your boat ... whatever consenting adults do is nothing to do with me'. On the other hand, Eve (N, 17, G) suggested (amid some embarrassment) that there might be a rather different sexual connotation: 'put the boot in, as in like put the penis in'. A few of the younger children were certainly aware of some sexual dimensions here: Alicia (N, 10, G) suggested 'she definitely wants to have sex with him' and Wesley (S, 12, G) referred to the fact that 'some men like that – with the whips and that'. A couple also expressed some disgust and shock (albeit rather delightedly) at the idea of penetration – 'imagine if that went up!' exclaimed Jed (S, 10, G). Nevertheless, many did not appear to have recognised this as a possibility: when asked directly about the headline, they tended to suggest that it was a matter of the boot going inside the jeans rather than anywhere else. 'Bums' for them had other associations: as Sean (N, 12, G) argued, 'it's disgusting putting your foot on a man's bum ... your shoe might smell'. Here again, the main issue for the younger children was simply the amount of bodily display – or, as Melanie (N, 10, G) put it, 'the bum-showing part' – rather than any sexual implication. In this case, several children argued, 'you can't see the rude bit' – and as such, they argued, there was no cause for concern.

As this implies, younger children are generally less likely to realise the sexual connotations of such images – and as such, one might argue, they are less at risk of any potential harm such images might be seen to cause. Thus, Tom (S, 17, G) argued that very young children (in his estimation, six-year-olds) wouldn't 'analyse' such material 'properly'; but that older children (like his nine-year-old cousin) who already knew about such matters would realise what the ads were getting at. As with the Opium ad, some of the children here did complain about the public display of such images: Morris (N, 10, G), for example, argued that 'little kids would be outside and they'd be seeing this rude stuff on the streets – but when it's on TV, it could be on later ... when the children are in bed'. Yet again, however, the 'little children' who are presumed to be at risk appear to be younger than Morris himself. Here we arrive at one of the *reductio ad absurdum* conclusions of the effects debate. If 'little children' cannot understand such material, presumably it does not affect them; and if older children *already* understand it, how can it affect them either?

In fact, much of the concern generated by the Lee jeans ad was not to do with children at all – as was apparent when a so-called 'men's group' picketed the ASA offices in protest against it. Familiar arguments about sexism in advertising were being reversed here, to the chagrin of at least some male viewers. As Darren (S, 12, G) put it, 'if the last one [Opium] was insulting women because a woman was naked, this has to be insulting men'. According to the advertisers in their evidence to the ASA, the ad was intended to reflect 'the prevailing "Girl Power" mood in Britain'. This was clearly recognised by some of the children here: as Nancy (S, 17, G) put it, 'this one certainly puts emphasis on a woman's power over a man'. As we have seen, some of the older boys appeared to be relatively relaxed about this, suggesting that some would see it – in the words of Jon (S, 17, G) – as 'more like seduction'. However, some of the younger boys found it rather more threatening: according to Darren (S, 12, G), the ad was 'saying that women can beat you'. Several children argued that a reversal of this – with 'a man abusing a woman' – would attract much more criticism; although others argued that this was justified, because most men would not take this ad seriously, or perceive it as 'degrading to men' (Glenn, S, 17, G). Some of the girls also suggested that the two were not equivalent, in that male violence against women was much more common in real life than the reverse. Yet however disturbing they may have found it, few children saw valid grounds for complaint on these grounds; and complainants were again dismissed, in Izzie's (S, 12, G) characteristically gendered terms, as 'stuck up old biddies that have nothing else to do'.

Looking at men

The issue of spectatorship was raised most powerfully in our discussions of two further ads, both featuring semi-naked male bodies. The first was part of the Levi's Jeans 'Twisted to fit' campaign. It features a man, wearing only a pair of jeans the wrong way round, standing in front of a woman. The woman is hidden except for the top of her face and her arms, which she has placed around the man, with her left hand in the front pocket of his jeans. This ad had also attracted complaints to the Advertising Standards Authority on the grounds of its sexual suggestiveness, although the complaints had not been upheld.

This ad was perceived to be less problematic than the Opium ad, at least on the grounds of propriety. As Bea (N, 10, G) succinctly put it, 'that one's okay because it's only showing the top half and men are allowed to show their top half'. Others argued that they might well see similar things in a hot summer, or at the swimming pool. The hand in the pocket was discussed by several children – as Darren (S, 12, G) noted, 'I think she's trying to reach his dick' – and the sexual 'suggestion' this gave was identified not just by the older children but also by some of the younger ones. In general, however, this was seen to be relatively mild – as Alma (S, 10, G) argued, 'if you moved maybe the hand nearer him, [it] might be more of a problem – but there's nothing wrong with the nudity there'. While some questioned whether this aspect of the ad was really necessary, it was mostly agreed that it was more legitimate than the Opium ad: as Ethan (N, 12, G) argued, 'you can actually see what it's advertising – the jeans'.

Several of the girls expressed a quite unashamed enthusiasm for the man's body – indeed, to a rather greater extent than had been evident among the boys discussing the Opium ad. Emma and Rebecca (N, 10, G), for example, spent some time admiring his 'six pack' and fantasised about how they would like to place their hands in his pocket; while Caitlin (N, 12, G) found him 'gorgeous' and expressed dismay that he still had his trousers on. Meanwhile, the presence of the woman in the ad seemed to allay any discomfort that the boys might have experienced. Henry (N, 12, G) argued that the ad was 'aimed at men because the woman's behind him ... there's that woman fancying him'; and, like several other children, he agreed that the message was unambiguously heterosexual – 'wear Levis and women will come on to you'. Rollo and Mia (S, 12, G) argued that if the man had been on his own 'he might look a bit gay' – although when pressed to describe what 'looking gay' might mean, they found this hard to define. Nevertheless, Theo (S, 12, G) actually covered his eyes when this image was revealed to the group; and when asked to explain this, he claimed it was because 'I'm a man' – and, he later added, 'I'm not gay'. He agreed, amid some laughter, that looking too hard at the picture might even cause him to *become* gay (a concern which also appeared to be a particular preoccupation for his father: see Chapter 8).

This issue became significantly more fraught in the children's discussions of another ad, for Calvin Klein underwear. The ad simply featured a male model posing in white briefs, with his hand on his hip, looking into the camera. In this instance, the ad had been included in a press story, which speculated about whether the contents of the briefs were all the model's own, or whether they had been padded. Readers were invited to phone in to the newspaper if they themselves had a 'bigger bulge'.

In this case, several of the boys claimed to be unable to look at the image for any length of time. Others squirmed with embarrassment or exclaimed in outrage. 'It's disgusting!' cried Joseph (S, 12, G), 'he should put some trousers on!'. 'It's demoralising to the public of England!' said Dale (S, 14, G), rather more ironically. In common with a couple of the girls, Joshua (N, 14, G) argued that boys might be 'jealous' of the model (presumably for his good looks, in addition to the alleged contents of his underwear); although this was strongly refuted by several other boys. The reason for their reaction, they argued, was self-evident: it was 'because he's a man' (Jacob, N, 12, G). 'I don't want to know about men!', Sean (N, 12, G) exclaimed: such things, he argued, were strictly for girls.

To some extent, the boys' anxiety was to do with being *seen* to display an undue interest (or indeed any interest) in such images; and hence with the possibility that others might accuse you of being gay. In the context of our interviews, this was bound to generate a degree of 'gender performance' (see Chapter 4): the stronger one's protest, the more hot-bloodedly heterosexual one would appear to be. As Dale (S, 14, G) assured us, reflecting a familiar idealisation of women's bodies, 'women are nice and you see all their body and their tits and their legs and their arse and that, but when you see a bloke you're like "urghhh!"'. Yet in some instances, as with Theo's reaction to the Levi's ad above, the boys appeared to believe that simply looking at such images would 'turn you gay'. Seth (N, 12, G), for example, said that his father would have torn up this picture: 'you don't want to be gay, do you, looking at other people?' (For further discussion of the family dimensions of these responses, see Chapter 8.)

In several cases, this concern was displaced onto the model himself. Several argued that they did not want to look at the ad because the model appeared 'gay' or 'like a poof'; while others argued that his long hair made him 'look like a girl'. This argument was also made by girls, such as Noelle (S, 12, G) who exclaimed 'look at his eyes! They look too gay!' – although here again, it was very hard for them to explain precisely what inspired such judgments.

As far as the girls were concerned, the Calvin Klein model did not match up to the Levis man. Heather and Abigail (S, 12, G), for example, argued that he was 'not sexy in any way whatsoever', although they also expressed a fear that he was 'too big' – 'it's massive – you could get it stuck up there!' Here again, simply touching the relevant parts of the picture brought forth the cry 'that's disgusting! You pervert!' Nevertheless, as in the discussion of the Page 3 models, they proclaimed their right to look at such images, if boys were allowed to look at similarly sexy pictures of women. Equal opportunity voyeurism was clearly the order of the day: as Sharmaine (S, 12, G) put it, 'boys like to see tits – and then girls like to see the other stuff, don't they?'

Yet the girls predicted the boys' uneasy reactions to this image, and clearly regarded it as a symptom of the differences between the sexes, which was also apparent in how they conducted their friendships:

> Lori (S, 14, G): If boys are seen looking at another boy, they'll say they're gay. But if women like compare themselves to other women or they look at them, then it's just seen as normal, because that's what women do.
>
> Jessica: Because like girls are really like close to friends and stuff and boys just, I dunno, they just ... If they're like seen like that with a, after another boy they'll think they're gay. Or if they look at pictures like that, they think they're gay.

Likewise, Lara argued that women 'are more comfortable with themselves', whereas men 'have got this big illusion that they have to have the biggest everything'. Nobody, they argued, would be likely to accuse them of being lesbians if they were looking at pictures of semi-naked women.

Interestingly, the boys did admit to some of these points. Sebastian and Jacob (N, 14, G) accepted that girls were, as they put it, 'more comfortable just looking at naked women'; although they saw this as a reflection of the fact that girls in general were more 'open-minded', and that 'they always stick together' as friends. Likewise, Pierre (S, 14, G) argued that 'women don't get embarrassed that easily'. However, part of the reason for this was seen to lie in the very ubiquity of images of women: as Holly (S, 14, G) put it, 'you can't get away from it, can you, it's everywhere'.

Nevertheless, the issue that continued to puzzle many of the children was that of the advertisers' strategy. Here we had an ad for a product intended to be worn by males that males themselves claimed they could hardly bear to look at. The article in which the ad was featured also included a small shot of the infamous 'Hello Boys' ad for Wonderbras, featuring the prominent cleavage of Eva Herzegova. Reena (N, 14, G) puzzled over this: 'but why do they have like a bra ... it's supposed to be for women, but why do they aim it at men, the advert, and why do they aim the men's advert at women?' One possibility here, which some children raised, is that women might buy such products for their male partners (or vice-versa); and it may equally be the case that the advertisers are targeting a gay audience. But it does raise the possibility that more might be going on for some male viewers than they are prepared to admit.

Bodies in motion

The three issues we have been addressing here – propriety, ideology and spectatorship – also threaded through the discussions of the final set of material we will be considering in this chapter, namely music videos. The issue of bodily display arose specifically in relation to three videos: Britney Spears' 'I'm a Slave 4U', Robbie Williams' 'Rock DJ' and the video of 'Lady Marmalade' featuring Missy Elliot, Christina Aguilera, Pink and Lil' Kim, made to accompany the film *Moulin Rouge*.

Britney Spears was, of course, well known to all the children in our study, not just from her music and videos but also from her frequent appearances in the celebrity gossip pages of the popular press. Her public stance on virginity – she had claimed that she would be 'saving herself' until marriage – was widely questioned and mocked. Many children referred to press reports that she had in fact recently lost her virginity, although many argued that, as Ethan (N, 12, G) bluntly put it, 'she'll already have done it, before she became a pop star', and that this stance was simply 'a publicity thing'. Others argued that her position was incompatible with her sexual public image, and that she was simply a hypocrite. In the words of Reena (N, 14, G), 'she don't act like a virgin and she don't look like a virgin'. This was partly about her clothing (or lack of it): 'she's saying that you shouldn't be having sex with a man, shouldn't be doing that, and then she goes on the stage with like nothing on' (Kelly, N, 14, G). However, it was also about her style of dancing: 'it's like she experienced doing, having sex before marriage before, 'cos the way she dances is like she ... she's like she really like wants to have sex and that' (Tania, S, 10, P).

Part of the difficulty here, as several children recognised, was that Britney was at a point of transition in her career, and in her public image. Her music was seen to be moving away from 'pop', but the most striking change was in her appearance: Britney, it was argued, had always been sexy, but the Britney of today was much more 'rude' and 'tarty' than she had been in her early career. As Rollo and Mia (S, 12, P) put it, she used to be 'pop star sexy', but now she was trying to be 'raunchy' – 'she's turned into Madonna'. The difference here was clearly to do with the implication of sexual experience – or, more precisely, to do with how this is culturally *signified*. Some argued this change was simply a matter of her 'growing up' and moving away from the over-protective influence of her mother; but others saw it as an attempt to reach an older (and perhaps also more male) audience.

In the process, however, she was seen to be giving problematic messages to her earlier fans, who were defined primarily as 'little kids'. (Indeed, several of the younger children here agreed with Tina's (S, 10, G) judgment: 'I liked the way she was before she changed'.) This was seen as particularly important given Britney's status as a 'role model'. As Lisa (N, 14, G) put it, 'she's basically influencing people to go and wear that sort of stuff'. Here again, however, the 'people' who were seen to be subject to influence were definitely younger than the children themselves. From her older vantage point, Melissa (S, 17, G) argued that 'especially when you're a bit younger, you definitely look up to like famous role models and you definitely like try to copy them'. Even younger girls like Rollo and Mia (S, 12, G) discussed how stars like Britney would encourage 'teenagers' to go on diets in order to look like her or wear revealing clothes, leaving them at risk of 'being attacked if they go out at night'. While they argued that some parents might not 'allow' their children to dress like this, they argued that 'some teenagers are a bit rebellious', and would do so precisely for this reason. Yet when asked about the age of the children in question, they rapidly came down from 'teenagers' to 'nine to ten' and then to 'like, six to ten' (they themselves were 12). Here again, several of the youngest children argued that this concern with propriety was simply a matter for 'grannies' (Stanley, N, 10, G).

For all these reasons, the discussion of a Britney Spears video appeared to cue some of the broader debates to do with the 'sexualisation' of children (or at least of girls) that had partly prompted our study. The video is a record of a famous (or perhaps notorious) live performance at the MTV awards, in which Britney dances on stage dressed in a skimpy 'slave' outfit that appears to be made of thin rags. In the background are various wild animals in cages; and at one point, Britney drapes a very large snake round her neck and parades around the stage.

Britney's appearance in the video appeared to confirm several children's prior judgment of her. As Abigail (N, 12, G) put it, 'she is a tart … have you seen what she wears? Like a skirt that's practically see-through!' And, according to Rollo and Mia (S, 12, G), 'the way she dances is like she is a pole dancer (…) she's always feeling herself and all that.'

Among the older children, this concern with propriety was compounded by a concern with ideology. Britney's dancing and style of dress were seen to contribute to a kind of objectification of women, which was reinforced by the lyrics of the song. The song itself was seen by some to reflect an almost prehistoric form of sexism: as Lisa (N, 14, G) put it, 'do you know how ages ago all women should respect men and do everything for them? It's basically what she's trying to say'. One group of younger girls flatly rejected the song on these grounds:

Melanie (N, 10, G): It's so unrealistic. It's like 'I want you back love … give me another chance'. It's like – shut-up! No, I won't. Get out of my life!

Alicia: Yeah, I'm not giving you another chance now. Go!

Melanie: Goodbye.

Alicia: I don't want you no more. Get out of my face!

As Melanie concluded, 'real life doesn't exist in the song – real life exists in real life'. In general, however, most children stopped short of outright condemnation, partly on the grounds that they did not believe it would be taken seriously.

For the older children, this argument was informed by a broader 'critical' perspective on the media, in which the video was seen merely as a commercial product, which had been calculated to attract a particular audience. In this account, Britney herself had very little control: as Glenn (S, 17, G) put it, even her stance on virginity was simply 'what her publishers have told her to do'. Yet while the younger children were less aware of the machinations of the music industry, they too were quite capable of criticising the media for 'selling sex'. Stars were not dressing or dancing in sexy ways simply in order to 'show off' or 'get attention' (as some argued), but also in order to make money:

> Heather (N, 12, G): Have you seen Kylie Minogue? She's been in America. She'd got these hot pants on her. And the only reason people bought the videos was because she was wearing these hot pants. And it's kind of the same thing. People … Especially boys. If it's a girl you know … A really nice pretty girl. And they're wearing things like hot pants and really small skirts. They buy the video. And that's how they make more money. So it kind of is an image. But it's making them money so they don't really care.

As with some of the criticisms of tabloid newspapers quoted above, Heather constructs a pathological (almost sexually 'depraved') male reader who is simply 'buying sex'. However, some boys were keen to distance themselves from such accusations, by offering a similar critique:

> Henry (N, 12, G): She's selling us her looks basically. I think she's not got anything in between her ears and um … And her voice isn't really that good either.

Here, alternative criteria for judgment are offered – to do with intelligence and musical ability – that are seen to outweigh those of sexual appeal; and in the process, Henry is able to distance himself from the delusions of the depraved male viewer. Some of the other boys here were less fluent in this discourse, however. Seth (N, 12, G) included a picture of Britney in his diary, describing her as 'smooth' – although he later claimed that he had been put up to this by one of the girls. Clint (S, 10, G) even began to fantasise – 'what if she *was* my slave?' – although he subsequently claimed that he no longer 'fancied' her.

Several of the boys seemed to find it necessary to put paid to such suggestions by protesting that she was 'ugly' or 'too skinny' – or, most significantly, that she was merely '*trying* to look sexy'. (As we have noted, boys' expressions of desire in these interviews were – for various reasons – rather less prominent than girls'.)

On the other hand, there were some interesting differences in how the older and the younger children perceived the sexual dimensions of the video. Some of the older children suggested that there was a 'kinky' aspect to the scenario – 'it's like S and M, submissive, tie me up' (Jeff, N, 17, G) – while others pointed (albeit somewhat ironically) to the symbolism of the snake: Jacob (N, 14, G) bravely explained that it was 'meant to symbolise ... a cock', while Jay (S, 17, G) speculated 'you can imagine where the snake might have travelled'. Here again, the older children were more aware of how 'sex' can be culturally signified – in effect, of a history of cultural representations of sexuality. For the younger children, this was less of an issue. For them, the main concern as regards the snake and the other animals was to do with possible cruelty: several groups debated at length whether the snake had been tranquillized or was somehow 'fake', and whether Britney should be prosecuted. As with the Opium and Lee Jeans ads, there was a sense that some of the younger children did not quite 'get' the potential sexual connotations here: Tina (S, 10, G), for example, told us that the song was simply about 'her boyfriend being lazy and she's doing everything for him'. However, it would be more accurate to conclude that these sexual implications were not actually what was most significant for them in the first place. This is an issue to which we shall return in our discussion of the final video below.

Our choice of the Robbie Williams video was primarily motivated by a wish to compare the children's responses to a male body on display. The video shows Robbie as a solo dancer, on stage in a club. He appears to be trying to attract the interest of the girls who are roller-skating around him, and of the female DJ (there are no other men featured in the video). Eventually, he begins to strip off, although this still does not appear to achieve the desired effect. He steadily removes all his clothes, and finally begins to peel off his skin, reducing himself to a dancing skeleton.

In this case, the issue of male display was somewhat complicated (or perhaps just confused) by two factors. Although we faded the video at the beginning of Robbie's self-dismembering (as had been done when it was screened on the pre-watershed TV show *Top of the Pops*), many children had already seen the whole tape, and were keen to discuss it.

There was considerable debate about whether this sequence was 'disgusting' and/or profoundly 'cool'; and whether or not it should have been shown when 'little kids' might be watching.

The second complicating factor here is that – as some of the older children specifically recognised – the video is in some respects an ironic critique of Robbie's own public image as a 'sex god'. As with Britney, many of the children were keen to discuss aspects of his persona in general, and brought this information to bear on their responses to the video. Since leaving the boy-band 'Take That', Robbie had gained a reputation as a hard-living, hot-blooded heterosexual: indeed, if some of the tabloids were to be believed, he was a 'sex addict'. This aspect of his persona was acknowledged by several of the children: 'he puts it about', said Abigail (N, 12, G); 'he loves the ladies' agreed Nancy (S, 17, G); 'he's always flirting' claimed Rollo (S, 12, G). Robbie's suspected relationship with former Spice Girl and UN Ambassador Geri Halliwell was discussed by several groups; and while Suzanne (S, 12, G) and her friends were quick to dismiss her as 'a tart', Kim (S, 12, G) described him as 'a dog', which she clearly saw as the male equivalent. Nevertheless, several – and particularly the boys – claimed that Robbie was 'arrogant' and 'cocky', and even a 'snob': 'he loves himself' said Glenn (S, 17, G); 'he thinks all the girls love him', argued Richard (N, 14, G).

Of course, it was precisely this aspect of Robbie's public persona that the 'Rock DJ' tape was seeking to satirise. Robbie's dancing and mugging in the video suggest a narcissistic over-estimation of his own sex appeal, which is confirmed by the fact that he sports a tiger on his underpants; and it is rendered ironic by the fact that he so clearly fails to gain the women's attention. In the process, of course, the video also confirms his status as somebody who likes to shock – he was described as 'mental' and 'outspoken' – and who is comfortable with a degree of self-mockery – as flora (S, 17, G) put it, 'he's the kind of person that can just take the mickey out of himself'. (And in any case, as Jay (S, 17, G) pointed out, this too was probably the record company's idea.)

Robbie's sex appeal was by no means uniformly confirmed by the girls. Heather (N, 14, G) asserted that he was 'gorgeous' (although she was teased for doing so), and Izzie (S, 12, G) simply said 'that was fine'; but both Phoebe (N, 14, G) and Courtney (N, 12, G) claimed to find his hairy chest 'disgusting', and Lara (S, 14, G) expressed disappointment about his lack of a 'six pack'. Some expressed disapproval of the stripping (even if, as Jake (N, 10, G) noted, 'it blocks off all the rude bits'): Caitlin (N, 12, G), for example, described how she had covered her little brother's eyes when they had seen this video at home. Nevertheless, their main complaint in this respect was that, as Chantel (N, 14, G) put it, he should have had 'a better body': 'if it had been Lee from [the boy band] Blue,' suggested Phoebe, 'that would be fine'. Perhaps the most damning indictment, however, came from Courtney (N, 12, G), who claimed 'my mum fancies him like mad'.

For the boys, this video was predictably more problematic. As with the Calvin Klein ad, some attempted to displace their anxieties onto Robbie himself, claiming that he was 'gay' – in some instances with quite obscure references to newspaper stories. When asked why he was stripping, Pierre (S, 14, G) asserted 'because he's gay' – a point that his friend Dale confirmed, throwing in for good measure the view that the women in the video were 'minging' and 'looked like men'. Another group of boys (S, 10) made vomiting noises, claiming that the video had made them 'feel sick', and quickly sought to distract attention away to the 'sexy chicks'. To some degree, however – as with the Levis ad – the self-evident heterosexuality of the basic scenario (and of Robbie's 'real-life' persona) undermined some of this threat. As Olivia and Louisa (S, 17, G) pointed out, the stripping was 'just a lark' – it was 'funny' rather than 'sultry', and hence a confirmation of Robbie's 'cheeky' persona. This argument also seemed to undermine any concerns about propriety: as Grant (S, 17, G) argued, the stripping was 'comical rather than serious': 'he's dancing in such a stupid way that younger kids I think would laugh at it rather than take much notice'.

Nevertheless, as with the advertisements, there were some striking contrasts here between the girls' and the boys' responses to these two videos. To a large extent, they reflect the heterosexual logic of spectatorship we have identified; but there was also a remarkable difference between the girls' apparent willingness to evaluate men's bodies (whether positively or negatively) and the boys' comparative reticence in doing so with women's bodies. The gender of the interviewer appeared to make very little difference here. Only some of the more working-class boys seemed willing to acknowledge the sex appeal of Kylie Minogue or Britney Spears. Of course, this does not necessarily tell us anything about the ways in which people view or read the media, but it certainly does say a good deal about the social etiquette that surrounds the discussion of such issues – at least in the context of our interviews and (by extension) similar social encounters. It may be that, in such contexts, overt expressions of desire on the part of boys are now decidedly politically incorrect; while equivalent expressions on the part of girls can be justified by appeals to a form of 'girl power'.

The final video we will discuss also proved to be threatening for some of the boys, albeit in a rather different way. The video was a spin off from the film *Moulin Rouge*, and featured the four singers/rappers in a whorehouse, both performing on stage and being dressed in corsets, suspenders, silk underwear and fishnet tights by various maids and attendants. The song was a version of the 1970s disco hit 'Lady Marmalade', with its chorus 'voulez-vous coucher avec moi, ce soir?' – a line that most of the children in our study were quite capable of understanding (even if some of them had had to ask their French teacher first). The video – like the film – was notable for placing into the mainstream images of more or less taboo or 'deviant' sexuality, complete with shots of whips and other S/M paraphernalia. It had attracted several complaints to the Broadcasting Standards Commission following its screening on *Top of the Pops*, before the 9 p.m. watershed.

Responses to this video among the younger boys in our pilot study verged at times on the riotous. One group of ten-year-old boys shrieked and covered their eyes, and two of them literally hid under the table. 'Don't look at the screen! Don't look at the screen!', they shouted. Even with the benefit of having seen the video at home, some of the younger boys in the main study expressed continuing discomfort: Morris (N, 10, G), for example, said he was 'disgusted' by the part where 'she started putting her hand all over her body', and (like some other boys) showed particular distaste for the fact that the models were putting 'make-up all over their face'. By contrast, some of the girls in this age group, such as Gina and Nerys (P, 10, G) argued that this kind of response was 'childish': according to Gina, children of their age 'should look at stuff [like that], 'cause they might be doing that when they're older'.

Here again, there is an interesting contrast between the responses of the youngest children and the concerns about propriety expressed on their behalf (albeit with some equivocation) by the older ones. Harvey (N, 17, G), for example, argued that the video was 'glamourising prostitutes', and feared that this would influence young girls; although his friend Adrian doubted whether they would 'dress up like hookers' as a result. Yet Maia (P, 10, G) – approximately eight years younger – expressed similar concerns, both about her nine-year-old cousin who had apparently sat 'with his tongue out' while watching this video on *Top of the Pops* and about girls who might 'start to wear no clothes' (or at least 'crop tops' and mini-skirts) as a result of watching such material.

On some level, the younger children clearly did 'get it' – in the sense that they recognised the sexually charged nature of the images. But when it came to the specifics, there was much they did not appear to have understood. The women, the ten-year-old children told us, were dancers, possibly strippers; they were in 'a big house' or 'a studio'; they had whips 'to show they're tough'; and they were dressing up in order to 'make themselves look sexy'. By contrast, the 12-year-old children recognised that the women were prostitutes, partly because (they claimed) they had seen prostitutes in the streets in real life, and because they had seen them in the media – in magazines, in films and on television. They were also familiar with S/M, on the grounds that this had also recently been featured in a (humorous) storyline in *EastEnders*. However, what was particularly striking here was that the children used sources like *EastEnders* and even another music video (by the group City High) to contrast with the 'unrealistic' view of prostitution in this video. Phil (N, 12, G), for example, echoed Harvey's comment above, claiming that 'it's showing prostitutes as glamorous, which it probably isn't glamorous, and something like they get paid to have sex with some fat old pasty alcoholic' – a scenario which Courtney (N, 12, G) likened to a recent story in *EastEnders*.

As with the Opium ad and the Britney Spears video, the older children were also more confident in locating the imagery of the video in relation to a history of other representations. They clearly recognised that these were prostitutes in a brothel; and that the video incorporated elements of S/M and 'fetish' clothing that 'some men' would like. The video drew upon what Tom (N, 17, G) referred to as a 'raunchy sort of French old Victorian brothel style', in which certain items such as suspenders were identified as 'really sexual'. Some of the older girls were also prepared to accept the idea (occasionally implied by us) that the video was showing 'powerful women', or a more assertive female sexuality – although this was partly carried over from the other work of the singers/rappers featured. Nevertheless, much of this was not recognised by the younger children: for Jessica (S, 14, G), for example, this was just a video aimed at 'men and teenage boys ... because they're women dancing around in their underwear'; while Dale (S, 14, G) predictably argued that it would only appeal to women 'if they're lesbians'. Paradoxically (or not), Jody and Lara (S, 14, G) even described how the boys in her school had harassed some of the girls by singing this particular song to them – 'they do it to be big in front of their mates (...) they're trying to act older and like they know about sex'. Despite the apparent challenge it might have represented, this video was ultimately accounted for in terms of the heterosexual logic we have identified: boys, we were repeatedly told, would like the video, while girls would just like the song.

Nevertheless, the evident sexual appeal of this video – or its 'suggestiveness' – did not appear to constitute sufficient grounds for censorship, as far as the children were concerned. Here again, regulation seemed to come down to a matter of how much flesh, or which specific body parts or actions, were on display; and in this instance, as Jessica (S, 14, G) put it, 'they're not wearing a lot – but you can't see anything, so I think it will be all right'. As our account implies, 'suggestiveness' is ultimately in the eye of the beholder. What viewers perceive to be 'sexual' depends both upon their knowledge of sex in real life, and on their experience of sexual representation more broadly. As we have suggested (Chapter 4), children use the media not only in learning 'facts' about sex, but also in learning what *counts* as sexual in the first place.

Conclusion

In this chapter, we have considered the children's responses to a diverse range of media texts. Like most of the material considered in the two following chapters, a good deal of this was pre-selected by us; and, of course, it was also encountered in the context of a project explicitly concerned with 'love, sex and relationships'. As such, the research itself inevitably defined or constructed a particular definition of 'sex'; although, as we have seen, the children did not necessarily accord with this or dutifully feed it back to us.

At several points here, the children were explicitly being invited to respond to the public debate about the regulation of sexual imagery – most notably through our choice of material that had attracted complaints to the regulatory authorities. In doing so, they were keen to define themselves as self-regulating consumers, and to displace such concerns onto others less competent than themselves; although in some cases, they clearly failed to recognise the sexual dimensions of the material in the first place. To some extent, then, this approach invited the children to produce 'opinions' for the benefit of public consumption. Yet their responses also raised some more complex questions about the role of such sexualised images, and the ways in which they are used. Our three main themes here – propriety, ideology and spectatorship – will be addressed in different ways across the chapters that follow, so this is not the place for a definitive conclusion.

Nevertheless, the analysis we have presented offers a challenge to several assumptions that are often taken for granted both in academic research and in popular debates about the media. Let us conclude by offering a brief 'provocation' in each of the three areas we have identified.

At least in the area of morality (or what we have been calling 'propriety'), discussions of media effects typically involve a form of displacement, in which it is always 'other people' who are seen to be more vulnerable to influence than oneself. Children are the most obvious targets of this form of displacement. Yet this research provides further evidence of the fact that children also seek to displace the effects of the media onto others – often younger, but sometimes older, than themselves. Of course, this does not mean that the media have no effects on them – but it should at least cause us to question some of the assertions that are often made in this respect, and the motivations that seem to inform them. Our research also suggests that arguments about media effects need to take greater account of the question of *understanding*. What children might learn from the media depends to a large extent upon what they already know – and, to paraphrase a popular cliché, it may well be that what you don't understand can't hurt you.

As we have suggested, concerns about ideology in the media also implicitly entail assumptions about media effects. In this case, these concerns typically relate to the issue of sexism – that is, the extent to which people's use of media images contributes to a more general imbalance of power between men and women. On one level, our research suggests that media images – and people's responses to them – are rather more diverse than this kind of analysis tends to suggest. It also suggests that children develop a form of 'media literacy' that enables them to recognise how media images are constructed, and the commercial interests that are at stake in this process – although it also appears to permit what might be seen as a form of political self-righteousness. Yet we found relatively – and for us, surprisingly – little evidence here of 'feminist' criticism, even when faced with such familiar targets as Page 3 pin-ups. Does this mean that such images have become so naturalised – and their values so comprehensively internalised – that any criticism has become impossible? Does it suggest that the media more generally have changed to the point where such traditional feminist criticism has become irrelevant? Or does it suggest that the media actually occupy a relatively marginal role in the formation of gendered identities and attitudes?

Finally, our research also raises some interesting questions about spectatorship – and particularly about the 'sexualised' nature of looking. To be sure, we found plenty of evidence of a libidinal 'male gaze'; although we also found many instances of an equally libidinal female gaze. 'Objectification' is a process that girls appear to engage in with equal enthusiasm to boys – and, if anything, they appear to be less reluctant to talk about it. Our research suggests that sexualised images of male bodies – which are arguably more prevalent, or at least more widely circulated, than they were in earlier times –can prove particularly troubling for boys, in a way that equivalent images are not for girls. As we have argued, children's responses to these images conform – or are made to conform, through a variety of social pressures – to a powerfully heterosexual 'logic'. Yet as we have also shown, this is very far from being a secure and guaranteed process; and from this perspective, we might even suggest that the media play a greater role in *disturbing* gender and sexual identities than they do in confirming them. These are provocative questions, to which we shall return in due course.

6
Dirty Laundry – Private Lives, Public Confessions

According to conservative critics, the media are full of people endlessly 'doing it'. In fact, it is still comparatively rare to find explicit representations of sexual behaviour in the mainstream media – and certainly in the media most children are likely to encounter. Of course, there is plenty of mild foreplay and strategic removal of garments. But even in primetime television dramas, researchers have found that there is much more talk about sex than visual representation of it (Kunkel *et al.* 2001). Indeed, if anything, it is the compulsion to *talk* about sex – rather than to actually display or witness it – that could be seen to dominate the contemporary media. In this chapter, we consider the children's responses to three media genres which particularly exemplify this 'proliferation of discourses'. We focus first on television talk shows, then on problem pages in teenage girls' magazines and finally on celebrity gossip in the tabloid press.

In several respects, these genres serve as perfect examples of Michel Foucault's arguments about the modern construction of sexuality, briefly discussed in Chapter 1. Foucault (1984) asserts that, since the seventeenth century, there has been a growing 'incitement' to speak about sex, 'a determination on the part of the agencies of power to hear it spoken about, and to cause *it* to speak through explicit articulation and endlessly accumulated detail'. In modern societies, he suggests, sex has been 'driven out of hiding', and forced to abandon its 'shadow existence'. It must now be spoken about *ad infinitum*, for it is in the discussion of sex that the truth of the self is seen to reside. However, this 'truth' is not simply given, and awaiting release or discovery, but one that is created and constructed in the act of talk itself. It is for this reason, he argues, that we cannot regard the increasing willingness to talk about sex, or to represent it, as simply a form of liberation from constraint.

Academic analyses of TV talk shows almost invariably refer to Foucault's discussion of the religious 'confessional' (see for example Dovey 2000; Gamson 1998; Shattuc 1997). It is in the confession, Foucault argues, that 'truth and sex are joined, through the obligatory and exhaustive expression of an individual secret'. While it may be sacrilegious, it is not difficult to see the relationship between the Christian penance and an appearance on the *Jerry Springer Show*. As Joshua Gamson (1998: 102) suggests, talk shows seem to define sex as 'a secret to be told, an ultimate truth to be endlessly discussed, dissected, and disclosed'. And as he argues, the talk shows are part of the active *creation* of sexual 'realities': they invite their guests to give witness, to expose their 'true' selves – even if they often simply hold them up to public mockery.

Perhaps the more obvious point of reference here is to psychological therapy – which could be seen as the contemporary form of the confessional. While the expert psychologist has now all but disappeared from contemporary talk shows, even the more outrageous examples of the genre seem to adopt a broadly therapeutic *stance*. There is an abiding assumption that talk is good for you – that speaking one's intimate secrets is a means to get in touch with one's true feelings, and thereby to achieve psychic health. Of course, it is a particular kind of 'health' that is being promoted here, and a particular type of expression of one's 'true self'. Critics argue that the shows espouse a 'religion of recovery', in which social problems are rendered in terms of individual psychology (Lowney 1999); and that what appears as 'self-actualisation' could equally be seen as another form of self-regulation (Shattuc 1997).

Despite these parallels, there are several respects in which they break down. While one might (at some stretch of the imagination) see Jerry Springer as a father confessor, it is rather harder to see him as a therapist (Shattuc 1997: 113): the 'agencies of power' of which Foucault speaks are no longer concentrated in a single figure, but are much more diffuse (Dovey 2000: 107). Talk shows also represent a highly *public* form of confession or therapy, in which a wide variety of 'advice' is offered to the 'patient', not all of which might be construed as particularly supportive. And the increasingly theatrical form of contemporary talk shows, with their emphasis on performance and confrontation, seems to invite viewers to regard them, not as a means of access to a form of psychic 'truth' or 'self-knowledge', but on the contrary as a genre that has much in common with more spectacular forms of popular entertainment.

Within Cultural Studies, much of the debate here has concerned the extent to which talk shows are 'empowering' for their participants, or for audiences. On one level, the shows do create a space for hitherto 'repressed' aspects of personal experience to be given voice – and for sexual identities that might be seen as deviant or marginal to be made visible. Yet in doing so, it is argued, they often reinforce conventional norms of acceptable behaviour, constantly re-drawing the line between what is 'natural' and what is 'unnatural' (Dovey 2000; Gamson 1998). However, such debates often seem to rely simply on the analysis of programme content. As we shall see, when one speaks to viewers of such programmes, they often claim that they cannot take them seriously. The idea that such programmes might be educational – or (in terms of our irritating question) that they might provide 'messages' about love, sex and relationships – often meets with scorn. As we shall indicate, similar responses were frequently voiced in relation both to the more overtly 'educational' genre of the problem page and to the entertainment provided by celebrity gossip. Crossing the boundary between the private and the public – whether willingly, as in the case of talk show guests, or unwillingly, as with some of the 'victims' of celebrity gossip – often seems to invite suspicion, mockery and summary judgment. Of course, this is not to say that young people do not *learn* from such material. However, it is to suggest that this learning may relate not so much to the content of the media (or their 'messages'), as to how they invite us to engage in the discussion of 'personal' life – and, by implication, to perceive or define the 'truth' about ourselves.

Talking the talk

By and large, TV talk shows did not appear to be a favoured genre among the young people in our sample. While there were a few enthusiasts – particularly among the girls – most claimed to watch such programmes by default rather than design. Some described how their mothers watched talk shows, leaving them no option but to watch with them: 'I always have to watch *Trisha* every Sunday morning when it's the weekend, because my mum likes watching it – and I hate it' (Clint, S, 10, G). When asked, several contemptuously asserted that these programmes were for 'housewives', who (according to Jessica, S, 14, G) would have 'nothing better to do' with their time. Of course, this impression was partly reinforced by the fact that such programmes are mostly scheduled during the day. According to Harvey (N, 17, G), this was a deliberate attempt to combat traucy: 'Obviously they want to get kids back into school. Put the really boring stuff on TV during the day, get kids back in school.'

However, most children appeared quite familiar with the conventions and routines of different types of talk shows, which might suggest that they were more interested in them than they were prepared to admit, at least in this context. In general, there was greater enthusiasm for the more confrontational style of shows like *Jerry Springer* than the more sedate approach of UK programmes like *Trisha* and *Kilroy*. Both boys and girls argued that boys mainly enjoyed the fighting on these shows, and that programmes like *Trisha* were more 'for women'; although in fact several girls also expressed enthusiasm for this aspect, along with the 'swearing'. Lysa (S, 10, G), for example, asserted that 'If there was more violence and they didn't bleep out the swearwords I would give [*Jerry Springer*] ten out of ten'. As the tone of her comment implies – and as several other children, both boys and girls, confirmed – the violence was generally regarded as 'funny' rather than serious. Yet while it was suggested by some that the audience for such shows was merely 'sad' (that is, pathetic), it was clear that many of the children had more than a passing acquaintance with the genre.

According to Laura Grindstaff (2002: 63), the most common reasons given by producers and critics for watching talk shows are as follows:

(1) people identify with, or want information about, the problem or issue being discussed; (2) people like hearing about the problems of others because it makes them feel better about their own lives ... ; and (3) people are drawn to watch guests say and do things that they themselves would never say or do on national television – the 'freak-show gawk factor', as it is known among producers.

These three motivations were certainly apparent, to different degrees, in our sample. When asked directly, a few were prepared to agree that such shows might be educational. As Jeff (N, 17, G) put it, 'talk shows are there to kind of inform but also help people who might have had similar problems, saying you're not alone here, these people know exactly what you're going through'. However, the word that was most frequently used to describe them – and particularly shows like *Jerry Springer* – was 'entertainment', closely followed by 'funny':

Kim (N, 14, G): They're trying to make it serious. And it is serious, like, in real life. But you're just laughing. Because you just think it's funny. And the [studio] audience are laughing. So you just start laughing. That's why I like it ... It is good entertainment – for us.

Reassurance (Grindstaff's second motivation) was also apparent in some responses: as Gina (P, 10, G) put it 'it's like, if [viewers] have problems they might think, well all right, they've got worse problems than me or something – and that might make them feel a bit better'. On the other hand, there were those who found this experience merely depressing, and felt that it might 'remind people of their own problems'. Rebecca (N, 10, G) even suggested that 'people who are watching, if they'd had an affair, it might make them feel guilty and then they might do something to themselves or something ... to stop themselves from going any longer. They might like do suicide.'

However, by far the most significant motivation to emerge from our interviews was the third on Grindstaff's list – what we might call the element of voyeurism. The humour described by Kim (above) derived very much from the opportunity to laugh at people's misfortunes and peculiarities, which might 'in real life' be taken seriously. Eve (N, 17, G) made an interesting distinction here between the talk shows and the 'embarrassing moments' revealed on *So Graham Norton*: 'when you're laughing with Graham Norton, you're laughing *with* the people, but when they're on talk shows you're kinda laughing *at* them'. As this implies, the participants in talk shows were very clearly defined as 'other'; and this appeared to permit a kind of *schadenfreude* – that is, a pleasure in others' suffering – whether in the context of the programme itself or in real life: 'the only reason these talk shows are so popular is because people like to watch 'em for a laugh. They wanna see other people, how crap other people's lives are' (Jeff, S, 17, G).

Of course, few of the children were likely to have experienced the kinds of problems featured on talk shows, and so the 'educational' or 'advisory' function might conceivably be less relevant to them in any case – although this argument might well apply to the majority of the adult audience also (cf. Shattuc, 1997: 177). For them, the pleasure and motivation for viewing such programmes was clearly premised on being able to adopt a very distanced perspective. If they wanted to watch these programmes at all, they did so in order to laugh at the humiliation and suffering of others, to enjoy violent and spectacular confrontations, and to feel safe in the knowledge that so many other people's lives were so much worse than their own.

Keeping your distance

Of course, this distanced response might well be seen as one that is implicitly invited – if not actively produced – by the interview situation. As David Buckingham has argued elsewhere (e.g.1993; 1996), adopting the 'critical' stance allows respondents to claim a kind of authority. It allows you to present yourself as superior to those who – for reasons of immaturity, perhaps, or mere ignorance – are perceived as impressionable victims of media influence. These 'media victims' are partly defined in terms of social class – and in this respect, the 'trashy' nature of talk shows is not incidental (Shattuc, 1997). They are also often defined as female – and here again, the fact that the audience of such shows is largely female is clearly significant. In this context, to admit to 'taking it seriously' would be to admit to a kind of emotional vulnerability or gullibility that is often seen to be characteristic of the 'mass' audience.

However, there were some significant differences here in terms of how specific talk shows were discussed. As numerous critics have pointed out, the genre underwent a remarkable shift in the mid-1990s with the advent of a new wave of talk shows, partly aimed at a younger, less female-dominated audience. Older shows, such as *Donahue* and *Oprah*, were at least partly intended to serve as a form of therapeutic self-help. They drew on liberal 'identity politics' (particularly liberal feminism), and sought to reassert broadly humanistic moral norms, both through the authoritative figure of the host and through the use of psychologists and therapists as visiting experts. *Ricki Lake*, first aired in the US in 1993, was arguably the first of a new wave of talk shows that adopted a very different approach. These new shows focused on sensational themes (often including crime and sexual 'nonconformity') and on verbal and sometimes physical confrontations between the guests. These shows were faster, louder, more visual and more 'full of attitude' than their predecessors (Grindstaff, 2002: 51). The hosts of these shows were generally less likely to make authoritative judgments on their guests' behaviour, and the therapeutic experts had largely disappeared. The emphasis was on the public baring of private lives – on sex, violence and personal tragedy – with much less explicit discussion of their moral implications. Some critics have suggested that the growing importance of the 'freak show' element in the new wave of talk shows represented a return to the origins of the genre in the circus sideshows and the tabloid 'yellow journalism' and 'true confessions' magazines of the nineteenth century (Gamson, 1998; Shattuc, 1997). As Shattuc (1997) argues, these new wave shows sometimes seem closer to TV wrestling (such as WWE – formerly WWF) in their emphasis on excessive style, confrontation and (particularly) audience participation than they do to the sedate, informative approach of the older shows.

As such, it may be harder for people to explain their enthusiasm for such material, particularly in the context of a research interview. However, it could also imply that the more distanced response identified above is to some extent *invited* by the genre – or at least by the new wave talk shows. Shattuc (1997) suggests that these shows have a strong element of 'camp', particularly in their theatricality, and their use of ritual and humour. They address an ironic, 'playful' viewer, who refuses to take them completely seriously; and this scepticism has been encouraged by the recurrent and widely-circulated allegations (several of which have been proven) concerning the use of actors or otherwise fake guests.

Some of these differences were certainly apparent in the children's responses to the two extracts from talk shows that we invited them to discuss. The first was from a British show, *Trisha*, which largely adheres to the therapeutic style of older-generation programmes such as *Oprah*; while the second was from an edition of the US show *Jerry Springer*, which (with the possible exception of the 'final thought', in which Jerry offers a closing homily about the issue at hand) effectively represents the new wave.

As we have noted, the children's stated preference was almost uniformly for *Jerry Springer*. *Trisha* was condemned by many as 'boring' and 'too serious'. In the words of Damian (N, 12, G), the programme was 'all talk and no action'; or, as Clint (S, 10, G) succinctly put it, it was just 'yap, yap, yap, yap'. Trisha herself was also widely mocked and rejected as 'irritating' and 'annoying'. Her more interventionist style was compared negatively with that of Jerry Springer, and rejected by some as 'biased' (in this instance, in favour of her male guest). According to Chantel (N, 14, G):

> Jerry just says it at the end in his final thoughts, whereas Trisha, she says her thoughts all the way through in different stages and then says one thing at the end, her final thoughts. But then she cuts people off when they're arguing and that. I think that's a bit mean, 'cause it's good when they're arguing and you're getting into it.

On the other hand, one of Trisha's few supporters, Jessica (S, 14, G), preferred her more authoritative approach:

> She acts like she wants to help and she like gives them all a chance to speak. Like, if they're trying to argue about it she'll wanna sort it

out, whereas Jerry just runs off to the back of the audience so he don't get hit with the chair.

At one point in our extract, Trisha compared the dilemmas of her female guest with her own marital difficulties, a move that was seen by many of the children as quite inappropriate. While some agreed that it gave her a degree of emotional authority or authenticity (as Jessica (S, 14) put it, 'it makes it seem real'), others distrusted this: 'doesn't Trisha not really bug you, that every single problem that's on that programme, she has had herself?'(Eve, N, 17, G). As Naomi (N, 14, G) argued, 'it's not *her* problems that they're trying to deal with'.

Yet despite this widespread rejection, the children's discussion of this extract was much more emotionally engaged than it was in the case of *Jerry Springer*. They spent longer talking about the extract, and in some cases even used the names of the guests featured. They were more interested in inferring the motivations of the two guests, and in making judgments about their behaviour. For example, while some felt the female guest – a jealous girlfriend – was unfairly 'shown up' by Trisha, most were keen to judge her as 'paranoid', 'insecure' or merely 'stupid'. Several expressed a degree of empathy for the boyfriend, who was generally perceived as an innocent victim who 'just wanted to live a life' (Darren, S, 12, G): some explicitly said they 'felt sorry' for him. Several children attempted to explain why the man then proposed marriage to her on screen – as Courtney (N, 12, G) put it, 'he was trying to propose to her to end all that and start new things, like opening a new book'. At the same time, the couple were widely perceived to be ill-matched: while the woman was judged to be 'buff' and 'fit', the man was condemned as 'ugly' and 'a fat slob'; and the man was also deemed to be far too old for her. Yet several children were inclined to judge the relationship on a more profound level, in terms of more abstract assertions about the need for qualities such as 'trust', 'commitment' and 'fairness':

> Chantel (N, 14, G): I mean there's no point having a relationship if you can't trust the person you're having a relationship with. So I don't think they should be together. It's not necessarily the age difference, it's more like the trust thing.

For some of the younger children, such as Emma and Rebecca (N, 10, P), this led on to stories about friends of theirs whose parents seemed to be always arguing. To this extent at least, it seemed to be possible for the children to relate the relationships shown in the programme to ones they had seen in real life.

The discussion of the *Jerry Springer* extract was quite different in tone. Despite many children's apparent enthusiasm for the show – and particularly for the elements of ritual and confrontation (several noted the studio audience's chant of 'Jerry, Jerry', and the interventions of Steve the bouncer) – it was also widely condemned as 'trashy' and 'fake'. In making these kinds of judgments, the children repeatedly drew attention to the *American* origin of the programme, arguing that it was simply representative of 'American society'. Thus, the word 'American' was frequently coupled with terms like 'uncivilised', 'violent', 'mad' and 'obese' (or even 'hyper-obese'). The programme was just 'a bunch of Americans like this in each other's face, yelling and swearing and everything' (Courtney, N, 12, G); or as Naomi (N, 14, G) argued, 'they're all inbred and just violent and aggressive and they're just stupid, they just sleep around with anyone'.

Particularly for the middle-class children, the 'Americanness' of the programme was a defining mark of its status as 'trash' – and indeed of the class position of its guests, who were implicitly and explicitly defined as 'common'. In this respect, according to Naomi (N, 14, G), the 'cheapness' of the programme's set was indicative of the cheapness of its participants – although, as Joseph (S, 12, G) pointed out, it didn't make much sense to have more than 'cheapo wooden chairs', given the destruction routinely wreaked by the guests.

However, these comments also reflected a general sense of the programme as 'fake' or 'set up' – a judgment which was frequently expressed right across the age range. Several children asserted that the guests were in fact actors; or alternatively that they were 'faking their problems' in order to get to appear on TV. Matthew (N, 14, G), for example, suggested that the guests were 'put up to it' and that 'they are told what to say'; while others described the events in the show as 'story lines'. Sharmaine (S, 12, G) even claimed that she had spotted the same actor twice:

> I saw once there was a person on it and his name was something like Paul or something and then ... a couple of months later I think they were hoping that we'd forget him, he came back on as somebody like George.

This distanced stance can be potentially disrupted, however, by moments of extreme emotionalism. In our extract, two sisters argued over their rights to the same man; and at a key point, one of the sisters broke down in tears, appealing to the man, 'forget about the *Jerry Springer Show*, this is *me*!' This is an instance of what Laura Grindstaff (2002), in an analogy with hardcore pornography, calls the 'money shot' (that is, the shot of male ejaculation): it is the point at which the emotional authenticity of the male encounters is somehow guaranteed by being shown in physical, bodily terms. The money shot makes visible the moment of letting go and losing control. According to Grindstaff, talk show producers go to great lengths in selecting and rehearsing guests, and in orchestrating confrontations, in order to create the possibility of displaying the money shot.

For some of the children in our interviews, this scene led them to question their belief that the programme was essentially 'fake':

> Jon (N, 17, G): I don't think it was [set up], because the wife, she had loads of emotion on her face. I don't know, she's either a very very good actor or she seemed to be almost in tears basically, she was very heartfelt (...) but some of them, you can sit there and you think this has gotta be set up, 'cause it's just ridiculous, what's going on. But I think that wasn't...

However, several other children suggested that this scene too was somehow faked. Sharmaine (S, 12, G) argued that the producers could have 'put some tear things in their eyes'; while Clint (S, 10, G) suggested that there was at least an element of performance here – 'she was crying even more 'cause she was on TV crying'.

Despite the greater intensity of this scene, as compared to the restraint of the *Trisha* sequence, the children's discussion here was quite dispassionate. There was some evidence of *schadenfreude* – Jonah (N, 10, G) said he thought the women's eventual rejection of the man was 'really funny ... 'cause in the end he was all lonely' – but in general there was little interest in probing the psychological motivations of the characters, or even in making moral judgments of their behaviour. Ultimately, as Joseph (S, 12, G) argued, the problems on such shows may serve merely as a pretext for the real business:

> I don't think [viewers] pay much attention to what's actually going on. They're just waiting for the fight. Because they know it's coming.

Even so, several children pointed out that the fights themselves were effectively choreographed in the interests of ratings: Jerry Springer was accused of 'stirring it up' – or at least 'just sitting there and letting them carry on' – because this would mean 'higher viewing figures and they get more money'.

Indeed, as we have noted, it was these elements of ritualistic, cartoon-like violence in *Jerry Springer* that received most approval. In some instances, the children drew attention to this, perhaps in an attempt to impress the interviewer: Seth (N, 12, G) knowingly asserted, 'violence is a good way to sorting out things', clearly expecting a teacherly reprimand in response. By contrast, *Trisha* was praised for helping her guests to 'sort out' their problems, and for offering 'good advice' – although here there was an opposite sense that the children were offering an 'approved' response. Yet ultimately, while *Jerry Springer* clearly possessed subversive appeal, *Trisha* was seen as worthy but dull – despite the fact that the children were more willing to engage with the emotional problems of her guests.

The talking cure?

Few of the children appeared to believe that talk shows served any particularly valuable functions for those who appeared on them. Many argued that there were better ways of sorting out your personal problems, and that appearing on a talk show would probably only make them worse. Perhaps the only argument that could be made here – as it was by some – was that going public might 'let the air out', as Sean (N, 12, G) put it. As Grindstaff (2002: 160) notes, this argument is often made by talk show producers in their attempts to convince potential guests to appear. For these children, however, 'getting things off your chest' (Phoebe, N, 14, G) on a talk show was not generally seen as a way to psychic health. The therapeutic 'talking cure' (cf. Shattuc, 1997) was almost universally seen to be less than effective in practice – at least in the context of the talk shows. As Joshua (N, 14, G) suggested, talk on *Jerry Springer* generally led not to 'sorting things out', but to more fights. Furthermore, the hosts themselves were generally distrusted as potential sources of advice; and the diversity of views among the studio audience would, it was argued, merely lead to greater confusion.

It was partly for this reason that the participants' willingness to 'go public' appeared to be so puzzling. Why, several children asked, would people *want* to go on these programmes in the first place? Some claimed that they did so merely in order to 'get attention' or 'get famous'; while others suggested that they were paid or given 'free flights', and that this would encourage them to 'make it up, just to get on' (Naomi, N, 14, G). Yet these potential attractions were seen to be outweighed by the requirement to 'embarrass themselves'. 'If you've got a problem,' asked Jay (S, 17, G), 'why would you go to a chat show in front of the whole nation to humiliate yourself?' Such people must surely be 'a bit stupid', argued Phoebe (N, 14, G), if they thought that going on the *Jerry Springer Show* would help resolve their problems. Many could not see any situation in which they themselves would do so. As Grant (S, 17, G) put it, 'personally, I'd be embarrassed to go on one of those chat shows with, like, that sort of problem. You wouldn't want everyone else viewing what goes on in your private life, would you?' – although as Ed (P, 17, G) suggested, these shows might be a viable alternative for those who were unable to afford therapy.

For some of the younger children in particular, this crossing of the boundary between the public and the private was particularly problem-atic. As Melanie (N, 10, G) put it, 'I don't think they should have these talk shows. I think they should just tell them privately without letting the whole world know about it.' However, few of the older children appeared to experience much discomfort about the apparent voyeurism involved in this situation. As Matthew (N, 14, G) asserted, 'it's good watching 'em humiliate themselves in front of thousands of people'. In this sense, the private suffering the guests described was compounded by the suffering caused by such public humiliation; although, for many of the children whom we interviewed, this served merely to accentuate their pleasure.

So to what extent might these shows be seen as a source of learning about personal relationships? When asked directly, many of the chil-dren rejected this suggestion out of hand: the shows were self-evidently 'entertainment' and nothing more. Nevertheless, others were prepared to argue that – despite their self-evident 'fakeness' – pro-grammes like *Jerry Springer* did tell you something about real life. Many children were keen to mock the programme's typical content – 'they're all in-breds, like raped by their fathers and stuff' (Chantel, N, 14, G); 'I had sex with my husband's boyfriend's sister's uncle' (Sebastian, N, 14, G). Yet however 'sick' or 'ludicrous' such content was perceived to be, it did at least 'tell you what happens'. On the other hand, some of the ten-year-olds argued that *Jerry Springer* was likely to be particularly harmful for young children, on the grounds that, as Rebecca (N, 10, G) put it, 'they were shouting, they were talking about sex and every-thing, they were swearing ... ' In practice, as we have seen, the focus of such concerns was invariably children younger than themselves – in

Rebecca's case, two- or three-year-olds who might watch such programmes at home during the day. As Gina (P, 10, G) asserted, 'children younger than us pick up things from the TV' – such as, in this case, fighting and swearing from *Jerry Springer* – although she was keen to emphasise that this argument did not apply to her or any of her friends.

Beyond this, however, there was little certainty about what – if anything – these programmes might be teaching. As we have seen, the hosts' attempts at teaching – for instance, in the case of Jerry Springer's 'final thought', or Trisha's interventions – were often mocked or criticised. Some children hesitantly suggested that the programmes might be offering negative examples, and thus implicitly be providing warnings about how *not* to behave – for example, about the dangers of under-age sex, or of obesity (!). As we have seen, some detected messages in *Trisha* about the importance of trust and commitment in relationships, or about the importance of talk itself; although others argued that, simply by showing such behaviour, the shows might encourage infidelity or an interest in sex without any consideration for 'feelings and emotions'. In general, however, the notion that such programmes might offer meaningful advice – whether to those who appeared in them, or to those in the audience at home – was seen as quite implausible.

This raises some interesting questions about the functions of such programmes for viewers, and indeed about their effects. As we have indicated, much of the academic discussion of talk shows has focused on their role as a form of surrogate therapy, both for participants and for viewers. In terms of Foucault's arguments, therapy – and the practice of the 'confession' through which it is applied – is part of a broader form of self-regulation that is characteristic of the operation of power in modern societies (see Rose 1999a). To put this a little more crudely, talk shows can be seen as means of encouraging viewers to internalise particular codes of moral conduct, and hence of reasserting dominant social norms. Yet these arguments apply much more easily to the older-generation talk shows (such as, in this case, *Trisha*) than they do to those of the 'new wave'. Here, it seems, viewers are not necessarily required to take moral or psychological issues seriously, or to engage with them in any depth. On the contrary, the extremes of private life – and indeed of private suffering – are held up as public spectacle, to be ridiculed and summarily judged. We do not need to engage or empathise with the participants in order to be entertained, nor do we need to think hard about how they might solve their problems – not least because they are probably faking or exaggerating to begin with. The potential consequences of this in terms of young people's developing 'sense of self' – or indeed of their conception of the relationship between the public and the private – are certainly worthy of further investigation.

Problems, problems

Like talk shows, problem pages and celebrity gossip also make aspects of private life available to the public gaze. In the remainder of this chapter, we consider the children's responses to these two media genres, and the extent to which they can be seen as sources for learning about love, sex and relationships.

Problem pages are a key feature of teenage girls' magazines – and, of course, of many women's magazines as well. In recent years, these magazines have repeatedly come under fire from conservative critics for contributing to the premature sexualisation of young girls. Academic studies of the genre have been relatively sparse; but in general, there has been a striking shift from wholesale condemnation to what often comes close to a form of celebration. Angela McRobbie's early work on *Jackie*, for example, accused the magazine of promoting an 'ideology of femininity', which encouraged girls to judge and define themselves in terms of their ability to attract the opposite sex. However, McRobbie's later work has tended to celebrate the more assertive, independent forms of femininity found in 1990s magazines like *More!* (McRobbie 1991; 1996; Winship 1985). These changes clearly reflect broader shifts in feminist debates about identity and popular culture, as well as in the magazines themselves. However, some critics continue to argue that such magazines have a profoundly negative effect on the development of young women's sexual identity and well-being. Garner, Sterk and Adams (1998), for example, in a rare historical study of advice columns in American teenage magazines, found that there had been little change in this respect over the past 20 years – although the magazines they describe appear significantly more conservative than their British counterparts.

Nevertheless, there have been very few studies exploring the responses of *readers* of these magazines. Those that have been undertaken – particularly Frazer (1987) and Kehily (1999) – suggest that young women are by no means passive recipients of the ideological (or indeed moral) values the magazines may be deemed to promote. Particularly when compared with the 'new wave' talk shows like *Jerry Springer*, the educational – or at least advisory – functions of problem pages are much more overt. Yet, as we shall see, this is not necessarily the way in which the children in our sample claimed to read them. On the contrary, the distanced – sceptical, but also occasionally voyeuristic – perspective adopted in relation to the talk shows was largely reproduced here.

Few of the youngest girls in our sample were regular readers of teenage magazines. For those who were, the problem pages were seen as a potentially valuable source of information – perhaps particularly about aspects of life they had yet to experience themselves:

> Rebecca (N, 10, P): Yeah, I like reading them, because it's like people write in letters about their worries and stuff. And then ... And then, um, they reply. It helps me learn about ... more about it.

Likewise, for Caitlin (N, 12, P), it did not seem to be difficult to empathise with the letter writers: 'I just think about what it would be like if I was in that position'. However, even in this age group, there was an emerging scepticism. Lisa (S, 10, P), for example, said of the advice on problem pages: 'I mean, like, don't always think that's like an excellent [idea]. You've got to be ... like, be prepared that it might not always be a good idea.'

By the time we reach the older girls, many of whom were regular readers of magazines like *Bliss*, *Sugar* and *Cosmo Girl*, this scepticism was the most striking aspect of the discussion. Like talk shows, the problem pages were frequently described as 'funny' and 'entertaining'. Several children suggested that the problems might have been 'made up' in order to fill column inches; and a couple even claimed to know people who had written in with fictional problems 'for a laugh'. The problems themselves were often described as 'ridiculous' or merely trivial. Like the guests on the talk shows, it was argued that people who wrote in to problem pages must be 'sad' (that is, pathetic). As Izzie (S, 12, G) put it, 'if you're sixteen, 'cause like you're nearly an adult, you can talk to like your friends or like someone else but not write in to a magazine. It is a bit sad, isn't it, like at sixteen!'

As with the talk shows, there were also elements of voyeurism here, along with a sense that viewing other people's problems could prove reassuring – both perspectives reflecting a fundamental distance from the reality of what is shown. Thus, Heather (N, 12, G) compared the problem pages with a fictional genre:

> They're a bit like soaps, I reckon. Because they're just like other people's lives. [...] And you're just, like, watching them. Or reading them. You're just like glued to it.

Meanwhile, as Naomi (N, 14, P) argued, 'reading about other people's problems that are more serious than yours' might also help to put your own problems in perspective. On the other hand, however, it might equally prove depressing. For Chantel (N, 14, P), this was a key difference between the talk shows and the problem pages, since the latter featured problems that were relevant to her age group: "Cause like they're people our age and they're just talking about their problems and moaning and it's common sense what they should do. And like it's not very, like, interesting reading somebody else's problems when you might have problems of your own. It's just stupid.'

As in Mary Kehily's (1999) study, the girls claimed to be much more interested in reading the problems than the answers – even though they agreed that the advice could be useful for some. There were several well-founded reasons advanced for this. Several children argued that the advice was too generalised to be of much use: there was insufficient detail, either to be sure that the advice was useful, or (as a reader) to enable you to apply it to your own life. As Lara (S, 14, G) put it, 'it's more universal advice, more than personal advice'; and as such, it was often difficult to put into practice – '[it tells you] how you should feel, but it doesn't necessarily mean that you're gonna do it'. As with appearing on the talk shows, few seemed to believe that writing in would actually help with your problems: as Kelly (N, 14, P) said, 'I don't see the point of writing in really, because you know they don't know you, so they can't really help you, can they? They don't know what's truthfully happened, do they?'

Similar complaints were raised in respect of a selection of problem pages we gave the children to read in advance of our final interviews. The children frequently suggested that the advice offered was 'just common sense' or 'obvious' – 'you should know it anyway' – even if the writers did 'add big words in, just to make it sound more scientific', as Phoebe and Naomi (N, 14, P) alleged. For example, one reply (to a letter headed 'I'm in love with a geek') suggested that the girl should ignore her friends and go out with the boy – a view that was disputed by Suzanne (S, 12, G), among others, on the grounds that 'you'd rather have all your friends than be with a boy for like a month or something'. Yet whether or not the advice was accepted, it was frequently accused of being too generalised: the best approach, it was argued, would depend on the people involved, and in that respect, you would do better to ask your friends for help. Several children were equally unconvinced by the magazines' strategy of seeking advice, not just from adult experts, but also from readers themselves;

and some even argued that these responses had been written (or at least selected) by the magazine editors, rather than by the young people themselves.

The question of age-appropriateness was also raised in several instances. Some of the younger children, like Kim (N, 12, P), found the content irrelevant for this reason: 'I'm a bit too young [laughing] to have any of those problems really like um ... "He doesn't wanna like have sex with me" and stuff like that'. However, several older children argued that the letter writers should already know the answers 'at their age', and expressed surprise that they seemed so ill-informed:

Nancy (S, 17, P): Like one of them said 'can I get pregnant through oral sex?' And I was like 'mm-hm' [sceptical]. And she's like sixteen. [...] I read things like that and I think well, do I know too much for my age?

Likewise, Lori (S, 14, P) argued that young people of her age had no reason to be ignorant, for instance about the risks of getting pregnant:

Really, they should know better. They should know in the first place. [...] Unless it was really and truly an accident. Like they didn't have a clue about it – which they couldn't, because there is like sex education in schools and things. They should know about it.

However, several of the girls were very attuned to the differences in the target age group of the magazines – a factor which was partly defined in terms of assumptions about their readers' sexual experience. Rollo and Mia (S, 12, P), for instance, had bought *Sugar*, but had stopped reading it on the grounds that it was for older readers: according to Rollo, 'it's more advanced, like "I've had sex with my boyfriend and I've done all this dirty stuff with my boyfriend" and you're like – that's just, they shouldn't put that in the magazine. Even for 16-year-olds, they should not put that in a magazine.' (Similar responses were recounted in Chapters 3 and 4.) Interestingly, Melissa (S, 17, P) suggested that the age at which particular problems were appearing had fallen over the years, for example in the case of girls worrying about sleeping with boyfriends: 'it's just, like, looking in magazines at the problem page, the age seems to be getting much younger as well, like you know, like 12 and 13 – when before when I was reading 'em, they were like 14 and 15.'

Here again, however, it is important to acknowledge that this relatively 'critical' – or at least disengaged – response may have derived from the influence of the interview context. Refusing to take the material seriously allowed the children to 'save face' in front of their peers. To some extent, this was also reflected in the children's accounts of the way in which the magazines were read. Here, for example, Ceri (N, 17, P) describes how she would read these magazines as a younger teenager:

> You'd just flick through the articles, read any that are of interest, you know, flick through the fashion or anything and then come to the problem page and just read a few problems and go 'ha! funny' and then just kind of put the magazine down or move on.

Several girls described how they would look through the magazines with friends, reading the problem letters aloud and laughing about 'how stupid it is'. However, some of the older children suggested that, in retrospect, this collective mockery might have disguised their embarrassment:

> Della (S, 17, P): Turn to the problem pages together in a group, like at school you just start off and do it. All read 'em together. All laugh about 'em. But then I think, like, deep inside we was all really thinking 'oh, what if that was me?' or but – all taking it in but no one would really talk about [it].

Perhaps predictably, this kind of response was even more apparent when we spoke to the boys about these magazines. Several claimed never to have seen such things – and some even affected surprise (followed by interest) in their sexually explicit content. While some of the older, middle-class boys were prepared to admit to having read them, most assured us that this was 'just to take the mick' (Richard, S, 17, P). At the same time, it was agreed that there was no possibility whatsoever of boys buying such a magazine themselves:

> Izzie (S, 12, P): Once when we went to a school trip in Bournemouth, I got the *Sugar*, I got two issues of it and all the boys are reading them and they said … They couldn't believe this is in a girl's magazine.
>
> Suzanne: And they were quite interested.

Izzie: Yeah, I think um ... What do they know, they couldn't exactly go and buy one. They'd look like poofs. [...] And they've got a reputation of knowing everything that they possibly can. So it would be a bit, like, shallow if they like went and bought one.

As Izzie and Suzanne argued – and as several of the boys in our interviews confirmed – being seen to read a girls' magazine was somehow incompatible with boys' public performance of heterosexuality, and indeed with their invulnerable self-image. When asked why there were no problem pages in boys' magazines, both boys and girls asserted that this would be unnecessary: as Izzie (S, 12, P) put it, 'boys don't really need a problem page, because they just don't usually have any big problems and things like girls have'. When asked what they would do to seek advice for their problems, Joshua and Matthew (N, 14, G) jokingly suggested they would talk to their teddy bear or their goldfish ('he's a good listener') rather than write to a magazine; and that if a boys' magazine had a problem page, 'the magazine would take the mickey out of 'em', or merely feature boys 'boasting that they have had sex'. As Lori (N, 14, G) argued, boys were 'too proud' to admit to having problems: 'they don't wanna get help from anyone'. As we saw in Chapter 4, the more overtly macho boys, such as Pierre and Dale (S, 14, P), claimed that there was no possibility that boys might experience any uncertainty here – although they also spoke at some length about the difficulties they had encountered in looking to other boys for help with their personal problems. As Joshua (N, 14, G) concluded, if boys have problems, 'they keep it to themselves' – and this was certainly confirmed by the way in which some groups of boys attempted to avoid discussion of these issues, even when encouraged by us.

To some extent, therefore, one can see the critical or disengaged response to the magazines as a kind of social performance – which, at least in some situations, is part of the broader performance of gender identities (see Chapter 4; and Kehily, 1999). As Melissa and Della (above) imply, what goes on in children's private reading of such texts may be quite different from the ways in which they are read or discussed with others (including adult interviewers). Yet it would be wrong to see the children's responses as simply a manifestation of a kind of superficial mockery. As we have indicated, they actually had good reasons to doubt the value or applicability of the advice that was offered – or in some instances, directly to challenge it.

Nevertheless, several were prepared to acknowledge that the problem pages might have a valuable educational function, particularly when compared with other potential sources. The anonymity of this form of communication was seen by many as particularly important in this respect (and here, there is an obvious difference from the talk shows). As Lori (S, 14, P) suggested, people might write in to a magazine ''cause they thought they haven't got anyone else to talk to, or they can't confide in anyone else, so they ask someone else that they don't know, and there isn't like any strings attached to it after'. Several children spoke of the potential difficulty of discussing problems with parents or doctors; although some were still concerned about the possibility of being unmasked if they were to write to a magazine. As we have seen, others argued that it might be helpful to read about other people with problems similar to your own – although these benefits were mostly hypothetical: only in one case (a minor medical problem) was anyone able to identify a useful piece of advice they had gained from a magazine. Yet the magazines were still seen to serve a more general educational function, that involved 'learning about other people's lives', as Caitlin (N, 12, G) put it. Indeed, it was argued that this should not be confined to girls: as Kim and her friends (N, 12, G) argued, 'boys should be made to read about it, to learn how to be nice to girls'.

Nevertheless, this potential educational value was undermined by the ever-present temptation to ridicule. For example, as Eve and Ceri (N, 17, P) argued, the problem pages sometimes contained sympathetic information about gay relationships; but the fact that people were likely to laugh at it meant that it was unlikely to 'change the homophobes' image of it'. Likewise, Sharmaine and Noelle (S, 12, P) related an embarrassing incident in which some of their schoolmates had been reading aloud a letter from a problem page in which a 12-year-old girl was concerned about her inability to stop 'touching herself' – which had resulted in a group of boys 'being really stupid' and ridiculing them.

Here again, there are interesting questions to be explored about the potential effects of such phenomena. There may be an element of perceived 'liberation' about the uncovering of the hidden secrets of sexual life. Making it possible to talk in public about such matters can be seen to remove the taboos that cause private suffering and fear. Yet if the arena in which such discussion is conducted is essentially one of mockery and ridicule, the nature and extent of that benefit is certainly debatable.

In the public eye

These issues to do with the boundary between the public and the private are writ large in the final area we shall discuss in this chapter, that of celebrity gossip. Few of the children were regular readers of newspapers; although – as the scrapbooks crammed with pictures of Page 3 models showed – the tabloids in particular were generally available, particularly in the working-class children's homes. Insofar as they were interested in them, the children claimed to read these papers for information about sports, entertainment and the TV listings; or alternatively to browse through when there was 'nothing else to do'. Nevertheless, they were undoubtedly aware of their sexual content – to the point where some argued that it was 'embarrassing' to be seen reading them in public.

There was a general argument, partly made on the basis of the nude models, that these newspapers were aimed at men; although the element of show-business gossip was seen by some (boys and girls alike) as being of greater interest to women. Gossip of this kind was described by several children as 'interesting', albeit with the proviso that it should concern very well-known celebrities, rather than (for example) minor actors from the soaps. Even in these cases, however, there were complaints about the triviality of some of the stories – 'Posh Spice takes Brooklyn to Tescos [the supermarket]' was one (perhaps imaginary) example mentioned.

While there was certainly a shared pleasure to be gained from this kind of gossip, there was also widespread distrust of the truthfulness of this material. To some extent, this was quite generalised – as Jody (S, 14, P) put it, 'I don't know that you can really trust everything that is actually written in the media' – but in several cases, it involved an understanding of how stories could be invented, or images could be 'faked'. Several children asserted that the newspapers frequently 'make up a load of rubbish' or 'blow things out of proportion'; and some were also aware of how images could be manipulated. For example, one of the stories we asked the children to look at featured paparazzi photographs of a topless Kylie Minogue. Most of the children recognised that the pictures had been taken with a long lens; and several were familiar with the term 'paparazzi', arguing that it was they who had 'killed Princess Diana'. Alternatively, Lee (N, 12, G) argued that 'computers' could have removed her clothes 'with editing and graphics and things'. In relation to this, Phil and Henry (N, 12, G) described how they had seen faked nude images of celebrities such as Britney Spears on the web: 'they put at the bottom [in] little tiny words "these are fake"'. Meanwhile, Zoe (S, 12, G) even doubted that it was Kylie in the first place.

This scepticism reflected the fact that newspapers – or at least tabloids – were seen as essentially a money-making business. Selling papers was the name of the game, and questions of public interest or protecting individual privacy were seen as secondary to this. As Reena (N, 14, G) put it, 'the newspapers don't care about people's feelings – it's about the ratings and how many papers they sell'. Likewise, sexual stories and images were heavily featured on the front pages 'just so people buy it': according to Krystal (S, 14, P), 'all they're after is their money and they wanna sell their papers'. Meanwhile, several children were aware that scandalous stories would be bought by the newspapers – by those whom Joseph (S, 12, P) referred to as 'cheque-book journalists'.

For some, the focus on gossip about the private lives of celebrities reflected a dangerous abdication of responsibility on the part of the press – or indeed of the celebrities themselves. Some argued that celebrities were expected to 'set a good example' or to act as 'role models', although there was some doubt about whether they were actually seen in that way. Lori (S, 14, G), for example, argued in a distinctly parental tone that the newspapers 'treat carefree sex as a joke, which doesn't set a very good example to people my age and younger'. However, she argued that such examples would not necessarily be followed:

> Lori: I wouldn't like do something like sleeping around or taking drugs. I won't just go and do it because they [the celebrities] are. [...] To other people, that follow them, like, it might but ... I don't think so. I don't think there are that many people who would just do things because people they admire do it.

As to some extent in the discussion of the talk shows, there was an occasional element of self-righteousness in these criticisms that might partly have resulted from the interview situation. Jody and Lara (S, 14, P), for example, engaged in a familiar lament about the way in which the newspapers allegedly relegated important stories in favour of celebrity trivia:

> Jody: Like sometimes you get stars on the front cover with just stories like um ... 'A star for wedding of the year'. And then in the

middle you get like the plane crash like on the Twin Towers or something. And something like so small is on the front cover ...

Lara: Mhm. I think that's quite bad when they do that. Because really the people should be caring more about like people being in danger and sorting out like wars and really getting that sorted out, than like pop stars and celebrities ...

This led to a situation in which, as Lara aptly put it, 'the *News of the World* has nothing about the world'. According to Lara, such material was often included on the grounds that young people were likely to be attracted by it; yet they placed the blame for this state of affairs on *adult* readers – like their own parents – who, they claimed, were more interested in such trivia.

The fact remained, however, that many of the children were interested in finding out about the private lives of celebrities (or at least some of them), and enjoyed discussing them, whether or not they believed the rumours were true. As Jacqueline Rose (1999) suggests, an interest in celebrity is often seen as somehow shameful; but the cult of celebrity provides a license for forms of curiosity that might otherwise be seen as voyeuristic, or even as positively 'ruthless'. Thus, despite their somewhat high-minded stance, Jody and Lara also engaged in a quite extended debate about what Victoria Beckham had allegedly said about Jordan, and how the latter was simply a 'slag'. Ultimately, however sceptical they may have been about the veracity of the stories, they were still keen to read them. As Ethan (N, 12, G) put it, 'it's like Harry Potter – you don't believe it, but you still read it ... 'cos you enjoy it'. Both in the interviews and in the diaries, many children were keen to exchange new gossip about celebrities. Snippets of supposedly authentic information were typically introduced with 'did you know ...', 'have you heard ...' or 'is it true that ...', for which the source was invariably the media. Abigail (N, 12, P), for example, expressed her shock at discovering that Will Young, the *Pop Idol* winner, was gay; while Suzanne and Mia (S, 12, G) engaged in an extended debate about whether Robbie Williams and Geri Halliwell had really had sex and were 'serious' about each other, or whether it was merely a 'summer romance'. There was much discussion of the possible name of the Beckhams' forthcoming baby, and of the troubled relationship between Britney Spears and her then boyfriend Justin. While there was certainly speculation about the veracity of the information that was being exchanged, there was clearly considerable pleasure to be gained from doing so nevertheless.

There was a similar degree of ambivalence when it came to discussing specific stories we had selected from the tabloids. In the case of the photographs of Kylie Minogue, for example, the children were mostly well aware that the images had been taken without her consent – and, most probably, without payment; and several suggested that she could 'sue' the newspaper on these grounds. There was general agreement that this kind of journalism constituted an 'invasion of privacy'. As Henry (N, 12, G) put it, 'they're raiding her personal life. She can't do anything without having a secret camera or long range camera watching her.' Several children said they 'felt sorry' for her, and that they would be 'really upset' if they were in the same position. However, others argued that this was simply the price of fame. As Lori (S, 14, G) put it, 'she's famous, so she should expect it. She knows that someone is gonna find out where she is and will be taking pictures.' Some went further, arguing that Kylie herself was partly to blame: 'if she didn't want to be in the newspaper about it, why did she take her top off?' (Naomi, N, 14, G). Others argued that she would be unlikely to be too concerned about the pictures, on the grounds that they were simply extra publicity: as Theo and Darren (S, 12, G) pointed out, 'she just gets more money when she gets her picture taken of her half naked ... and more men get attracted to her. Some of them will buy her CD, buy her posters.' Indeed, the stars were seen by some to have little grounds for complaint here. As Holly (S, 14, G) argued, 'I don't think she was that bothered though – look at the little tops she wears all the rest of the time.' Likewise, Phil and Henry (N, 12, G) argued that stars like the Beckhams deliberately courted publicity, and made money, for example by selling pictures of their wedding; and so they could hardly complain when 'faked' pictures of them appeared on pornographic websites.

Another story, featuring the former *EastEnders* star Martine McCutcheon, was viewed with similar ambivalence. Here, the actress – now apparently 'lonely' and single – had been spotted at a London nightclub, allegedly 'snogging' (and being rejected by) three different men. Her status as a 'D-list celebrity' (as Izzie (S, 12, G) put it) made this story less immediately engaging, and its veracity was widely questioned. Seth (N, 12, G), for example, asserted that 'someone in this sick world has made this up and got money for it'; while others suggested that the events had been exaggerated, or that the story had been 'twisted' as it had circulated – 'like Chinese Whispers', according to Courtney (N, 12, G). Some noted a contradiction between the story – which alleged that the star had left the club in tears – and the accompanying picture, which showed no such thing. Few, however, felt much pity for her. Some claimed to be 'disgusted' by her behaviour; while Gareth (S, 14, G) described her as a 'sad bitch'. As was clearly the intention of the story, several children felt a degree of *schadenfreude*: Seth (N, 12, G) laughed at the fact that 'so many people stood her up', while Izzie (S, 12, G) also said she found it 'funny' – "Cause she's been rejected and she's crying – I mean, there's lots of other men in the world, it's not like it's the end!' Here again, several children argued that there had been an invasion of privacy, and that the tone of the story was 'unfair'. As Dale (S, 14, G) complained, 'if she wants to go out clubbing, that's up to her. If she wants to go and kiss boys, then it's up to her what she does. She don't have to have the mick taken out of her for it.' Yet here too, it was argued that celebrities should expect this to happen, and that Martine herself might not have been unduly concerned about it.

A rather different example, which was introduced by several of the children rather than by us, concerned the model Jordan's intention to have the forthcoming birth of her baby transmitted live on the internet. This story had been widely featured in the tabloid press, and some children included examples of this in their scrapbooks. In this instance, the courting of publicity was clearly seen to have 'gone too far': it was generally condemned as a 'publicity stunt', or as 'sick' – and as something that was just being done for the money. According to Dale and Pierre (S, 12, P), 'she'll get millions of pounds – just to open her legs and force something out!' – although others expressed some doubt about the likely size of the audience. This approach was seen as symptomatic of Jordan's 'excessive' public persona. Most children knew about her multiple breast implants – Ethan (N, 12, P) suggested she would 'melt in a fire' – and some commented on her 'thick' make-up. In this sense, the stunt was seen as further evidence of the fact that she was, in the children's words, 'manky' or a 'nutter'. Some expressed concern about the possibility that her child would be 'embarrassed' in later life: as Courtney (N, 12, P) put it, 'if I was that little baby, would you wanna be slapped across every single newspaper and looked at on the internet – looked at when you're having your umbilical cord chopped and everything like that?' In this instance, therefore, there was general agreement that the boundary between the private and the public was being violated, and that, as Ethan and Seth (N, 12, P) put it, this was 'a private thing ... between you and your boyfriend or husband and your family'. Interestingly, however, this was one case where few of the children expressed any doubt that the story was true – which may partly have reflected their dislike of Jordan in the first place.

As Ian Connell (1991; 1992) has argued, this kind of ambivalence may be characteristic of readers' relationships with the popular tabloids, and with celebrity gossip in particular. On the one hand, there is a straightforward curiosity: we want to see or know about such things, particularly where they relate to people whom we admire or lust after – or alternatively despise. Yet there is also a kind of resentment, which can be expressed in an apparently uncaring pleasure in others' suffering: we want these glamorous people to suffer because we envy their wealth and good fortune, and because we know we will never enjoy the kinds of lives they lead. In some cases, this can lead on to a kind of moral condemnation – a censorious rejection of the irresponsibility or selfishness of the celebrities, or their failure to conform to the standards required of would-be 'role models'. And yet, underlying all this, there is a doubt about the veracity of it all – a suspicion that perhaps the stories may be invented or at least exaggerated after all.

The final stories we would like to mention here – and which we gave the children to read in advance of our interviews – were not concerned with celebrities but with private citizens. The first of these, the story of the Canadian teacher who had sex with her students, has already been considered in Chapter 3. In that case, the children seemed largely unconcerned about the level of detail in which the events were described: this was seen as merely a necessary aspect of the public shaming of the teacher, and the boys involved were not identified. The second story was rather different: it concerned a woman who was offering her virginity for sale (at £10,000) on the front page of a Sunday newspaper. As far as the children were concerned, this was tantamount to 'prostitution', and they were unanimous in condemning not just the woman herself, but also the newspaper for running the story in the first place. There was some debate about whether the newspaper had paid for the story (with the aim of increasing sales), or whether the woman had paid for what was effectively an advertisement for her services. Either way, both were effectively accused of 'selling sex'; and, as Lisa (N, 14, G) asserted, 'sex isn't meant to be sold'.

In different ways, and for different reasons, all these stories appear to blur the boundary between the public and the private. The Canadian teacher was implicitly seen to have forfeited her right to privacy by committing a criminal act; while the woman selling her virginity had voluntarily surrendered hers in the interests of financial gain. These are people whose private lives have now become legitimate public property, albeit for different reasons. In the case of the celebrities, there is more room for debate about this. Kylie Minogue and Martine McCutcheon have had their privacy violated, without their apparent consent; although in the case of Jordan, the opposite is true. Yet either way, the fundamental issue here is whether the privileges enjoyed by celebrities effectively deprive them of the right to privacy, or whether they are bound to live their private lives in the public gaze (cf. Rose 1999a).

Here again, there are interesting questions to be raised about the potential consequences of all this in terms of young people's learning. Like the talk shows, much celebrity gossip could be seen to depend upon (or to assume) a level of prurience or voyeurism on the part of its audience. Yet, as Ian Connell (1992) suggests, such stories can also be read as 'cautionary tales', which reveal what happens when people violate moral norms – for example, by committing adultery or engaging in promiscuous sex or behaving 'indecently' in public places. As such, this material must be seen as a highly ambivalent source of learning about personal relationships: it can be seen to convey quite different 'messages' to different readers, or indeed to be interpreted in several different ways simultaneously. In this respect, the media may allow us to have our cake and eat it: we can – if we wish – revel in the details of others' private lives, while simultaneously deploring and condemning them. Children may indeed be learning about things from these sources that they might not have known about in earlier times; but that does not necessarily imply that they are being led to approve of them, or even to tolerate them as acceptable – much less to copy them. The relationship between sexual knowledge and sexual behaviour is, to say the least, rather more complex than that.

The interesting question that remains here is to do with the fact that so much of the material we have discussed in this chapter did not seem to be taken seriously. We accept that some of the critical distance – and indeed the ridicule – with which this material was discussed can be seen as a consequence of the interview situation. As some of the children themselves acknowledged, much of the mockery and hilarity that surrounded everyday discussions of such material was merely a disguise for their embarrassment – and it was possible that it could be taken much more seriously when encountered in private. Even so, the responses the children recorded in the more intimate medium of their diaries were not significantly less sceptical or satirical. As we have suggested, the children often had very cogent reasons for their refusal to take this material seriously, or to use it as a guide for their own behaviour. Furthermore, much of this material does not *demand* to be taken seriously – and indeed, some of it seems to demand precisely the opposite.

In this respect, Foucault's argument about the confession may be in need of some adaptation, at least in this context. In some areas of the contemporary media, there is indeed an incitement, even a compulsion, to speak about sex – to bear witness to intimate secrets that might previously have been hidden away. Yet the idea that it is through this process of confession that the 'truth of the self' is revealed – or rather that what is revealed is *believed* to be the truth – would seem to be rather more questionable. If guests on talk shows or celebrities or those who write letters to problem pages are indeed being compelled to confess, they are doing so in a public arena in which fewer and fewer people are likely to believe what they say. They are holding themselves up, not so much to an inquisition designed to uncover the truth as to a form of open mockery and humiliation. Foucault's argument is that this public discourse – in this instance, about sex – has significant implications, not just in terms of the regulation of social behaviour, but for the individual's personal sense of self. Yet if audiences – including children – seem disinclined to regard what they hear or read as true, and instead to see it merely as a kind of entertaining performance or show, the potential implications for their sense of self are at least more ambiguous and difficult to define.

7
Show and Tell – Learning from Television Drama

Ray (parent): Would you invite two people in your home to take drugs? Or would you invite two people into your home to have a fight in your living room? Would you invite people into your home to – maybe it would be two women – to kiss each other, or to hold hands? Would you invite them into your home to do that? (FG2S)

Like many critics of television, parents like Ray tend to regard the medium as an unwarranted intrusion into family life. Indeed, part of the problem of television is that the 'guests' it brings into our homes are, precisely, *not* invited. For Ray, drugs, sex and violence on television are somehow the same as they are in real life – as if such things might actually leap out of the television screen onto your living room carpet. This is perhaps a particular concern when it comes to television drama, which is the focus of this chapter.

If talk shows and problem pages give young people access to *discourses* about personal relationships, television drama purports to show them as they actually unfold. Via the small screen, we meet people whom we come to know over weeks or months, and possibly years. We have privileged access to the thrills and crises of their love lives. We eavesdrop on their private conversations, witness their intimate moments, share their secrets, doubts and fears. And while a good deal of television drama merely tells us about the physical details of these relationships, or refers to them in ways that children are assumed to be unable to understand, at least some of it actually shows us what happens in considerable detail.

According to critics like Joshua Meyrowitz (1985), television gives us access to 'backstage' behaviour that would otherwise be hidden from view. This, he argues, has particular consequences for children. It is no longer so easy for adults to keep secrets from children, or to ensure that they will not learn the undesirable facts of adult life. For example, the television sitcoms of the 1950s largely presented an 'official version' of family life, in which parents (and particularly fathers) always knew best. By contrast, modern family sitcoms show how parents behave when children are not around; and much of their humour derives precisely from acknowledging the gap between what parents ought to be and what they actually are. Likewise, much of the pleasure of contemporary soap operas and drama series lies in their revelation of 'secrets' about adult life. Even those that purport to focus on professional working life – such as crime shows or medical dramas – seem preoccupied with intimate, personal relationships. And much of their emotional appeal derives from the revelation of aspects of private life that would previously have been considered taboo.

Among the children in our research, these aspects of adult sexual behaviour were often recounted with considerable fascination. From the psychotic rapist in *Clocking Off* to Janine selling her body for drugs in *EastEnders*; from Linda Green visiting a lesbian nightclub in search of sex to discussions of 'doing it doggy style' in *Gimme, Gimme, Gimme*; and from the prisoners' strip club in *Bad Girls* to heaving buttocks on a snooker table in *Footballer's Wives* – television appeared to be revealing adult secrets with wild abandon.

David Buckingham's earlier study of the television soap opera *EastEnders* (1987) found that this aspect was central to its popularity with young people. Being privy to the characters' most intimate secrets – and speculating about how and when they would be revealed to other characters – created a powerful form of complicity between the programme and the viewer. 'Gossip' – that is, the public circulation of private knowledge – was a key source of narrative pleasure, both within the programme and outside it (in the popular press as well as in viewers' everyday conversations). Young viewers were not primarily interested in the younger characters – who were often judged to be lacking in authenticity – but in the adult characters, whose private secrets were much more vivid and sensational, and potentially more far-reaching in their consequences.

Of course, this is not to imply that viewers regard such material at face value. Alongside their heated speculation about what particular characters will do when they find out 'the truth', viewers often display a powerful scepticism about what is shown. In the *EastEnders* study, the young people were well aware of the constructed nature of the programme; and they knew that the narrative was manipulated precisely in order to achieve the effects we have described. They also made judgments about what they saw by comparison with real-life experience, and by invoking more generalised beliefs about what was psychologically plausible. This became particularly difficult when the programmes addressed social issues, such as drugs or racism. Children suspected that such issues were artificially imported into the programme, and they resisted its attempt to convey overt messages – in effect, to use the characters as a means of preaching to the viewer. Despite its claims to realism and authenticity, the programme was ultimately seen as *entertainment* – and hence as something that should not be taken too seriously.

Television drama is undoubtedly an important source of informal learning about love, sex and relationships; and in some instances, it can also set out explicitly to teach. In this chapter, we will focus specifically on this process of teaching and learning (or 'pedagogy') in television drama series, including soap operas, situation comedies and children's/teen series. As we shall indicate, the pedagogy of television drama is often problematic, for two main reasons. The first of these is to do with the question of *modality* – that is, the extent to which viewers perceive what they watch to be realistic. The extent to which television is capable of teaching particular messages (whether 'good' or 'bad') largely depends upon how far it is seen to be plausible; and plausibility, at least in the case of drama, is far from easy to achieve. The second, related issue here is that of the relationship between 'education' and 'entertainment' (which of course are problematic terms in themselves). To take a medium that is largely perceived as 'entertainment' – such as television drama – and recruit it for the purposes of 'education' is a strategy that, we suggest, is fraught with difficulties.

Soap, sex and secrets

Television soap operas have long been celebrated and criticised for their emphasis on personal relationships. Much of the genre's appeal lies in its exploration of the intricacies of romance and family life: the everyday desires and wishes, the lies and deceptions, the unspoken longings, the uncertain feelings and nagging anxieties, the mundane domestic routines – these are the stuff of soap opera. Meanwhile, moral conservatives have frequently condemned what they regard as the soaps' unremitting focus on the seamier side of human relationships – infidelity, promiscuity, 'deviant' sexuality, prostitution, sexually-transmitted diseases, domestic violence and the rest.

In our research, these elements were obviously to the fore in the children's discussions; although there was evidence to suggest that this was not simply invited by us. As Olivia (S, 17, P) pointed out, much of the appeal of the soaps was the fact that 'you come into school [the next day] and then talk about who's sleeping with who'. This was particularly the case with the British soaps, especially *EastEnders*, which will be the primary focus of attention here. According to Keira and Alma (S, 10, P), *EastEnders* 'actually show them having sex', unlike the Australian soaps *Neighbours* and *Home and Away*, which (according to them) 'just show 'em going into the bedroom and don't show anything else'. Likewise, Clint (S, 10) singled out *EastEnders* for mention in his diary, arguing that the sex in it was 'wicked', and that 'if it didn't have sex in it, it wouldn't be so interesting'. There were some dissenters here: Kim (N, 12, P) claimed that the sex in *Coronation Street* was 'disgusting' – 'I just change over, me, and then I keep flicking back to see if it's finished yet'. In general, however, the sexual content of the storylines was a topic of considerable fascination for the large majority of the children here, particularly the girls. These events were often described in the manner of a catalogue of serial relationships: 'Steve slept with Sam (...) Steve was going off with Sam because Steve wanted to get back at Phil. 'Cause then, um, Mel and Phil, um ... Steve were going away with Lisa and Mark, but Mark can't go now 'cause he's got HIV...' (Clint, S, 10, P). Who fancied whom, who had slept with whom, who was having whose baby, and who did and didn't know – these were the focus of intense speculation and debate.

Despite their enthusiasm, however, it appeared that some of the younger children did not quite understand what they were watching. The recent storyline in *EastEnders*, in which Kat had confessed to Zoe that she was her mother and not her sister (see below), seemed especially confusing to some. As Rebecca (N, 10, P) confessed, in relation to another story about sexually-transmitted disease, 'most of it I'm just really confused about, 'cause I don't understand most of it'; while Jay (S, 17, P) recalled 'I wasn't even sure what exactly infidelity was when I was like 10 or 11. I was like "what's all that about? Are they just like good friends or something like that?"'.

As in earlier studies of audiences for soap opera, we found a marked degree of ambivalence here – a phenomenon which Christine Geraghty (1991) has aptly termed 'an oscillation between engagement and distance' (see also Buckingham 1993: Chapter 4). On the one hand, there were instances of intense emotional empathy with the characters. Several children, both boys and girls, described how they identified with characters by projecting themselves into the programme: 'if I had a husband and he died in a car crash ... I'd be upset' (Sharmaine, S, 12, P); 'if I was to fall pregnant when I was 13 and I chose to give it away, I wouldn't give it to my mum and watch it grow up as my sister' (Della, S, 17, P). Others described feeling sad when favourite characters had died, or relationships had broken up: Alma (S, 10, P) even said that her mother had forbidden her to watch *EastEnders* because she had been so upset (at the age of six) by Melanie jilting Ian on their wedding day.

In some instances, these storylines were regarded as necessary, even if they were painful to watch, as in this discussion of the Kat and Zoe story:

Sharmaine (S, 12, P): I think that's really bad because..., just to think about it, because you have things in everyday life and you think those are really bad. But I just thought to myself, I thought that ain't entertainment. If that happened to me I'd feel really bad.

Noelle: I thought Kat's situation was bad. I've never heard of anything happened like that before, getting raped by her uncle. And also nobody cares for her at home especially. I've never heard of any case like that or anything.

In this instance, the girls are able to empathise with the characters ('if that happened to me ... ') even though the events that are shown are much worse than their own experience, or simply beyond it altogether ('I've never heard of any case like that ... '). While this was not 'entertainment' in their view, they did describe it as both 'interesting' and potentially 'helpful' – both terms that would imply some kind of educational value.

On the other hand, however, there was a great deal of criticism of the soaps on the grounds of modality. These criticisms were particularly voiced by the older boys – many of whom tended to reject the soaps outright – but they were common across the age groups. Part of the concern here was to do with the pace and repetition of narrative incident, not least in the frequency of 'affairs' between the characters. As Grant (S, 17, P) put it, 'you get relationships, sooner or later one of them's going to have an affair, just to make a better story line'. The stories, we were frequently told, were 'predictable' and 'corny', and the soaps routinely 'copied' stories from each other, or extended stories in order 'to keep people watching'. For example, Rebecca (N, 10, P) complained that, while such stories were 'exciting', 'all different soaps have affairs all at the same time'; and she reserved particular criticism for

Coronation Street on these grounds – 'Sandra was having an affair with that other man and Janice is having an affair with Dennis and it's like way too many affairs going on'. These kinds of stories were also condemned on the grounds of implausibility. For example, according to Grant (S, 17, P), 'it ain't exactly real life, when he drags her round to the alley way and just you know... She only had to talk to him and he just had sex with her. It don't really happen, does it?'

These criticisms were partly reinforced by the children's knowledge of the production process. While there was a good deal of praise for *EastEnders* on the grounds of its realism, there was no doubt whatsoever that it was fictional. Rachel (N, 10, P), for example, praised the acting – 'they use good facial expressions and they look like they really mean it' – while Alma (S, 10, P) argued that the producers were responsible enough not to upset viewers unduly – 'the people – even though it's pretend and everything – I thought that they wouldn't do that for the little people who watch'. As with advertisements and other media, several children recognised that 'sex sells', and could be used to build audiences. This seemed to be the case even where the stories were seen to have some kind of educational function. Rory and Skye (N, 10, P), for example, recognised that the story of Janine selling her body for drugs was 'realistic', and could serve as a 'warning' against drugs; but they also argued that 'it would get people watching it'. Likewise, Heather and Caitlin (N, 12, P) argued that the story of Mark's HIV was 'another storyline to get people interested, glued to the TV, so they can get more money' – although they seemed rather vague about how what they called the 'money business' of television actually operated.

The pedagogy of soap

This 'oscillation' had interesting consequences in terms of the *pedagogy* of the soaps. When we asked the children if the programmes were offering them 'messages' about love, sex and relationships, many agreed that they were. As we suggested in Chapter 2, our search for 'messages' was one we began to regret, not least because it appeared somewhat at odds with the children's experiences of these programmes – or at least with some aspects of them. It seemed to encourage them to reduce the storylines to moral fables or health education warnings. Encouraging them to identify the 'messages' also seemed to position them as 'children', who were merely the passive objects of patronising adult attempts to show them the path to righteousness – and in asking the question, we ran the risk of becoming complicit in this.

Nevertheless, the children did recognise that some of these programmes had educational *intentions*, and that these were of different kinds. It is worth distinguishing here between what might be termed 'overt' and 'covert' pedagogy. By overt pedagogy, we are referring to clearly defined moral or health-related 'lessons' that viewers perceive the programmes to be putting across. Covert pedagogy refers to more general attitudes or beliefs about relationships which viewers infer from their viewing, whether or not they see these as intended on the part of the producers.

As we shall see in more detail below, soaps positively invite moral debate; and as such, the children were able to draw moral conclusions from the programmes without having the sense that they were being explicitly taught – even if these conclusions were often somewhat vague. In a few cases, the children disapproved of the moral messages they perceived: Angela (N, 17, P), for example, argued that *Coronation Street* was 'giving the wrong message to kids' about extramarital affairs; while Morris (N, 10, P) felt that *EastEnders* was encouraging violence, and that this 'shouldn't be shown on TV'. In general, however, the soaps were seen to be promoting values such as fidelity, respect and trust – not least by showing the consequences for people's relationships when these values were lost or abandoned. As Glenn (S, 17, P) pointed out, affairs in *EastEnders* always ended in tragedy. Izzie (S, 12, P) argued that the programme taught you not to 'give in to temptation'; while Clint and Leo (S, 10, P) agreed that the programme taught the dangers of 'two-timing' – 'you shouldn't do things that you don't mean ... and be happy with what you've got'. According to the soaps, we were told, ideal relationships involved unselfishness and commitment: 'it's not like me, me, me, in relationships. You've got to think about the other person as well' (Joseph, S, 12, P). Similar messages were detected in *Coronation Street*: as Caitlin and Heather (N, 12, P) put it, 'when you get married you have to really think about if you really love this person ... You've got to be ready for it, basically – you've got to be committed'. Others argued that the programmes taught people to be aware of the consequences of their actions: as Sharmaine (S, 12, P) argued, 'you shouldn't like treat people like they're just like something on the bottom of your shoe, because they can treat you back and you won't like it'. In many instances, these judgments seemed to imply that morality was not primarily a matter of following externally-imposed rules, but rather of taking personal responsibility for ensuring your own fulfilment (cf. N.Rose 1999a).

In addition to these covert messages, children in all age groups identified much more overt teachings in the soaps relating to issues such as drugs, HIV-AIDS and teenage pregnancy. Thus, we were repeatedly told that *EastEnders* was 'warning' children in particular about the dangers of drugs: according to Damian (N, 12, P), for example, the story of Janine was telling you that 'if you go on drugs, it'll just ruin your whole life'. The messages about teenage sex were perceived in similarly stark terms: 'don't get pregnant if you're a teenager' (Ethan, N, 12, P); 'certainly don't have under-aged sex – and you should use a condom' (Wesley, S, 12, P). It could be argued that the programmes' 'messages' are in fact more complex than this; and that the long-running nature of the storylines allows such issues to be dealt with in a more multi-faceted way (see Buckingham 1987). Yet these injunctions to 'just say no' are messages that children are very familiar with, often to the point of overkill; and in recounting them, they often appeared to reduce the programmes to little more than health education propaganda.

Some children explicitly commented on the value of this kind of teaching. Richard (S, 17, P) said that he had first learned about HIV-AIDS from *EastEnders*; while several girls argued that they had gleaned more general messages about safety from the soaps – as Nancy (S, 17, P) put it, 'I think that's the message there – like when you go out, don't make yourself completely vulnerable to your surroundings'. Izzie (S, 12, P) was one of many who approved of the ways in which soaps could give 'warnings' about likely dangers: 'sometimes you don't find out until it happens to you, and then if you like find out [from TV] then you kind of know and you know the consequences as well.' Rollo and Mia (S, 12, P) said they preferred learning about issues like under-age sex from television than from teenage magazines, where explicit information often appeared unexpectedly: while Caitlin (S, 12, P) also expressed a preference for 'having a play right in front of you on TV'.

However, several children appeared to believe that the programmes were preaching at them, and some of their comments displayed a certain impatience with this. Several suggested that the programmes were sacrificing realism in order to reinforce particular messages. Sharmaine and Noelle (S, 12, P), for example, implied that it was too predictable for teenage sex always to result in pregnancy:

Sharmaine: So Sonia like takes him upstairs and then like they start. The end.

Noelle: They do everything and then –

Sharmaine: And the next thing you know, she's pregnant.

Noelle: Exactly. It's the end of that episode. And then the next episode she goes to see the doctor.

Sharmaine: 'I'm pregnant.'

Noelle: 'Oh you're pregnant. Oh no. Okay then. Bye.' Walks out the door. 'I'm pregnant.' Okay then. Then like about a few weeks later 'Oh look, I've had the baby.'

Sharmaine: 'I'm going to give it up now!'

Others argued that these kinds of storylines were included on the grounds of salaciousness – and in order to attract more viewers – and that the 'messages' were simply a pretext for this. Kim (N, 12, P), for example, felt that in *Coronation Street* there was too much 'picturing' of the sex itself – or at least too much for 'this age group' (her own) – and not enough of the 'message': 'they kind of take the sex bit a bit too seriously and then there's kind of like a little bit of a message at the end, instead of like a bit of sex and then a big message at the end would be better, because it's kind of teaching something'. Likewise, Lori (S, 14, P) argued that characters were made to do such things without 'considering the consequences' simply because this made for a good storyline.

For several children, this educational approach was essentially incompatible with the soap opera form. TV drama, they insisted, was fictional, and as such it was merely 'entertainment'. Heather (S, 12, P), for example, argued that such programmes might be trying to teach, 'but you don't really take it in'. Likewise – and in contrast to Rollo and Mia's positive comments above – Sharmaine (S, 12, P) argued that showing such events on television somehow undermined their educational potential: 'to watch 'em is totally different to hear about 'em, you know. Because if you hear about 'em you're like "oh that's really bad". But if you watch it, it's like entertainment, ain't it?' Some of the older children recognised the educational intentions of the soaps, but argued that this was unlikely to coincide with viewers' motivations for watching, which were seen as primarily to do with entertainment. Tom (N, 17, P) was particularly forceful in his criticism of this approach:

You know, [there was] *Coronation Street* with a girl who's supposed to be 13 and she slept with someone for the first time and got pregnant and it's not like 'OK, I didn't use a condom, it's my own fault'. It's 'oh, I didn't know you could get pregnant on your first time', and all of that. It's just so obvious. It's like the words have been put in the mouth from social workers. (...) It's like there's pressure from the Government. It just feels like if a girl has sex with somebody it's like 'oh you can't have this' and she enjoys it, 'well, this will teach our youngsters to do something wrong', which is considered wrong. Only it's like they feel they're obliged to give this moral thing. It's like people do sleep around but you know it can be very bad and they don't show that you can just sleep around and enjoy it. Which a lot of people do. And that's really irritated me.

Despite this, Tom's rejection of this approach was somewhat ambivalent: he was prepared to believe that such overt messages might have an educational function for others, even if not for himself. And of course, rejecting such overt messages does not necessarily imply that soaps (or the media in general) do not have a more implicit educational role, even if this is not always apparent to viewers themselves.

Making judgments: blaming and explaining

Both directly and indirectly, soaps invite an ongoing process of moral judgment. As Chris Barker (1998) has indicated, young people's moral discourses about soap operas appear to take two main forms. On the one hand, they condemn 'inappropriate sexuality', both in terms of its representation (where it seen as too explicit) and in terms of the 'immoral' actions of the characters themselves. From this perspective, the emphasis is very much on *blaming* individual characters for their moral shortcomings. On the other hand, they may also seek to understand the characters' behaviour in the broader context of their social circumstances and relationships. The emphasis here is more on *explaining* why characters behave the way they do – and often on 'forgiving' them for their misdeeds.

To some degree, the balance between blaming and explaining depends upon the storyline, and (in some instances) on the pedagogic intentions that viewers perceive to be informing it. In our research, certain characters were clearly in line for blaming. Most soaps tend to have characters who are marked out as 'baddies', although there is often a degree of relish in their villainous deeds: *EastEnders'* Steve Owen, for example, was condemned for his mistreatment of his wife Mel, but (as Della (S, 17, P) put it) 'he was adventurous, and he always had something good up his sleeve'. Others, such as Janine, were dismissed as merely 'stupid' or 'a slapper': 'what sickened me is like when she had no money and she just like unfastened her blouse to that drug addict and he's just like "that's a start". And then he gave her the drugs just because she did that, and it was disgusting. I just sat there going "I think I'm gonna be sick"' (Abigail, N, 12, P). Stories such as this appeared to be perceived as 'cautionary tales', that might have some straight from a Victorian moral primer. The story of the wife-beater Trevor and his victim 'Little Mo', for example, was seen to have a very obvious message: according to Emma (N, 10, P), the story was teaching you 'to be strong' and to refuse your husband's unreasonable demands. Several of the younger girls argued that Mo was right to 'stand up to him' and fight back, and in some instances, this message appeared to have been reinforced by other family members: 'the first time that he hits [her], my mum says to me, "if a man ever hits you, Lysa, don't ever give him a chance 'cause he'll do it again"... Some people in our family're going "Yes! Kill him! Kill him! Down with him!"' (Lysa, S, 10, P).

In many other instances, however, the motivations for the characters' actions were less than clear. On one level, this simply encouraged children to speculate. Did Steve have sex with Sam just to get back at his business rival Phil? Did Sam really believe that Steve would leave his wife for her? In some instances, the fact that certain aspects were not shown clearly encouraged this. Were Mark and Lisa really having a sexual relationship or not? And if they weren't, was Lisa more likely to go back to Phil when she got the chance? This kind of speculation often led to predictions about future plot developments – in some instances, encouraged by revelations in the popular press. Mark, we were assured, was bound to find out about Lisa and Phil, and Mel would find out about Steve and Sam – and in both cases, things were bound to end badly.

This uncertainty, both about the characters' present motivations and about the future, clearly encouraged moral debate about what *should* happen. The story of Sonia and Jamie, two of the younger characters, exemplifies this. In the weeks preceding our interviews, Jamie had suddenly proposed marriage to Sonia, and she had accepted – despite the fact that she knew he had slept with both Janine and Zoe. The motivations on the part of both characters were not wholly clear at this point, which led some to find the story implausible. This is apparent in Neville's (N, 14, P) account:

> He had sex with someone else because they'd had a fight, and she found out about it. And then he just proposed to her because she dumped him and then he figured out that he loved her and he proposed to her. And then she just instantly forgave him for having sex. Which I thought was a bit weird. Because she was really, really mad at him. And then as soon as he proposes then she instantly forgets about it, and says she wants to get back together with him.

However, other children were able to offer explanations of these apparently sudden reversals: Jared and Russell (S, 14, P), for example, suggested that Jamie was feeling guilty, whereas Sharmaine (S, 12, P) argued that he had finally realised that he did not want to lose Sonia.

Opinions about the advisability of the marriage were quite diverse, however. Several of the boys argued that it wouldn't work out, simply on the grounds that Sonia was 'ugly' and 'fat' and Jamie was not; and on these grounds, they found it quite implausible that he would abandon the more attractive Zoe. On the other hand, several of the girls argued that she should not accept because Jamie had 'cheated' in the past, and was unlikely to stop; although Jessica and Lori (N, 14, P) argued that Sonia had also behaved unreasonably towards Jamie, particularly when he brought up the matter of the baby which she had given up for adoption – 'every time he tries to help, she just pushes him away'. Others argued that marriage at a relatively young age was ill-advised in itself, particularly as they had so little money; and Melissa (S, 17, P) suggested that showing such behaviour might encourage people to think it was a good thing. For all these reasons, most of the children seemed to believe that the relationship would end badly – not an unreasonable expectation, given the conventions of the genre.

Similar debates occurred in relation to another story of marriage, albeit one of a rather different kind. This concerned the relationship of Dot and Jim, an elderly couple. This story was handled in much more overtly comic terms, although here again, the basic motivation of the characters was partly left unclear. Dot had agreed to marriage, although (as several children pointed out), it was far from certain that she loved Jim, or even that the feeling was mutual. According to Rollo (S, 12, P), this was evident from their body language: 'cause like in a normal relationship they wouldn't back off away from each other –

and Dot and Jim, like if they see each other in the street they talk as if they're friends and they sometimes back away from each other, like they're not married'. This led some to speculate – yet again – that the relationship would not last, not just because they were 'such different personalities' (as Rollo put it), but also because (as several children argued), they were simply 'too old'.

While a few children argued that the relationship was 'sweet', many found it rather disgusting to speculate about elderly people's sex lives. This was an issue that the programme had clearly placed on the agenda: at the time of our interviews, Dot had insisted that the couple sleep in bunk beds, although Jim had obtained some Viagra. Alma (S, 10, G) was not alone in arguing that 'watching old people' in such a context was 'disgusting ... because you see the wrinkles'. By contrast, others argued that there was a positive message here: if elderly people wanted to get married, they argued, this was 'up to them' – 'it doesn't matter how old you are'. Nevertheless, this was somewhat undermined by the fact that the story was largely played for laughs: both Dot and Jim were essentially comic characters, and other characters were seen to be laughing at them.

As with the children's discussions of Jamie and Sonia, the debate about whether the relationship would last thus invoked a whole range of potentially contradictory arguments. On the one hand, there were generalised assertions about what makes for good relationships (were the characters too young, or too old? should good-looking people marry ugly people?), as well as specific judgments about the characters' personalities and behaviour (are they compatible? do they treat each other well?). On the other, there were judgments that derived from a knowledge of the genre (relationships rarely last for ever in soap operas) and from a reading of these specific storylines (for example, the elements of comedy). On the one hand, viewers 'read through' the programme, as though the characters are real people; and yet they remain aware of the fact that it is fictional, and that it tends to follow particular conventions.

Ultimately, the invitation to moral judgment – and particularly to moral *explanation* – has a covert pedagogic function. We might even say that it offers children a form of applied training in morality; although the word 'training' is perhaps misleading, if it implies that children are mechanically ingesting a series of fixed messages. In some instances – as in the overt imposition of moral lessons to do with drugs or under-age sex – this may appear to be the case; although it is precisely this kind of approach that leads some viewers to perceive the soaps as preaching or lecturing, and to reject them on these grounds. The pedagogy of the soaps is more effective where it is less overt – where it encourages viewers to make their own judgments, rather than simply commanding their assent. Of course, this apparent autonomy may be misleading, since the programmes do nevertheless seek to define the *terms* within which such judgments can be made: the moral universe of the soap is bounded, and some judgments are clearly much more possible than others (see Buckingham, 1987). Yet as Chris Barker (1998) points out, the moral discourses in which young people position themselves are diverse and sometimes contradictory: there is not necessarily a single explanation for why people behave the way they do, nor is there always a single right course of action. Nevertheless, the persistence and complexity of these moral debates challenges the idea that we live in an amoral society: as Barker argues, far from being 'without moral resources', young people appear to place such considerations at the centre of their lives and identities.

Yet soap operas are not educational texts. As several of the children in our study reminded us, 'it's just entertainment, isn't it?' While they recognised the presence of educational 'messages' in the programmes, they argued that this was not their primary reason for watching. To this extent, soap operas walk a precarious line. If viewers are to learn from them, they must take them seriously on some level. Realism is crucial here: as soaps veer towards comedy (on the one hand) or melodrama (on the other), they run the risk of sacrificing their pedagogic authority. Yet an excess of seriousness may undermine their status as 'entertainment'. Viewers may be happy to learn from such programmes, but they do not wish to feel that they are being taught.

In the following sections of this chapter, we consider two areas of television drama that strike this balance in a rather different way. We turn firstly to comedy, and specifically to the US sitcoms *Friends* and *The Simpsons*; and then to children's or teen-oriented drama series, in the form of *Grange Hill*, *Dawson's Creek* and *As If*.

Just for laughs?

Like soap operas, situation comedies may convey both overt and covert educational messages. Comedies clearly do provide specific representations of the social world, and much of their humour derives from implicit assumptions about 'normal' and 'abnormal' behaviour. Comedies may also promote more overt moral lessons – for example in the homilies about trust or sharing with which more traditional US sitcoms tend to conclude. Nevertheless, the defining characteristic of comedy is precisely that it is not to be taken seriously. If comedy teaches, it must surely seek to do so with a very light touch.

With the exception of a few older boys, the US sitcom *Friends* was universally popular with the children in our sample. It was mentioned in several of our initial interviews, and we selected two different episodes (for different age groups) for inclusion on our videotape. On one level, the basic situation of *Friends* has a self-evident appeal for children in the pre-teen and teenage years. As Liesbeth de Block (1998) suggests, comedies like *Friends* and the British show *Men Behaving Badly* seem to be popular with children partly because of their focus on personal relationships within non-family settings. Whilst their portrayals of relationships between male and female characters are fairly stereotypical (and indeed intentionally exaggerated to provide much of the comedy), their portrayal of adulthood is rather more intriguing. On the one hand, the characters appear to have some of the desirable trappings of grown-ups – such as independence, money, and control over their own space and time. Yet, unlike characters in more serious adult soaps or dramas, the characters in these comedies are not portrayed (or indeed perceived by children) as particularly mature. As de Block suggests, their appeal rests largely on the fact that they are adults behaving like children.

In this research, some of the children appeared to see the lives of the characters in *Friends* as a kind of idealised fantasy of their own futures. As Rhiannon (N, 17, G) put it, 'it's just easy to watch it and just imagine what your life is like when you're like 20, if you're living in a flat with your mates and stuff'. In addition to the fantasy of lasting friendship, the characters were seen to enjoy a degree of independence that was not yet available to them: as Caitlin (N, 12, G) put it, 'I am looking forward to the independence. I mean, you can just go out in town on your own and nobody will say "oh. I'm coming with you", or "you're not going out on your own". You can do what you want.'

Of course, children's projections of the future are bound to involve an element of fantasy: one group of ten-year-old boys told us how they wanted to become a professional footballer, a Formula One racing driver and an archaeologist when they grew up, while another assured us that he would be 'driving around in a Ferrari' during his later teenage years. Yet the children's enthusiasm for the ideal future of *Friends* was tempered by a recognition that it was far from unproblematic. For example, some argued that the lives of the *Friends* characters was too 'hectic', while others felt it would be boring 'just sitting on the couch' in the café. Others worried about the lack of privacy. Interestingly, several children criticised the characters for being incompetent and 'childish': 'Rachel can hardly do her own washing' (Naomi, N, 14, G); 'they don't seem to be able to look after themselves' (Caitlin, N, 12, G); 'Ross has been divorced, like, three times now' (Chantel, N, 14, G). Indeed, there were several children like Ethan (N, 12, G) who explicitly rejected our suggestion that the programme might be offering them a vision of life in their twenties, arguing that, on the contrary, it was 'just comedy'.

More significantly, many children argued that the programme was unrealistic, and that real people in their twenties did not live like that. Some pointed out that the characters rarely seemed to leave the house or go to work; while others argued that they were all so different, they would be unlikely to remain friends – particularly after some of them had previously been lovers. Others argued, in relation both to *Friends* and to other US sitcoms such as *Saved by the Bell*, that while this might be 'American real life', it would be unlikely to happen in the UK. Interestingly, the *Friends* characters who were most popular were the least psychologically plausible, Joey and Phoebe – who were variously described as 'crazy', 'dopey', 'stupid' and 'thick'. These, it was agreed, were characters you would laugh *at* rather than *with*. By contrast, Ross was generally rejected as 'boring' and 'too serious'. Some of the older children also argued that the characters were one-dimensional and stereotypical – although Jon (N, 17, G) argued that the sex-obsessed character of Joey was 'a parody rather than a stereotype' of a 'typical male', and that this was the source of the humour. Meanwhile Eve and Trevor (N, 17, G) criticised the show on the grounds that all the characters were 'pretty' – unlike in British sitcoms where 'a lot of the characters are ugly on purpose'.

Yet this unreality was generally seen as a precondition of comedy as a form. As Joshua (N, 14, G) succinctly put it, 'that's why it's funny, 'cause it's unreal' – a point echoed by several of the other children. For this reason, our attempts to encourage the children to identify 'messages' in *Friends* largely fell on stony ground. As Melissa and Della (S, 17, G) asserted, they didn't watch the programme 'because of issues', but because it made them laugh. Likewise, Jay (S, 17, G) pointed out several ways in which the programme was 'a bit too fake', but added 'it's meant to be, 'cause you're not meant to take comedies seriously'. Some did attempt to identify likely 'messages', particularly to do with the presence of lesbian and gay characters (who appeared or were mentioned in both the episodes we used). Rebecca (N, 10, G) and Sean

(N, 12, G) both noted that there were relatively few such characters in other programmes; while Lara (S, 14, G) praised it in this respect for showing 'all different types of life'. Richard (N, 17, G) referred to the storyline in which Susan, Ross's lesbian former wife, had been trying to conceive a baby, and argued that such scenes could 'open your eyes with humour'. Likewise, Chantel (N, 14, G) and Dale (S, 14, G) praised one scene in the episode we used, in which Phoebe's formerly gay husband described how he had 'come out' as straight: as Chantel put it, 'they're turning it round, and normally it's you want to be straight to fit in and you don't wanna be gay but [here] it's the other way round – so that was a good perspective'. According to Kim and Abigail (N, 12, G), *Friends* could 'make the embarrassing aspects funny' through their coverage of such themes, and thereby make people less 'afraid'.

Yet aside from this, the children seemed unable to think of any other examples of 'serious issues' that had been covered in the programme. They were prepared to believe this in principle, but in practice this was clearly not what their experience of *Friends* was about. As Melissa (S, 17, G) argued, you did not expect to 'come out learning something' – 'it's just there for entertainment, isn't it?' Here, as at several other points, we felt that our pursuit of 'messages' was at least inappropriate: as Bret (P, 10, G) observed, 'in things that are supposed to be funny you don't look for any messages'.

It is also worth noting here that most of the programme's treatment of sexual relationships is conveyed through talk rather than through explicit display. As Jake and Jonah (N, 10, G) pointed out, the characters would almost always be interrupted as things were about to get serious. Without exception, the children appeared to understand the sexually-oriented situations in the episodes we used, and to pick up on some of the more obvious jokes. Nevertheless, some of the more 'adult' humour was rather lost on the younger children: none, for example, could adequately explain why the rampantly heterosexual Joey should find it so 'cool' that Ross's wife was a lesbian. As Eve (N, 17, G) pointed out, the programme manages to have such a wide audience largely because it has 'jokes on different levels'. Here again, some of the more specific sexual content of the programme requires a level of prior knowledge if it is to be noticed in the first place; while, conversely, as Rebecca (N, 10, G) put it, 'if you already know about them things, then the messages won't be sent because you already know them'.

Similar issues were raised by another programme included on our videotape, an episode of *The Simpsons*. Here, Marge and Homer attempted to revive their flagging love-life by discovering the joys of having sex in public places – in a barn, and subsequently on a 'crazy golf' course. Events became farcical when they were forced to run naked through the streets of Springfield, eventually exposing themselves to a church congregation and to the crowd at a football game. Like *Friends*, *The Simpsons* is a programme whose humour functions on different levels, ranging from basic slapstick to complex satire. Some of the older children doubted whether the younger ones would pick up on the sexual content – Trevor (N, 17, G), for example, argued that 'the only thing they'd see is how he's naked', while Nancy (S, 17, G) suggested that 'if we was a couple of years younger, we wouldn't get some of the jokes'. In fact, however, several of the youngest children were quite clear about what was happening in this episode: as Will (S, 10, G) explained, it was 'the fear of getting caught' that made them 'feel more excited'. For Jed (S, 10, G), as for many of the other ten-year-olds, it was 'the sex' that was the most amusing part. Here again, it was hard to dispute the conclusion that, as Jared (S, 14, G) put it, 'if you understand it then it's all right, but if you don't understand it then it's still all right, because you're not learning anything'.

In fact, *The Simpsons* has attracted considerable criticism from conservative critics – indeed, from President Bush Senior himself – for its 'negative' representation of family life. The children acknowledged that Marge and Homer had a 'bumpy' relationship, and cited several other episodes where they were not getting along: Homer in particular was seen by some as a 'bad husband'. There were also 'messages' here: according to Courtney (N, 12, G), this episode showed how 'if your relationship's going down the drain, you can do stuff to brighten it up and make it better'. Several children claimed that *The Simpsons* was realistic, despite the fact that it was a cartoon. 'It shows what happens in families,' said Courtney (N, 12, G); 'they're doing the same, what a family acts like', agreed Sharmaine (S, 12, G). Others detected similarities between the characters and their own family members; while in the case of this episode, several commented on Bart's disgust at seeing his parents kissing – a reaction which they had clearly experienced themselves. On the other hand, some children noted that problems between the characters were always quickly resolved: 'it's predictable. Like, he's just gonna go back to Marge so ... you know what's going to happen' (Joshua, N, 14, G).

In general, however, as with *Friends*, the children rejected the idea that the programme should be taken seriously, or that it contained 'messages' of the kind we were seeking. This was partly to do with its status as a 'children's programme', and as a cartoon – as Kelly (N, 14, G) exclaimed, 'they're yellow! It's just cartoons!' It was also to do with its status as a comedy, and (more broadly) as television. Here again, our earnest enquiries about 'messages' were repeatedly met with the observation that 'it's just funny' or 'it's only TV, isn't it?' Indeed, it was precisely its *lack* of serious intent that accounted for its appeal: as Matthew (N, 14, G) argued, 'it's easy to watch. You don't have to think about it.'

Of course, it would be quite wrong to conclude that people do not learn things from such programmes just because they claim that they do not take them seriously, or fail to completely understand them. 'Understanding' something or 'taking it seriously' is not a matter of all-or-nothing. Depending on how one chooses to interpret it, *The Simpsons* might indeed be seen as an attack on the sanctity of the American family – or alternatively as an ironic, but ultimately sentimental, reaffirmation of family values (see Wells 2002). And for all its apparent liberalism about gay and lesbian relationships, it could well be argued that *Friends* simply reinforces a narrow conception of heterosexual gender roles. Yet the problem with such arguments – as the children in our study repeatedly reminded us – is that they are in danger of forgetting that such programmes are, precisely, *comedies*.

Teaching through drama

In this final section of the chapter, we move on to consider three programmes that are characterised by a much greater degree of educational seriousness. All are targeted at a children's or teen audience; and all contain more or less overt 'messages' about love, sex and relationships.

Grange Hill is the UK's longest-running children's drama programme. Set in an outer-London comprehensive school, it has a history of tackling 'controversial' issues, including some (such as teenage pregnancy, child abuse and sexually transmitted diseases) that are relevant to our theme (see Jones and Davies 2002). The programme is broadly in the social realist tradition of the British soaps, and typically contains several continuing storylines. For this research, we used an edited storyline focusing on the relationship between two pupils, Leah and Tom, who are in school years 10 and 11 respectively (and hence probably aged 15 and 16). Their relationship develops over several weeks, and eventually Leah and Tom have sex in a bedroom at a friend's party. There is no indication that Tom forces her, although Leah subsequently makes it clear that she had sex reluctantly, and attends sessions with a rape counsellor. The storyline also features the couple interacting with their respective groups of friends, who offer a variety of perspectives on what took place.

We used this tape with the two youngest age groups only: despite its apparently mature subject matter, *Grange Hill* is definitely perceived as a 'children's programme', and as such is widely dismissed by the majority of teenagers. Some of the girls in our sample were quite enthusiastic about the programme – particularly Caitlin (N, 12, G), who described herself as a 'soapalistic person'. However, several children found the story quite difficult to follow, and complained that (at around 45 minutes) it was too long. Some of the boys in particular expressed a wish for less talk and more action.

Compared with the adult soaps, very few children raised questions about the realism of the programme. There were a few passing criticisms of the acting, but several children affirmed that the programme gave a fairly accurate representation of life in secondary school. Of course, the characters in the programme were somewhat older than our interviewees, but they were seen as authentic 'teenagers' nevertheless:

> Courtney (N, 12, G): It's just as if it's ... actual people acting, but in real life. It could happen any day, for certain. And it's all around and like people spreading lies about it and it gets round the school and tales get twisted. It just shows what happens at high schools and how teenagers are.

The children's discussions of the Tom and Leah story were characterised by some quite intense moral debates. There were some heated discussions about whether Tom had in fact raped Leah. While it was clear that she had been reluctant, several children pointed out that she had not protested at the time – although others claimed that this did not make any difference. On one side, for instance, was Noelle (S, 12, G):

> I think she was raped ... because he should have asked her. And it doesn't matter what they think of you afterwards as long as people don't think it's rape. Because if you just turn round and say 'look, do you want it?' Then they can say yeah, or no. But if you just say 'come on' like he did, then that counts as rape. Even though she didn't say no.

For others, both boys and girls, the absence of physical force (or the threat of violence) – combined with the fact that they were already in a relationship – meant that it could not be seen as rape: according to Henry (N, 12, G), 'he said, "Do you want to come in again?" And she said, "Yeah." And so she didn't say no. He didn't attack her, or force her to do anything.' Yet many children argued on both sides, agreeing that in some ways it was rape, while in others it was not.

In various ways, this debate was invited by the programme itself, not least by the comments and criticisms of the other characters who surrounded Tom and Leah. Yet, as we noted above in relation to *EastEnders*, uncertainty about the characters' motivations or intentions is a crucial generator of debate. This uncertainty was compounded here by the fact that, of course, the programme had not actually shown them having sex (they were seen disappearing into the bedroom, and subsequently getting dressed). This left open several crucial questions, to do with why Tom had failed to ask Leah and why Leah had failed to resist. In relation to the first question, it was argued that Tom was simply 'embarrassed' or scared of being rejected by her; or alternatively that he believed she really wanted to have sex. Others pointed to the role of peer pressure: Courtney (N, 12, G) suggested that 'he was scared that the answer was going to be no and then he'd have a bad reputation 'cause, "oh you got let down by a Year 10", like ... That gets dragged round the school as well.' For her part, it was argued that Leah was 'scared', either of being 'dumped' by Tom or of the threat of violence: as Rebecca (N, 10, G) suggested, 'she was like panicking what he'll do to her. When you're really scared, you can't talk, you just open your mouth and nothing comes out.' Some argued that she had changed her mind at the last minute, and that she had been trying to say no; some that she was 'drunk' or 'confused'; while others simply suggested that 'she didn't know what to do'. She too was seen to be influenced by peer pressure – in this case, by a friend who had been boasting about having had sex with an older boy. On the basis of the programme, all these explanations are plausible: but the crucial point is that the programme itself does not offer any single answer to these questions.

Ultimately, some of the children were concerned to allocate blame: either it was Leah's fault for not saying no (or for going into the bedroom in the first place), or it was Tom's for not asking. (And it should be emphasised that this was by no means neatly divided along gender lines.) Some saw the difference in age as a deciding factor – at least on the grounds that Leah would be likely to be more scared of an older boy – although others asserted that this did not matter. Yet the majority of children argued that both of the characters were to blame; and several claimed that they were 'on both sides' of the debate. The children's discussions explicitly and implicitly invoked broader assumptions, both about how and why people behave the way they do, and about what was moral or ethical. To return to Chris Barker's (1998) distinction, discussed above, this story clearly invited 'explaining' rather than 'blaming' – both because of the diversity of views presented in the programme, and because the characters' motivations (and the precise nature of what took place) were left uncertain.

Pedagogically, the story appeared to function on several levels. At the most basic level, it was read as a warning about the perils of under-age sex: and if there was one aspect of the relationship that the children recognised as unequivocally wrong, it was the fact that one or both of the characters was under the age of consent (their ages are not made fully clear in the material we used). More generally, it was read as a warning, particularly to girls, about the risks of 'going to parties and going into a room and having sex', as Bea (N, 10, G) put it. Particularly among the younger children, this was perceived in quite stark terms, as in the case of some of the discussions of the soap operas: as Alma (S, 10, G) argued, 'it was teaching you not to do it'. However, others suggested that the message was a little more complex than this: it was about the importance of communicating and 'taking it slowly'. 'It tells you to speak your mind,' said Rebecca (N, 10, G); 'it teaches you to ask', argued Sharmaine (S, 12, G); 'ask a person if you want to do something, don't just assume they want to', asserted Leo (S, 10, G). More broadly, there were messages about the importance of not giving in to peer pressure to have sex, or rushing into relationships before you were 'old enough to understand'. According to Courtney (N, 12, G), the programme told you not to 'go too deeply into a relationship before you know the person'; while Kim (N, 12, G) said it showed that 'sex has to be for a reason'. For these children at least, the message was not simply of the 'just say no' variety.

As this implies, the programme clearly set parameters to the debate: the issue was not so much about whether or not to have sex (that is, about whether to obey externally-imposed codes of conduct), but about when and how to have sex at the time that was psychologically 'right' for you as an individual, or for the relationship. Nevertheless, the programme 'worked' pedagogically because it enabled the children to think the situation through, and to empathise with the characters' dilemmas, rather than simply offering abstract warnings. As such, they argued, it would help them to deal with such situations as they might arise in future: as Bea (N, 10, G) put it, 'like, you watch that and then it actually starts happening to you. You know that, what you've got to do. It helps you.' Likewise, Courtney described how the programme might be used to resolve difficulties in real life:

> Courtney (N, 12, G): It's like if a Year 10 is going out with a Year 11 and the Year 11's asked her if they want to start going to the ... another level, basically. If she sees that [programme], it makes her think more and it makes her ... 'just hang on a sec, what if this happens to me, if I get forced into it?' Then she could go to her boyfriend and say 'look I don't want to be nasty or anything, but I don't want to do it yet'. And it shows like that they could get the courage of doing it, if someone else has.

Nevertheless, Courtney clearly sees the situation she is describing as one that lies several years in the future, rather than a dilemma she has to face now. It was partly for this reason that a few children in our interviews argued that this kind of material was inappropriate for a children's programme. Rollo (S, 12, G) suggested that, as 'the kids' soap' watched by younger children, *Grange Hill* was 'getting a bit too mature'; while Izzie (S, 12, G) asserted that young children 'shouldn't really be thinking about that', and that they were being 'forced to grow up and learn the consequences of what you're never going to do'. As ever, the girls' primary concern here was for children younger than themselves; although they are certainly correct to point to the mismatch between the age of many of the characters in the programme and the age of its principal audience.

Similar issues were raised in the older children's discussions of the US teen drama *Dawson's Creek*. This is another long-running series, which has followed the lives of the same group of characters over adolescence and into early adulthood (see Nixon 2000). Here again, we edited one storyline out of a longer episode, and showed it only to the older children (aged 14 and 17). The story focuses on a school trip, and follows the relationships of two pairs of characters: Joey (female) and Pacey (male), who after several months of waiting, finally consummate their relationship; and Jen and her gay friend Jack, who get drunk and seem to be about to have sex together, but ultimately draw back.

In general, responses to this programme were very negative. It was widely dismissed as 'boring' and 'ridiculous'. This was particularly the case among the older children, and the boys. Neville (N, 14, G) argued that this programme was 'more for girls', on the grounds that 'it's all about relationships all the time, that's all they ever do'; while other boys concurred, accusing it of being 'soppy' and 'lovey-dovey'. Yet even the girls who appeared to enjoy it described it in a relatively distanced way, as 'sweet' or 'cheesy'. Several children described how they had laughed out loud while watching particular scenes.

Perhaps predictably, the primary grounds for criticism were to do with modality. Some of the children claimed that the programme could 'relate to real-life situations' (as Grant (S, 17, G) put it), but only in a fairly abstract way. For most, the setting and the characters were highly implausible and 'far-fetched'. The actors, it was argued, were 'too beautiful', but also far too old for the parts they were playing (some alleged they were in their thirties, or even older). The school was unlike any in these children's experience, and the location was described as a 'dream world'. The script was seen by several children as unnecessarily literary: Eve (N, 17, G) argued that 'you just wouldn't come out with the stuff that they come out with. It's the kind of stuff that you read in books.' And the sex scenes were judged as ridiculously coy: 'when they do have sex, it just shows two heads. It shows them getting into bed with their underpants on. How are you going to have sex like that?' (Matthew, N, 14, G). All these factors seemed to be compounded by the programme's 'Americanness': Ceri (N, 17, G) argued that the stereotyping was indicative of 'American culture', while Adrian (N, 17, G) was less forgiving, dismissing it as merely 'American drivel'.

To be fair to *Dawson's Creek*, these elements of 'unreality' partly reflect the intentions of its creators. According to the writer, Kevin Williamson, the series reflects a self-consciously nostalgic idealisation of youth in small-town America (Nimmo-Jones 2001). Jessica (S, 14, G) may partly have recognised this when she described the programme: 'it's not aimed at teenagers, but it's like acted out and it's a bit like an adults' programme, the sort of thing an adult would watch.' Nevertheless, this perceived lack of realism seriously compromised the programme's pedagogic intentions, to the point where it was widely perceived as quite patronising.

The children detected several 'messages' in the episode we selected. The story of Joey and Pacey was perceived to be a lesson in the virtues of virginity – or 'true love waits', as it is promoted in the US. As various children argued, the fact that they had sex in the end – albeit outside of legal wedlock – was justified because Joey 'saw that he [Pacey] was faithful and that he had been waiting so long' (Kelly, N, 14, G). Embedded in this storyline, however, was a rather more ambiguous 'safe sex' message. In one scene, Joey discovers that most of the boys have brought condoms with them on the school trip – as indeed has Pacey, although he does not wave them around boastfully like the other boys. On one level, this scene was believed to promote 'safe sex' messages; yet in the context of the episode, it also seemed to reinforce the view that, as Reena (N, 14, G) suggested, boys are 'always up for it'. (A scientific statistic widely quoted by the girls in our research was that 'boys think about sex 23 hours out of 24'.) On the one hand, the children said that they were being told to 'be prepared' for any passing eventuality, while on the other they were being told that sex 'means something' and was not to be engaged in lightly. The storyline involving Jen and Jack was also seen to contain pedagogic 'messages', although here again these seemed somewhat ambiguous. While some argued that the story might promote greater understanding of gay people, others found it merely confusing and implausible: Grant (S, 17, G) argued 'maybe what's it's trying to say is if that's how you are, that's how you are – there's no point trying to force yourself to change it'; while according to Trevor (N, 17, G), the story simply showed that 'sexuality just depends on how drunk you are'.

Yet despite this sense of ambivalence (or confusion), several children clearly felt that the programme was preaching at them. While it contained 'good messages', they were seen to be conveyed in a 'patronising' and 'obvious' manner. Harvey (N, 17, G) argued that, as in other dramas aimed at teenagers that purported to deal with social issues, the message was 'rammed down your throat', and argued that this 'insulted your intelligence'. His friends Tom and Jon were equally scathing:

Tom (S, 17, G): It should have had a sign saying 'Don't have sex until you're ready'.

Jon: Sponsored by Durex condoms!

Others complained that the problems in such programmes were always too quickly resolved, and that they were dealt with in a humourless way – and here again, this was seen to be particularly true of 'American' shows. Chloe (N, 17, G) argued that this approach was unlikely to change her opinions about such matters; while Jay (S, 17, G) explicitly rejected some of the programme's messages: 'I guess they were [saying] like you shouldn't be so promiscuous at that age and that. But still that's the whole idea of growing up, isn't it, to discover things for yourself rather than take... That's just one person's opinion, the writer's'.

The final programme we will consider here adopted a much less overtly pedagogical approach. *As If* is a Channel 4 drama series that follows the interconnected lives and relationships of a group of characters in their late teens and early twenties. The episode we used – only with the Year 12 children – focused on the issue of infidelity, particularly as it affected one gay relationship.

As If was generally well received, particularly by the middle-class children. There was praise for its 'cool' camerawork and editing, and rock music soundtrack; although some found the complex interweaving narratives and the use of flashbacks rather hard to follow. It was also described as a 'realistic' representation of young people, and as psychologically plausible. For example, Trevor (N, 17, G) praised the fact that the programme showed characters being 'petty' and 'lying' to each other, and displayed the gap between 'how people were trying to portray themselves and how they really were'. Several young people compared the programme favourably with *Dawson's Creek* in this respect: according to Melissa (S, 17, G), 'they look like real teenagers, whereas in *Dawson's Creek* they're all stunning'. Harvey (N, 17, G) went further: '*As If* is like it could be a documentary about the life of these people or like a fly on the wall and, you know, *Dawson's Creek* is just false, it's just so obvious.'

This 'obviousness' – or lack of it – was particularly manifested in the pedagogic style of the two programmes. For many of the young people, *As If* did have a distinct message, to do with the acceptability of gay relationships. Jon (S, 17, G) summarised this as follows:

> [The] bisexual and the gay bloke, that was the main story line ... I think a good point it showed is that like the way gay love is. It's like the guy was like 'Oh, I really do love you' and all this, and you know you can get that with like a male/female relationship ... But I think a lot of people don't think that gay love's like that. I think they think it's just like a sexual thing. But I think it's showing a good view of ... There is actually love and feeling and emotion in gay relationships and it's not just like a sex thing.

However, there were some striking differences between the middle-class and working-class groups, and to some extent between the boys and the girls, in how they responded to this. As Jon's comment implies, the middle-class young people clearly saw the 'message' as being to do with tolerance: the programme was seen to be promoting the idea that gay people were 'just like us', rather than dangerously promiscuous. Trevor (N, 17, G), for example, argued that the presence of the gay characters was evidence of the programme being 'very liberal': 'it's not at all a taboo, it's just, it's on exactly the same level as the heterosexual characters'. For some, the fact that the bisexual character is unfaithful with a woman, rather than another man, was seen as a 'shock'; and this was seen to have some kind of educational function, as Saul (N, 17, G) implied – '[the fact] that [the gay character] had a problem with the fact that he was both was interesting'. Yet once the sexuality of the characters was discounted in this way, it became possible to view the message of the programme as being about the importance of fidelity: as Eve (N, 17, G) put it, 'it's really tight of me to go off with anybody – it doesn't matter if it's a bloke or a woman, just don't do it!'

In general (and as we have seen in Chapter 4), the middle-class young people were keen to proclaim their own 'open-mindedness' in this respect. Some argued that the programme's tolerant message was confirmed by their own experience: Tom (N, 17, G), for example, claimed that there were gay people in his circle of friends, and that people within the group accepted this, even if outsiders might not. Others sought to present this tolerant attitude as evidence of their own 'maturity': according to Trevor (N, 17, G), for example, it was only the younger students in the school who were 'homophobic'. There was also a sense expressed by several of the young people here that society was gradually becoming more liberal in this respect, even if this might be slower to manifest itself in their town than in bigger cities (and the sexually 'explicit' nature of cosmopolitan series such as *Queer as Folk* and *Metrosexuality* was cited as evidence of this: see Chapter 4). However, there was also a clear class dimension to this tolerant self-image: the outsiders who might hold such prejudices were identified as 'scallies' and 'townies' (which in current slang means working-class youth). In this respect, it might be argued that the tolerant middle-class characters of *As If* offered the middle-class young people in our sample a somewhat flattering self-image.

By contrast, some of the working-class young people – and particularly the boys – were keen to reject this message. They recognised that the programme might have been 'trying to promote homosexual awareness', as Richard (S, 17, G) suggested; and some of the girls clearly picked up on the point that love 'happens the same [for gays] as it does between straight people' (as Olivia (S, 17, G) put it). But for some of the boys, this was too much to take:

Jay: Well, I just think it's still an issue that everyone's a bit shaky about, they're not really keen, that's why I don't really like it. I mean I don't have a problem with homosexuals. I just don't particularly like watching 'em on telly. It [makes me] cringe.

Like most of the other boys, Jay struggled somewhat here, attempting to displace his discomfort onto 'everyone', and taking refuge in the classic line 'I don't have a problem but ...'. Others also claimed not to be prejudiced, but ultimately just did not 'want to know'. Richard, however, was more forthright:

Richard: I didn't really like listening about the queer and his boyfriend and all that, and they were getting all serious chats and stuff. You know I was like ... It was just making me feel sick ... and probably a bit angry as well.

The notion that, as Jay put it, the gay characters were being 'pushed in my face' clearly reflected a broader concern about the 'promotion' of homosexuality that is still prevalent on the political Right in Britain (see Epstein and Johnson 1998):

Richard: It really promotes homosexuality. And the more there is of it on TV, the more it will be accepted within society, and it should not ... It's getting worse and worse over the years.

As with the middle-class boys, there was certainly an element of self-presentation here. Glenn (S, 17, G) acknowledged that boys in particular would be likely to reject *As If* for this reason: 'it shows that they're masculine – "oh I'm not watching that, it's got poofters in it".'

These different views led to rather different estimates of the effectiveness of the programme's pedagogic style. For the middle-class young people, there was a striking contrast between the overt, preacherly style of *Dawson's Creek* and the more implicit approach of *As If*. They appreciated the fact that there was no 'clear-cut ending', and that a range of views was presented: as Jeff (N, 17, G) put it, 'it's not trying to lecture... it's more about considering different perspectives and trying to think out for yourself, make up your own opinions rather than being given anything'. The fact that the lead character addresses the camera directly was also seen as effective:

Harvey (N, 17, G): I think it involved the viewer much more. Like in *Dawson's Creek* you sort of watch it, then you could turn off and go and have a cup of tea and not think anything of it for the rest of your life. But with *As If* they sort of ... the way they talk to the person, you know directly to the camera and the way he didn't quite resolve his issue, I think it made the viewer think a lot more about how they would feel about it. Without saying you should feel this way. It was saying 'how do *you* feel' and I like that a lot.

Tom: It wasn't trying to like force a moral on you.

However, some of the working-class young people clearly felt that the programme *was* trying to force a particular 'moral' on them; and even those who were inclined to be more sympathetic to this doubted whether it would be effective in terms of changing people's views. Della (S, 17, G), for example, argued that it was good to see such relationships represented on television, but that 'people who don't like gays wouldn't wanna see 'em on TV anyway. So I can't imagine [them] thinking "oh well, I'll watch it and maybe I'll accept 'em".' Some of the evidence quoted above would certainly support this.

Ultimately, it is hard to say whether the differences in our sample reflect the different attitudes towards sexuality of different social class groups, or simply different preferred styles of self-presentation. What is interesting, however, is the relationship between the young people's professed attitudes towards the issues and their responses to the pedagogic style of the programme. The middle-class group saw the programme as adopting tolerant attitudes, in line with their own, as well as a more 'open' pedagogic style. The working-class boys were less sympathetic to the attitudes they detected, and also saw the programme as more 'closed' (or even didactic) in its pedagogic style. The middle-class young people argued that the programme was not preaching; but in a sense, they would be less likely to notice this, since they were already the converted – and were keen to let us know this. By contrast, some of the working-class young people had a rather different self-image – and one to which the programme ultimately failed to speak.

Conclusion: a preparation for life?

In this chapter, we have focused explicitly on the *educational* dimensions of television drama – although, as we have indicated, these are inextricable from its functions as 'entertainment'. This emphasis was also apparent in our line of questioning in the focus groups – in some cases, as we read the transcripts, rather awkwardly so. As we have suggested, a great deal more is going on for young people in watching these programmes than simply the identification and retrieval of 'messages'. To assess them in terms of teaching and learning is thus, in some sense, inevitably reductive.

Nevertheless, there are some interesting conclusions that might be drawn about this process – not least in response to those who see television drama as promoting messages about love, sex and relationships that are in some way false or misleading. It is very clear from our research that questions of ethics and morality are central to how young people read these programmes. The children here were able to engage in complex moral debates about characters' behaviour, and about how they conducted their personal relationships. They were concerned not just with summative moral judgments, but also with understanding people's motivations and with thinking through the kinds of ethical choices they have to make. They wanted to develop plausible explanations, not merely to allocate blame; and their observations were informed by a strong sense of broader moral values, for example to do with qualities such as trust, mutual respect, co-operation and self-reliance. This is not, we would argue, simply an artefact of our research method, or of our somewhat earnest pursuit of 'messages'. And, as Chris Barker (1998) suggests, it very effectively refutes the idea that the media are leading us all towards a moral vacuum.

While this might be seen as a positive conclusion, our second point is rather more ambivalent. As we have shown, the process of teaching through television is a complex and difficult one. Programmes that are perceived as realistic clearly possess a higher degree of pedagogic authority than those that are not; but there are many grounds on which realism can be challenged or undermined. As the children repeatedly insisted, television is ultimately about entertainment; and in seeking to entertain, television producers are perhaps bound to be led towards comedy or melodrama – modes that are perceived to be lacking in the legitimacy of realism. Furthermore, viewers are likely to resist programmes that appear to *use* dramatic entertainment for educational ends; and this may be particularly true for children, who are routinely addressed as passive recipients of warnings about the dangers of various 'unhealthy' practices – warnings that are often delivered in exaggerated and absolutist terms. For those who would seek to use the media for the purposes of sex education, sugaring the pill is therefore unlikely to prove an effective strategy.

8
Family Viewing – Embarrassment, Education and Erotics

Joseph (S, 12, P): We usually get videos Friday nights and that's one night a week like we spend it as a family. Other times it's just, my brother is going out and everything. (...) For all we care like it could be the worst film ever. But it's the fact that we get to spend that one night with each other.

Rachel (N, 10, P): Mine's more like a teenage magazine but my mum lets me read it ... the first time I wanted to get it she read it all through in Asda [supermarket] and so we were late coming back and dad started moaning cause he hadn't had his tea – but yeah she said it was OK cause it wasn't that bad and I'm fast at growing up.

Alma (S, 10, P): I was grounded last night (...) My mum told me that I had to go to bed and then she started talking with my dad and they started saying 'If you keep talking to us and looking at us like that, then you're just gonna have to have your telly taken out your room and you're not allowed to watch TV, you gotta go to bed early and you're not allowed to watch *Home and Away* for the whole week' and I started screaming saying 'that's not fair' because I love it.

In talking about their media usage, children were also painting vivid and often affectionate portraits of their family lives. We can hear in their voices the cadences of texts such as *The Simpsons* that enable them to narrate their family life (sometimes self-consciously and ironically) as situation comedy, with its imperfections, quirks and punishments on display. Although home and family are easily romanticised as places of emotional and material security, neither is simply given: they have to be worked at and brought into being through practices and through the stories families tell about themselves. As such, television, as Roger Silverstone remarks, is both a 'focus of family activities and a resource', and how it is used within the home can provide insights into family interactions more generally (Silverstone 1994). Research by Morley and Gray has emphasised the overriding contextual nature of any kind of media use, particularly in respect of gendered power relations in the home (Gray 1992; Morley 1986; Morley and Silverstone 1988). As other research has shown, children's viewing is more commonly social and interactive than solitary (Palmer 1988): in our survey, 60 per cent of children stated that they tended to view with others and only 27 per cent that they preferred to watch in their bedrooms.

We have explored in previous chapters how young people learn about love, sex and relationships through their media consumption. In this chapter, we explore what they might be learning about family roles and relations – about what mothers, fathers, carers, children and siblings are like and what they do – through collective viewing of sexual media content. The home is often assumed to be a place where individuals can escape the disciplinary practices that govern everyday life. But gendered and sexual identities are performed and come under surveillance at home, particularly for young people who may have less power within the family and are subject to parental rules and intrusion of privacy. Moreover, families' uses of media must be set in a wider context, in which young people are economically dependent on their parents for longer than in the past: in this context, it is argued, the culture of childhood and youth is increasingly being controlled by parents and taking place in supervised and protected spaces rather than on the streets (Livingstone and Bovill 1999).

However, roles in the family are not assigned once and for all, but continuously contested. Being a younger sibling, for example, can be a source either of special privileges or of lesser status, and this can vary over time. Further, in relation to family rules and regulation – discussed in more detail in the next chapter – we are not looking at a simple case of parental enforcement and children's acquiescence. Both media use and its regulation within the home are complex, negotiated, enacted and resisted practices. In our discussion of embarrassment, of education and of 'erotics' we will see how family viewing practices help to construct sexual identities and gender roles in the home. Our wider argument is that different styles of interacting with the media – and specifically with television – serve to mediate its content in a way that undermines facile assumptions about media influence.

'It's so embarrassing ... '

As we noted in Chapter 3, many parents were keen to insist that they were more open with their children about sexual matters than their own parents had been with them. Nonetheless, the most common words used by both parents and children to describe their experiences of encountering sexual material in the media, especially on television, in the company of family members, were drawn from the lexicon of embarrassment. (As we saw in Chapter 3, this was also how children described their experience of parental attempts to discuss 'the facts of life' with them.) Most participants described the physiological experiences of embarrassment and the responses it provoked – sweating, shuddering, getting 'all shy' or 'squirming', feeling 'uncomfortable', staring ahead as if transfixed, sitting in complete silence, and so on. Only a few rejected the idea: Dale (S, 14, P) argued that 'They're all your family, so how can you get embarrassed in front of your family?' – while Pierre (S, 14, P) avoided the possibility by always watching in a separate room from his mother.

These tales also sometimes sounded almost ritualistic, in that participants recounted them with relish and in similar terms, without necessarily being able to provide many specific examples of problematic material. We need to emphasise that we are dealing here with *accounts* of embarrassment, not actual events. Claims to feel embarrassment, as we will show, are conventionally structured in order to make claims about identity, status within the family, and maturity; they may represent a demand for recognition of sexual identity or for its invisibility.

Parrott and Harré (1996) describe embarrassment as an 'emotion of social control' that is necessarily social in that it is not felt on one's own – just as our interviewees agreed that the feelings they described were not generally experienced when viewing alone, but specific to viewing in company. They draw on Goffman's argument that embarrassment expresses 'the judgement that other people will think that something about us or something we have done is improper in the context'. Displaying embarrassment serves as an apology for that real or imagined fault but simultaneously demonstrates one's awareness of social mores and thus one's commitment to membership of society. Parrott and Harré describe three 'regions' of embarrassment. The first draws on Goffman's dramaturgical theory: 'embarrassment is a flustering expressing our perception that our performance has been spoiled, that we have lost our grip on our role and that we cannot regain our role or adopt a new one' (op. cit. 46) and its symptoms are social discomfort and unease. A second usage suggests that embarrassment expresses a 'perception of loss of self-esteem' consequent to feeling that others judge us as inadequate or incompetent. A third theory maintains that displays of embarrassment express 'social anxiety' stemming from the belief that other people have formed an undesirable impression of us, the focus here being on anxiety about how others are assessing us rather than our own loss of self-esteem. All of these, Parrott and Harré argue, implicate the sense of self-worth we call 'character': 'the importance of these styles of social behaviour in social life lies not so much in the feelings they betray as in the characters they disclose' (53). These authors also repeat the familiar cliché that embarrassment is 'endemic to adolescence'. There are certainly grounds for arguing that adolescent sexual roles are particularly open to contestation and redefinition; and that this lack of clarity about social roles or perceptions may be more likely to give rise to embarrassment.

Elements of the usages Parrott and Harré describe did appear in our interviewees' accounts. However, they do not discuss examples related to sexuality and their account needs to be made more specific to this. Theorists of sexuality, by contrast, have in recent years focused on how mechanisms of shame (a social emotion closely related to embarrassment) are used to stigmatise, silence and control identities and are crucial in understanding how gender works (see e.g. Munt 1998; Sedgwick 1993).

Descriptions of embarrassment fell into a number of categories. On the one hand, some parents recounted their own embarrassment. Julie-Anne recounted the following anecdote amidst much hilarity from the rest of the group, some of whom had heard it before:

> I remember my little boy (Joey) when *Forrest Gump* was on. And you know the last part of the scene where he gets on, where he eventually ends up sleeping with Jenny. And bearing in mind he was only six at the time. And he was, he sat and he went 'Mum, this bit is making my willy go hard'. I didn't know what ... [laughter and unclear passages] – 'off the couch and come and have a drink'. I didn't know what to say really, do you know what I mean? 'Don't watch it then'. I was so embarrassed. As I say I feel awful now. I should have dealt with it better but ... Now when anything comes on he says 'I can't watch this bit now, can I mum?'. And he won't watch it now. I feel awful. [laughs] (FG5N)

As we saw in Chapter 1, there is a widespread belief in children's fundamental 'innocence', which is often equated with asexuality. Joey's reference to his physical response seems to defy the latter, whilst simultaneously confirming the former, thus contributing to Julie-Anne's confusion. Her regret touches on another dearly held belief, that young people have a right to 'healthy' sexual self-expression, which her response unfairly suppressed.

Parents frequently represented their discomfort as translating into regulation on children's behalf, often without the anxieties about doing so that Julie-Anne described. Howard (FG3N) described how with his 12-year-old daughter 'if something comes on that I'm not comfortable watching with her, I go "you're not watching this" and change channels or something like that'. His phrasing suggests that parents' concerns about the negative effects of television may occasionally be something of a smokescreen for their own difficult emotions, at least in relation to sexual material. Moreover, his reaction reveals and reinforces his relative power within the home over his young daughter.

Parents and older siblings also asserted their authority or greater status within the family by teasing children: 'the jokes'll come in ... just cause we're there' (Flora N, 17, P). In fact, some parental responses as reported by their children were far removed from the maturity to which those in the focus groups laid claim. Thus, Rebecca (N, 10, P) said that 'when people kiss on TV my mum goes "ooh look Rebecca they're kissing" (...) as a joke. 'Cause I used to always look away when people were kissing on television'. Meanwhile, Jacob (N, 14, P) claimed that his mother 'goes "Hey you don't wanna be looking at that" and when they're all like doing it she goes "Oh Jacob cover your face up, don't look at that."'. Sometimes such teasing provoked considerable resentment or indignation from interviewees who claimed that their embarrassment was engineered by others. Seth (N, 12, P) recounted how his sister would tease him:

Like it could be I'm watching a film, watching it all the way through, and a bit will come on like that and she'll sort of say 'look at Seth watching it' but I've been watching the film all the time.

Ethan: Oh Esme yeah she'll say look at Seth gawping at it.

Seth: I know but I'm just watching it and all.

He and Ethan claimed the same experiences at the hands of their mothers:

> Ethan (N, 12, P) If you're watching it like on your own in your bedroom it's just normal but when your mum's there you're like ooh er.
>
> Seth: Yeah, that's the one! [...] Sometimes she says 'oh you best be watching this because you know, then you'll know what to do when you're older', but then you're like 'mum! shut up!'.
>
> David: [...] Do you think your mum's embarrassed?
>
> Seth: No. No. She's doing that to make me shy.
>
> Ethan: Yeah.
>
> David: Oh right. OK. So she enjoys making you shy.
>
> Seth: Yeah.
>
> David: Why ... Why does she enjoy that?
>
> Seth: ... Women thing!

Naomi and Phoebe (N, 14, P) also identified this as something mothers did:

> Phoebe: The dads don't ... they're all right. They just let you watch whatever you want. But your mum ... If your mum's there. They look at you and you're like. 'What, just let me watch TV!'. They keep just staring at you. You're like ...
>
> Naomi: 'Mum!'
>
> Phoebe: 'Ok. I'm going to go upstairs now. Because you all keep staring at me.' [laughs] ... They just keep staring till you get a reaction.

One can only speculate here whether parents might be projecting their embarrassment onto their children or vice versa. However, such teasing and staring not only creates an unwelcome visibility for their recipient, but implies that their response to sexual material might be somehow inadequate or problematic. The indignant tones of these accounts counter such implicit accusations by transposing the alleged inadequacies onto parents instead.

However, parental embarrassment – or more accurately, representing parents as embarrassed – enabled some young people to demonstrate their own greater sophistication. Seamus (N, 14), for instance, described in his diary 'one particular moment [in *Footballers' Wives*] where Jason Turner had sex on the snooker table with another footballer's mum, which doesn't affect me but for some reason my parents.' Likewise, Melanie (N, 10) wrote 'two of the characters were kissing and I didn't think this was very rude but my parents didn't like it. (...) I didn't think it was rude I thought it was very entertaining'. In interview she presented herself as more able to cope with such material than her parents: 'They keep being stupid about things like that, I'm like "mum and dad, it's not that rude. I mean, get a grip, it's not that rude!" [laughs]'. She claimed both that she thought it was 'just entertainment' and – like many children, as we have seen in Chapter 3 – that in any case she knew about 'it' already – 'Huh. Four brothers, one sister. I think I do!'. Her co-interviewee Alicia added sagely: 'It's just life. People want to do what they want to do'. Of course, it may have been particularly necessary for Melanie, as the youngest in her family, to assert her sophistication in this way.

Some young people, however, did describe their own embarrassment, claiming that it was inherent to the situation of watching with parents: Rhiannon (N, 17, P) argued that 'you get embarrassed [giggles]. Somebody naked I'd be like [gestures looking away] (...) It's not that I didn't wanna watch it or it offended me, it, just because I was sat with my mum and dad ... I felt like I shouldn't be watching it. It's just like try and not watch it [laughs]'. Given their status within the family, they often had to remove themselves from the scene or from the sight of the source of the embarrassment, so they recounted covering their eyes, hiding behind cushions, leaving the room on the pretext of getting a drink, and so on. Some engaged in moralistic discourse as a defence:

Nancy (S, 17, P): Go make a drink. 'Cause you can't watch it. Even though you could watch it by yourself, when your parents there it just feels ... Even now sometimes. Now it's a bit ...

Olivia: Yeah. I still get embarrassed now.

Sara: Do you. Mm. So what do you do now if you get embarrassed?

Olivia: Go 'Oh god there's too much sex on TV now'. And she'll go 'yeah, you're right'.

Nancy: Yeah – 'That's disgusting'. [all laugh]

Where younger children did not want to watch sexual material in the media at all (and many interviewees referred to this as something that had been the case in the past rather than the present), their rejection seemed to represent a refusal of the world of adulthood itself. Embarrassment, however, came to mean something different, confirming children's identity as different from that of their parents, but at the same time often representing a demand for recognition of their growth towards adulthood. Thus, parents and children appear to construct their identities through what we might call 'embarrassment exchanges'. Melissa (S, 17, P) mused on the embarrassment she had felt previously: 'I was about 14, 15, and that was on, and it was a bit like I used to get ... 'Cause you know, you're going through that yourself and it is a bit embarrassing'. Similarly Grant (S, 17, P) offered the following justification for why he did not like watching sexual material in the company of his parents: 'You don't actually involve your parents in that sort of activity, do you. You've got a separate life to them. (...) It's just, sitting down and watching it in the same room he's in at the same time, sort of thing, 'cause you don't use that language in front of your parents'.

Underlying their accounts was often a developmental model of adolescence in which teenagers go through specific experiences and have particular needs – for instance, for sexual information – as they grow into adulthood. Sometimes it was important that teenagers felt their needs for such information (and hence their right to access potentially 'embarrassing' material) were recognised, as Kim (N, 12, P) suggested:

> Kim: My mum doesn't really mind me watching things like that (...) She thinks that in a way I can watch a bit of things like that, 'cause it's kind of like growing up and that and she knows it's important that I know, like, what's what. But she doesn't like, let me watch anything porno or anything. But I don't even wanna watch something like that.

In Chapter 3 we saw how young people countered their parents' discourses about children's vulnerability with their own discourses in which parents were construed as 'over-protective' (this was also a theme of discussions about regulation, as we will explore in the next chapter). They also argued that parental embarrassment reflected parents' unwillingness to allow them to grow up or to recognise their maturity. Many then claimed that they posed as more ignorant of sexual issues than they actually were, in order to protect their parents:

> Nancy (S, 17, P): Even though I've known from quite a very young age what is what. (...) But even I still sometimes say to my parents – and they go like, 'so what do you think on that then?' I'll go 'I haven't got a clue what that is. Dunno. So what's that?' (laughs). But mind you my mum does admit, my mum does say like I could probably tell her more than she could tell me. I was like, 'No mum. Of course not!'

As this implies, collective viewing was a forum in which revelations of knowledge could be made or suppressed. Ceri (N, 17, P) remarked 'some of the things that you'd laugh at, your parents go "Why do you know about that?" (...) I would rather leave them with a nice little mental image of me being 12, if that is what they want'. Similarly, Gareth (S, 14, P) remarked 'on *They Think It's All Over* or something, when they say something, I'll laugh and my mum just looks at me thinking like "oh, he knows what that means" (...) Sometimes when I watch it upstairs with my brother, I laugh then, but when I'm downstairs I try to not laugh at some of the things which I shouldn't really know'. Such accounts present a self-image as knowledgeable and sophisticated, to the detriment of parents who are then painted as 'naïve'.

In this respect, we can see children's media choices and active display of choosing potentially embarrassing media as constituting a 'coming out' to one's parents as sexual. Chloe (N, 17, P) described her mother's shock the first time Chloe bought a teenage girls' magazine at the age of ten: 'she just didn't realise that I wanted to read more about stuff like that, rather than comics like the *Beano* and stuff'. Her friend Angela added 'it's you growing up'. Conventionally, parents are seen as unable to handle their children's maturity and sexuality – particularly fathers in relation to daughters (see Chapter 3).

If embarrassment constructed age boundaries and identities, it also helped construct gendered roles. Rebecca (N, 10, P) commented that she was more embarrassed with her father, 'because he's like the only man in our house and I prefer talking to women about these kinds of things'. She represented her embarrassment in such a way as to underscore a feminine identification developed in opposition to masculinity (her father). She also projected herself as nearly grown – as needing to talk to 'women' about such matters. She added ' ... but I get embarrassed talking to my mum about it as well', which might suggest that she perceives two appropriate valences of embarrassment here – that of feminine propriety in relation to men, and that of modesty about the subject matter itself. She subsequently recounted, however, that her mother would sometimes laugh at her when she did attempt to raise questions about relationships. This might indicate that making claims to feel embarrassed are important for the identity work they involve (as here, Rebecca is working to build an identity as both feminine and mature) regardless of the actual experiences to which they refer.

Many others gave accounts in which embarrassment varied according to the gender of the parent with whom they were watching:

> Abigail (N, 12, P): But sometimes I'll just be watching something downstairs on the TV with me mum and it might have like a bit of sex in it and my mum and me just have a giggle about it but if me dad's there he'll go 'huh huh' [throat clearing noise] like that and just turn over (...) with me and my mum it's different because like we're both girls and we just have a laugh about it but when it's just like me and my dad we're just like – no way. I can't laugh at anything.

In this way, Abigail underscores gender solidarity between herself and her mother, against her father. Although such alignments within the family were generally with same sex parents, Chantel (N, 14, P) argued that she was not embarrassed about going to see *American Pie* even though 'that's about sex and like virgins and stuff that haven't had sex before. And I was watching it with my dad and my dad just said when he came out "do you not feel a bit embarrassed going and seeing it with your dad?" I didn't actually! Cause my dad's like my friend. But my mum's like my mum because she nags me all the time'.

A consequence of embarrassment was that young people developed definite senses about which programmes they would watch with parents, and which they would watch in their own rooms if they had a television there. Whilst it was generally agreed that the main living room contained the best quality television, and many young people sought out the pleasures of watching with others, at other times it was not worth the embarrassment of doing so. On many occasions, such decisions would have to be made during a programme, where children would disappear upstairs to continue watching in peace. It seemed that parents would operate a 'don't ask, don't tell' policy on this, where they knew what was happening but preferred not to challenge it. In these ways, media content and preferences about contexts of watching contributed to the demarcation of private and public spaces in the home.

Watching with mother

As we will see in the next chapter, many parents argued that good viewing practices around the television could mitigate its allegedly negative effects. Rather than simply watching or forbidding potentially embarrassing or 'difficult' material, parents (and mothers in particular) tried actively to construct it as an occasion for debate and discussion with their children. The genre most frequently referred to in this context was soap opera, and at the time of our research, two current storylines about teenage pregnancy on *Coronation Street* and *EastEnders* elicited considerable comment: both were seen by the parents as containing clear messages or warnings. For example, Moira (FG6S) commented: 'yeah, like to actually let them watch how she's struggling, how she can't go out with her friends 'cause she's got to look after this baby, how she's missing out on (...) So I suppose that way it's good because you're actually giving them a warning, you know, it's a warning to them not to do it'. A group of mothers praised the story as a sensitive and realistic treatment:

Heidi: They've made that quite clear that, you know, how difficult it is for a young girl still at school. With a baby and you know. So they're giving the right message there. That you know it's not all ...

Penny: It's not being glamourised. (...)

Wendy: Yeah. And then *EastEnders* give a different view, don't they, when she give up her baby. (...) Because she took it really bad and wanted the baby back then, didn't she? (...) It's different views, isn't it.

Heidi: Yeah. I thought the *Coronation Street* one was well done really. It was just, like you say, one simple mistake and that's what can happen you know. And you know you can't ... she can't just go out and please herself with her friends (...) Because my daughter (...) looks at baby clothes all the time. 'I wish I had a baby'. (...). I'm trying to explain to her that it's different when you have a baby, you know, they are keeping you up in the night. And so when she sees that and I say 'see ... That's what it's really like'. It worked. It worked. (FG4N)

Here the 'best' programme is defined as the one which confirms parents' own moral teachings and acts as a support to them. The hectoring or even punitive tone parents sometimes adopt, as when Moira notes 'it's a warning', and Heidi slips between 'you' and 'she' – 'you can't ... she can't just go out and please herself with her friends' – indicates how parents apply the moral messages they identify in soaps to their own children and perhaps even how they might project their own disappointments in life in these admonitions. However, some parents did note that some stories might be aimed at parents rather than their children, citing a storyline about school bullying in *Brookside*: 'I think that's to bring to put parents more in the picture because some parents are naive about, I dunno, a lot of things. They don't realise they're happening'.

At the same time, parents did not necessarily agree with the messages in soaps, nor did they passively accept them. They were quick to point to gaps in soaps' coverage of issues. For example, some were particularly critical of the double standard where soaps failed to give enough attention to the man's responsibility in relation to sexual issues or pregnancy, and focused primarily on women's responsibility for contraception and on the consequences for women if they became pregnant. Thus Jan (FG3N) praised a storyline in *Hollyoaks* about a male character with a sexually transmitted infection because it challenged the idea that 'it's normally the women who are slags'.

However, the exact nature of the 'message' was often seen as irrelevant, in that the conditions of reception – during family viewing time – meant that parents could maintain their own values in relation to it. Most parents felt confident that they could make use of or combat the 'messages' they identified in such programmes. For instance, Latisha (FG9S) argued that she found it 'totally wrong and disgusting' to show story lines with gay characters in what she described as 'normal programmes that we would watch with our children' such as soaps. Yet she simultaneously recognised that many people 'do agree with it' and that the producers were trying to remove taboos in order to promote 'equal opportunities' and to show 'that this is part of our society now'. She therefore continued to encourage her children to watch soaps because she found the discussions they provoked useful, claiming that in any case her children followed her views in finding such storylines offensive and would switch over if they were screened. Tania Modleski has argued that the soap viewer is positioned as an 'ideal mother', who 'identifying with each character in turn, is made to see "the large picture" and extend her sympathy to both the sinner and the victim' (Modleski 1982). Here, however, parents presented themselves as valuing the active role they could adopt in relation to the text, actively propagating their own moral values in relation (and sometimes in opposition) to its perceived messages.

Our research may provide evidence that soaps are 'open' texts whose messages are comparatively optional, or through which different meanings can be produced. However, it also suggests that soap viewers are successfully constructed as 'ethical subjects', who can deliberate, make choices and adopt a range of positions for themselves. There is rarely a voice of 'correct' knowledge or absolute moral authority within the fictional space of the soap, which potentially allows audiences (and here, parents) to occupy it themselves. As a genre, soaps value talk over action and this may resonate with the practice of 'talking about it' that parents depict themselves as trying to encourage in their children. The genre might thus be seen as successfully negotiating the problematic issue of raising moral dilemmas in a pluralist society (as we discuss in Chapter 7).

Again, we should note that our research is not based on participant observation: we are dealing with accounts that may have reflected what parents hoped for or felt *should* have been the case as much as what actually happened. It was apparent that some of the time they relied on their children not understanding or asking about storylines, particularly where they were difficult to explain – such as a rape in *Coronation Street*, or prostitution in *EastEnders*. As one parent commented, 'Well I felt I had to answer them [his questions] because I allowed him to watch it. I mean if I was concerned about it I should have turned the TV off but some of the things do go over his head (...) But on that particular – he really picked up on it and he wanted to know'. As we saw in Chapter Seven, the use of the media as a source of moral 'messages' or 'warnings' favoured by parents was often resisted by young people. Many parents admitted that such talk around issues during viewing fell short of their hopes:

Moira: Yeah, we did talk about it, but whether, you know, whether it goes in or not.

Rod: (...) But the subject has been broached and you can you know, you can sort of enlarge on that.

Harriet: I can remember saying you know 'you don't want to be getting yourself in that situation, you know. You want to be going out, having a good time, looking forward to your life. That all comes later on'. [imitating her daughter] 'Yeah, yeah, yeah'. [laughter] But you just hope it goes in. (FG5S)

Children's own accounts often indicated that embarrassment was caused by precisely the strategies of talking about sexual material that parents claimed to value:

> Jacob (N, 14, P): When that Sarah Lou got pregnant and my mum went 'When you're her age you'd best not come home with any girls pregnant' and stuff (...) I just got dead embarrassed when she was, tried saying that to me.
>
> Sebastian: Go, 'mu-um! Shut up!'
>
> Sara: And did you kind of like leave the room or anything?
>
> Jacob: No. I just thought I'd better shut up.

As well as illustrating the difficulty of such discussions, these reported conversations suggest that some parents use the text to promote relatively fixed moral positions. They contrast strikingly with the picture parents painted of their intentions when they encouraged debate about television programmes, which we consider in the next chapter.

As might be expected in relation to a genre that is still coded as a 'woman's genre', there were also gender differences in degrees of acceptance of these viewing models. Some men (who tended to claim they did not watch soaps anyway) were more inclined to dismiss the notion that soaps were providing a public service, arguing instead that controversial storylines were 'all for the ratings'. One issue repeatedly raised was that of the helpline numbers published at the end of programmes, the significance of which was hotly debated. For some, it was evidence of the broad-casting institutions' desire and ability to fulfil a social role; while for those who insisted on the 'ratings' perspective, it was a cynical move to evade criticism of sensational storylines. Whilst the latter can be seen as a moral stance in itself, it tended to close down debate about soaps as texts by denying their role in generating moral perspectives. Women's involvement with these genres gave them some power and a 'voice' in the interviews – which may be why men asserted their disengagement.

Parents readily acknowledged that an approach that worked in the context of soap opera worked less successfully with programmes outside family viewing time that provoked more divergent responses between parents and children. Audience segmentation leads to divergent taste communities. For instance, *Club Reps* or *Ibiza Uncovered* arguably address their audiences as hedonistic consumers of pleasure; and whilst some parents clearly found them enjoyable, others objected to them – although they also acknowledged that older teenage children, at least, had a right to watch them. Heidi related rather ruefully how her attempts to talk to her daughter about *Ibiza Uncovered* fell on stony ground:

> I'm trying to get through to her that this isn't a normal way to behave. You know like saying, 'What do you want to watch this for?' You know all this – so I say 'I don't know what you see in it at all, it's not the way you should be behaving'.
>
> Sara: And what does she say to that?
>
> Heidi: She just, oh … You know the sort of thing. I'm old and old fashioned and that … [laughs] I think. Like I say I don't think she is the kind of girl who would grow up like that. But … (FG 4N)

Gender and regulation

In many instances, mothers and fathers were reported to adopt rather different positions with respect to sexual content in the media, as Sharmaine described:

> Sharmaine (S, 12, P): My dad just sits there. Flicks it on to something like rude and it's sort of like five o'clock in the afternoon and he just puts it on. And there's all this sex stuff. And my mum's going, 'the kids are here!' He's going, 'you're needing sex education'. 'Cause he's just like one of them blokes, isn't he? And my mum gets the hump with him because he turns it on.

Her father adopts a more 'radical' position on the question of children's needs for sexual information, which both conveniently enables him to carry on watching what he wants and, for his daughter, confirms polarised gender identities – that he is 'one of them blokes'. It appeared that, in general, mothers were more likely to adopt a role towards their children in which they attempted to raise broader issues of ethics and personal conduct. Boys did not generally recount the same conversation with fathers as with mothers – Ethan's remark that 'with my dad it's all about football' (N, 12, P) was typical. Often, fathers' involvement in issues to do with relationships seemed to extend mainly to teasing about girlfriends (cf. Frosh *et al.* 2002).

It also seemed that children would receive varying amounts of ethical 'nurturing' according to their gender. Different viewing practices in themselves offer different opportunities for talk – many boys appeared to be watching football and sport rather than soaps, and so might have been less available for the discussions mothers described. Moreover, while children were divided on the question of whether mothers or fathers were stricter about their viewing, many boys perceived such concerns as feminine. Phil (N, 12, P) commented: 'it's my mum, *like all mums* they don't like some stuff that the kids watch, but my dad wasn't that bothered' (our emphasis).

Regulation within the home contributes to the shaping of identities. As is evident from the sexist language interviewees used to describe those who complained about media images (as 'old ladies', 'old biddies' and 'stuck up grannies', 'over protective mothers' who should be 'chucked out the window'), ethical concerns are often perceived as feminine. Some boys therefore define themselves in opposition to their mothers' endeavours, sometimes with the active collusion of their fathers. For instance, Phil (N, 12, P) claimed that when he ran up a large phone bill while looking for porn on the internet, his father condoned his interest and simply told him off for getting caught. Dale (S, 14, G) remarked in relation to a discussion of the Opium advertisement (Chapter 5) 'mums would be "no, don't look", dads would be "go on, son!"'. Clint (S, 10, P) seemed to be developing a masculine identity that required an explicit repudiation of his mother, at least insofar as she was understood as representing an undesirable discipline and control:

> Clint: I think it's just because, like some of the people that are my friends, they listen to their mum too much.
>
> David: And that's a bad idea?
>
> Clint: Yeah. Especially if you're like me and Luke! (laughs)

Parental control and regulation thus has effects on young people that extend beyond simple passive acquiescence. Young people might assert their independence and resistance to parental efforts to encourage their ethical development by focusing on 'their' programmes and media choices that parents might either disapprove of or find incomprehensible. In their interviews, they depicted mothers as ineffectually commenting on their media choices but having little power to do anything about them. This depended in part on their age – parental control declined as they grew older – but also on their gender. For instance, Naomi (N, 14, P) described keeping her pin ups in her wardrobe and not on her wall, because her mother would 'kill' her. Whilst her mother still exercised authority over her, however, she added that it was rather different in relation to her older brother who had 'pictures of naked women up on the wall.' She speculated that this was because her mother was not allowed access to his bedroom – 'She only goes in to get his washing then comes out again'. Joshua's account of his mother's response to his viewing suggests she was similarly powerless to impose her views:

> Joshua (N, 14, P): The older generation don't seem to ... like them kind of pictures. (...) She never really says like 'don't watch it', or 'I am not letting you watch that'. She just seems to be like, 'Oh you're not watching that are you?'. She doesn't seem to want me to watch it. (...) I was watching a video called *American Pie* with my brother. And she came in and said 'Ooh what's this?' And I say 'it's *American Pie* the movie. It's really funny'. And she starts watching the thing and said 'Oh I don't like the look of that'.

Watching programmes and films of which parents disapprove may enable young people to carve out space for themselves within the home, and confirm their separateness, more progressive values and greater skill as media readers in comparison to their parents. In turn, this material suggests that when mothers adopt a moralising voice (which in practice frequently emerges as simply a disapproving one) they may be trying to re-assert their (waning) power within the home as much as to guide their children's spiritual growth.

Enacting 'erotics'

So far we have argued that family viewing makes visible a range of performances of emotion – as for example, embarrassment can be incited not just by the television but also by who is present. Family viewing is also a place where children learn gender-appropriate styles of media consumption and displays of desire. That is, parental and sibling responses to media texts, rather than the texts themselves, might help acculturate children into particular styles of femininity and masculinity. For instance, for Reena and Chantel (N, 14, P), discussing styles of viewing and audience behaviours served to rehearse gender identities:

> Reena (N, 14): There was this film on telly and it had these two people having sex and [my little brother] he's like, he's going 'look at them, look at them' and like you know looking at them like that and it was embarrassing.
>
> Sara: And what do you think's going on for him that's making him do that kind of thing?
>
> Reena: He's just … He's a boy. He's just … stupid, yeah. They're supposed to do that and it's like something in their heads and …
>
> Sara: So if he's supposed to do that 'cause he's a boy, how are girls supposed to watch it?
>
> Reena: They just watch it.
>
> Chantel: Yeah. They're more emotional so they don't just like let out stupid things. They're just like talk to their mates about it. So. I slept at my friend's house last night and we started talking about stuff like that!

Many interviewees related family jokes about their parents 'fancying' celebrities. Caitlin (N, 12, P), for instance, commented on how her mother liked Mel Gibson in *What Women Want*: 'She was getting really excited at that bit [a shower scene]. She was sort of like shaking!'. However, fathers appeared to have more rights to assert forms of sexual desire within the home. Lara (S, 14, P) described her father putting up a Page 3 pin-up:

> Lara: Sometimes [my mum] does like flick through [the *Sun*]. She reads like the little problems and they laugh at us because my mum's like the typical like little woman that likes to talk about problems. But my dad he like … Like … You know like page three in the *Sun*. You get the naked women … But sometimes as a joke one day, (…) he had a poster of these Page 3 girls. He had like her tits

out and everything, and he put it on the wall (...) We don't take
that as serious. And I don't say 'oh you ... (...) These are really disgusting'. I think he's just mucking around. And he's showing that
he don't take it that seriously. He's just ... Because he said 'well I
think she's really pretty' and my mum was saying 'fine'.

On Lara's account, practices of reading the *Sun* are interpreted quite
differently within her family. When her mother reads the problem
page, she confirms gender stereotypes – that she is indeed 'the
typical little woman'. When her father puts up a poster of a Page
Three model, however, both she and her mother protect him from
the potential accusation that his behaviour might be objectionable
or hurtful.

For Courtney and Phil (N, 12, G), exchanges about fanciable celebrities were used to reinforce codes of behaviour and regulate desire:

Courtney: My mum fancies him [Robbie Williams] like mad. That
gets my dad mad though. (...) She's like, Robbie Williams comes on,
'oh, look at him. Isn't he a hunk?' And my dad's there like, 'You're
married to me you know, come on'.
Phil: Yeah, but my mum ... my mum fancies Angel and my dad
don't mind Buffy so like when she's going on about Angel, me and
dad just go 'shut up, Buffy's better', and stuff like that ...

Even jokingly, Courtney's father interdicts desire beyond the institution of marriage. Phil and his father counter his mother's expressions
of desire and mutually reinforce their own heterosexual identities.
Indeed, Phil suggested a (mock?) competitiveness between him and his
father:

Phil: I was in Las Vegas, I've been twice and I was in the casinos and
you know how the girls have like short skirts up to here. Me and my
dad were on our own so walking through, 'mmmmm!'. And (...) my
dad sees me looking, he goes, 'Oi you, turn round. That's my job,
not yours!'

In the next chapter we will discuss how some mothers focused on gay
representations in the media as a powerful symbol of their own
changing, more progressive, views. However, some fathers in the
parent groups expressed anxieties about their sons turning 'gay'.
Indeed, Louis listed this as a main reason why he would regulate his

four sons' viewing: 'the root of it is I don't want my kids or my sons to be homosexual. That's my feeling. And I don't want them to say it's okay in case one day they'll say "dad, I'd like you to meet Simon". [laughter] I dread that.' It seemed that children quickly picked up what would or would not be acceptable, even if this was conveyed at implicit or unconscious levels, as Rod's exchange with his ten year old son suggests:

> Rod: I really hate the thought of it, like I said before I mix with a lot of gay people but I wouldn't like Jack to be gay. So I try to steer him away to that. But I opened up the computer one day and there's a file and it's got 'poofter' written on it. [laughter] So I opened it up and he'd downloaded a Will Young MP3 and he labelled it 'the poofter'. So he knows his words and he knows ... I think he knows why a man loves a man (...)
>
> Sara: Did you say anything to him about it? Did you sort it out?
>
> Rod: Yeah, I did and we laughed. [laughter] You know 'cause I thought, God, you know, how do you stop kids from learning about these things? They pick it up. (FG6S)

In many cases, heterosexuality was simply assumed and bolstered. For Ross, what he construed as his young son's early expression of hetero-sexual desire was a cause of pride and reassurance rather than the mortification Julie-Anne described above:

> Ross: He used to come in here and watch pretty girls on the telly didn't he? And then you weren't supposed to watch him watching. One ... I can't remember what advert, he'd be right up the telly [mimes tongue hanging out]. Yeah, real pretty girl on. And then, you know, he'd notice that he ... that he likes pretty girls and then he'd go, 'my thing keeps standing up'. I said 'Oh don't worry about it'. (FG7S)

In other cases, fathers worked hard to extirpate potential marks of non-masculine behaviour in their sons. One group of mothers shared stories of how their husbands had banned their boys from playing with 'girls' toys from a young age. Some children were subjected to explicit anti-gay messages and even exhorted to help scrutinise their siblings' behaviours for marks of deviance. Krystal (S, 14, P) gave a disturbing example of the lengths to which fathers would go:

One thing with my dad, 'cause he's not too fond of gay people and neither is my mum actually. (...) he made me watch a film and I felt sick. And he told me all these things that he'd do and how his friends had rectoral [sic] bleeding and he had to cover for him and the way they had to put tampons sometimes up their arses. I felt *sick*. I felt literally sick. And he was saying 'this is why you shouldn't do this da-da-da-da-da-da. So if you see your brother acting a bit weird tell me and set him straight'.

Our interviews did, however, suggest how different practices might be developed within specific subcultures or communities. For instance, in order to correct the gender imbalance of our parent focus groups we sought out a group of men who had formed a support group for male carers (who looked after children professionally or were the main carers within their own families). Perhaps because they had been able to develop within this group ways of challenging gender ideologies in their own occupations, they self-consciously rejected homophobic views on masculinity and sexuality. They remarked acerbically that any men who were anxious about their sons' sexual orientation or about gay representations on television clearly 'had some issues about their own sexuality' (FG10S). Similarly, a group of lesbian mothers discussed how varied their children's gender performances could be, when not constrained by parental anxieties about homosexuality. One gave this account of her two-year-old son's response to *Shrek*:

> Marion: He loved the princess. He *was* the princess! He wants to lie down and be the princess and I have to wake him up and we have to have a kiss of true love (...) For a while he really wanted to be called princess all the time, wherever we were. (...) in the playground with the other parents, in the street, everywhere. (...) I noticed one or two second glances when they twigged he was a boy. I think usually they just assumed if they heard me saying princess, I was talking to a little girl (FG8S)

We would speculate that many parents, should they so choose, would be able to recount similar examples where their own children might have exhibited gender 'inappropriate' identifications and passions, but that these are likely to be screened out. Marion is able to relate this story because she is unafraid of behaviour that might be judged by others to be a mark of gender 'deviance'. She illustrates by contrast how deep-rooted homophobia is within many families – a view that contrasts with the more optimistic claims about lesbian and gay identities made by our interviewees elsewhere in this book.

Conclusion

As we have seen in this chapter, practices of media consumption within the home may be seen a means by which gender and sexual identities are performed, negotiated and confirmed. Their meanings are further determined by the cultural resources available for interpreting them. When children claim to feel embarrassment, for example, they are actively making claims about their own identities relative to others in the family and to imagined 'norms' of development and age. Meanwhile, parents enact moral positions through regulation of their children's viewing, and in many cases co-opt resources from the media to help to construct their moral perspectives. These seem to vary according to the gender of the parent, and young people react to such 'nurturing' in a range of ways according to their investments in particular gender positions.

Clearly, we cannot make assertions about media influence without considering how media texts and styles of use are negotiated within the home. However, practices of family viewing do not consist solely of 'role modelling', if by that is meant a rational process through which children are socialised into gender-appropriate identities. Interviewees' accounts frequently suggest that there are powerful fantasies and unconscious processes at work in family interactions, over which individuals may have little control. As we will see in the next chapter, this complicates parents' own descriptions of their aims and intentions in regulating their children's viewing.

9
Governing the Living Room – from Morality to Ethics

Sharmaine (S, 11, P): I watch *CBBC*. When that's finished I watch *Neighbours*. Then by six, 'cause it finishes at six, I watch *Home and Away* and then about half an hour on to an hour then *Emmerdale*'s on so also I watch that. (...) Everybody's talking about *EastEnders* as well, (...) everybody's like 'oh yeah did you see *EastEnders* last night' and all that. (...) 'Cause I've grown – I've grown up with like, going downstairs, watching *EastEnders*, cause my mum, my mum absolutely loves it. My mum loves *Emmerdale*. And she used to turn it on to *Coronation Street* when that was on, for us. So we would watch that. And we'd also watch like erm silly things like *The Simpsons* and that ...

The home is popularly perceived as a private and deeply personal realm, with television correspondingly represented as an intrusion that must be guarded against and controlled. Yet as we saw in the previous chapter, and as Sharmaine's account of her evenings at home suggests, television has been domesticated and become part of the basic organisation of family life, including how we handle time and space. It actively helps shape our routines, mealtimes and rhythms of the day, and the demarcation of public and private space in the home. Interactions with family and friends often take place around and through the television set. Some of these appear more legitimate than others, as Sharmaine indicates when she hesitates before reporting that her family watches *The Simpsons*, and terms it 'silly'. Television can become part of the moral economy of the household, as when children are denied it as a punishment; and even attempts to limit its role have implications for the siting of the set in the home (Leichter *et al.* 1985). Moreover, as James Donald comments, how broadcasting (through its scheduling, regulation and discourses) defines and addresses its audiences ' – as the nation, the private citizen, as the family, the developing child – has played an important part in making these into operative social categories' (Donald 1992). He argues that its effectiveness in shaping individual capacities and collective ways of thinking and behaving depends precisely on how it mobilises us, becomes interwoven into our everyday lives, for instance as a matter of what we 'absolutely love', rather than by manipulating or coercing us.

Media regulation is an interesting example of these processes at work. Although technology has until recently allowed 'appropriate' subject matter to be determined centrally, broadcasting institutions have long attempted to train audiences in their domestic uses of the media, encouraging them freely to adopt certain modes of feeling and conduct towards them. The practices of regulation are not therefore only negative or repressive, nor are they clearly distinct from the texts to which they are applied. Rather, they actively constitute the media in particular ways, suggesting how texts (and their audiences) are to be understood, defined and talked about (cf. Kuhn 1988). Putting an age-related classification on a video, for example, marks it out as a potentially unacceptable object and encourages moral concern about children's access to it. It simultaneously addresses media audiences, exhorting them to act responsibly. The nine o'clock watershed, too, offers a tool for rational viewing in a partnership with the audience, who in making use of it perform their civic duties as concerned parents. It is an example of how the 'little routines of social citizenship and civility' are implanted into each 'private family', and social obligations into the soul of each free citizen (Rose 1999b). The home should therefore be thought of as a site in which we practise what Nikolas Rose has called the 'arts of connection', between individual habits and the wider society.

Arguably such 'arts of connection' are particularly crucial at this point in time. New technologies such as video, cable and the internet mean that control is passing to the audience rather than being left in the hands of centrally directive bodies. Market segmentation has led to the construction of divergent and incompatible 'taste communities' (Collins 1995) that pose new problems for regulatory bodies who must rule in the name of all (Thompson and Sharma 1998). However, we should not see these changes in a determinist way, as only a consequence of technological change, but set them in a social context. Many commentators have argued that traditional agencies of moral authority – issuing authoritative guidance and external, binding, moral codes – are in decline, and are being supplanted by individualised values of personal autonomy, self-realisation and free choice. Rose conceives this as a shift from 'morality' to 'ethics', that is, from obedience to an externally imposed code of conduct and values in the name of the collective good, to the active and practical shaping by individuals of the daily practices of their own lives, in the name of their own pleasures, contentments and fulfilments (Rose 1999c). As individuals become 'entrepreneurs of themselves', the centralised control of the media comes to seem anomalous and problematic.

In this chapter we continue to consider the accounts children and parents give of media consumption practices in the home and the regulation of children's access to sexual material. In the previous chapter, we explored the emotional dynamics of collective viewing and suggested how these might be bound up with the actual experience of or motives for regulation. In this chapter we explore how children and families are managing their own 'practices of freedom' as we move from centralised control and morality to individualised ethics. We ask whether we can identify changing ways of thinking about and acting in relation to sexual material in the media. We consider how far the weakening of centres of power involves new or expanded roles and responsibilities for audiences in relation to media materials, such as greater parental vigilance over children. We also aim to capture some of the nuances that might lie behind the findings of recent attitude surveys, of the kind identified in Chapter 1.

Parents who care

Research on the family audience for television and other media has often been highly value-laden, taking the practices of middle-class families as the norm. It has implicitly or explicitly adopted a prescriptive stance towards media consumption, favouring an information-retrieval or active pedagogic approach to television usage, in which each encounter with television is turned to cognitive account and used as a learning experience. It often stresses the need for parents to limit their children's viewing and prevent them getting access to particular types of material. In the process, less vigilant families, or those who have an 'entertainment orientation' to media usage (often assumed to be working-class families), have been stigmatised. For instance, psychologists have created distinctions between 'socio-' and 'concept-'oriented families. The latter refers to more 'democratic' families who adopt 'approved' viewing practices, such as discussing programmes critically and conveying family values, the former to authoritarian ones that do not discuss television but use it to promote family harmony and avoid conflict – which is often condemned as unhealthy (Buckingham 1993; Walkerdine 1997: 107–37). As Valerie Walkerdine has remarked, there is little space in these models to consider unconscious processes and fantasies – such as those hinted at in the previous chapter.

However, such research has also pointed to anomalies, particularly between what parents say and what they do. David Buckingham's previous research in this area (Buckingham 1993; 1996) compared the different accounts given by children and parents when interviewed separately, depicting television viewing as a site of struggle, where parents try actively to regulate their children's viewing, but where children also resist and subvert – or claim to subvert – family rules. He argues that such a picture more accurately reflects the messy compromises of family life than the idealised accounts some parents offer in interviews. In this instance too, we found some limited but revealing disparities between the perceptions of parents and of their children on this matter. Ethnographic research or participant observation into the actual uses of television in the home would undoubtedly uncover further contradictions.

Nevertheless, the aim of our parent focus groups was not to catch parents out in moments of hypocrisy. We were interested here precisely in how they *talked* about parenting – the discourses through which they accounted for themselves as parents, the authority they called on in doing so, how far they felt able to challenge others with whom they disagreed and so on – and what this reveals about current definitions of good parenting. For instance, one parent, Lynda (FG2S), said, 'we're here [in the interview] because we care about our children – but there's many parents out there that don't care. They wouldn't come to a meeting like this'. On this understanding, a willingness to admit and offer for scrutiny their own parenting practices marks individuals out as caring, and a refusal of or indifference to self-examination signifies the opposite. This perhaps shows how deeply individuals have internalised social norms of 'good parenting', as well as how our focus groups ('meetings') were viewed by participants.

In one earlier study by David Buckingham (Buckingham 1993), parents – interviewed in school – propounded very anti-television views, but this was not generally the case in our focus groups. This may have been the impact of context: most of our groups took place in people's homes, seated round the TV, accompanied by drinks and snacks to help make the atmosphere informal. By asking interviewees to name their favourite television programmes as they introduced themselves, we tried to establish an atmosphere in which TV could be considered as a source of pleasure. Nonetheless, some participants would apologise for their tastes as they did so, even if jokingly – 'I'm afraid I'm a soap queen' – as if feeling, like Sharmaine, that certain preferences were likely to be unwelcome in the context of the research.

Regulation of sexual material differs from regulation of bad language or violence, the other two concerns most frequently mentioned in survey research. Whilst parents might argue that they regulate violence or bad language because they do not think it should be a part of their children's lives at all, such a position is virtually impossible to sustain in relation to sex. Although views differed as to timing, all participants acknowledged that they would have to cope with their children's questions and desire for knowledge about sex, and eventually with their active sexuality. (This notion of the child as having a 'natural' curiosity about sex is itself relatively recent, as noted in Chapter 1.) The discussions therefore touched on parents' own sexual selves and pasts; they tended to be just as much about 'sex' as about 'the media', and about what kind of men and women they wanted their children to grow up to be. As will be seen, parents divided roughly into those who saw the media as an ally or as an obstacle in this process.

Parents talking about effects

Parental regulation depends in part on how parents conceive the media as 'objects' and their effects on children – and in turn this raises broader issues to do with the nature of childhood, the utility or desirability of providing information on sexual matters, which forms of knowledge might be acceptable, and the 'proper' source of such knowledge. In our focus groups, some parents expressed concerns about children's 'loss of innocence', describing them as 'mini adults', commenting that 'a lot of children don't seem to be children somehow', 'they seem to grow up too quickly', and comparing children's knowingness with their own naivety at a comparable age. (The conventionality of such perspectives was brought home by the fact that they were echoed by several of the older teenagers in our sample.) As we saw in Chapter 3, our interviews with children told a rather different story.

In some cases, television figured in parental explanations as a foreign element or invasive force, with the power to defile a natural authenticity of childhood (as well as the sacredness of the home and parents' authority). It was depicted through violent metaphors – as 'garbage' 'forced' or 'shoved down our throats', 'just literally ramming it down these kids' throats', for example. However, for some, children's awareness was a source of pride. Many of the parents were actively critical of their own parents for withholding sexual information from them, and felt they were not repeating these mistakes with their own children. In welcoming greater openness, they allied themselves with the forces of progress in society. Moreover, the composition of our parent groups was such that some mothers were able to recall their own memories of dressing up and dancing like pop stars, which they claimed had been fundamentally innocent. They thus challenged the notion that such activities in their own children were necessarily precocious or overly eroticised.

In one previous study by David Buckingham, parents expressed concerns about violence in the media not because they thought their own children might copy it, but because they might find it upsetting or disturbing (Buckingham 1996). One comparable issue mentioned here was body image, where glamorised images in the media were seen as damaging to self-esteem. Howard and Sandra (FG3N) recounted how their 12-year-old daughter was already concerned about her size, which they attributed to the 'abnormal' models in the media, the sense that 'you have to be a size 10' (FG3N). Vikki (FG5N) was also distressed by her daughter's response to teenage magazines: 'My daughter does listen to all that. She reads all that. She thinks that's how she should be. She gets dead upset, you know. She gets very withdrawn. "Mum, I'm too fat"'. No one articulated similar concerns in relation to boys, perhaps because they are seen as less vulnerable in this respect than girls. However, many parents expressed a general sense of the media pressurising their children to behave in certain ways:

> Penny: Every newspaper you open now, every magazine, it's got a nude body on, or somebody's, pop star's, sex-life or –
>
> Wendy: – Yeah. Famous people.
>
> Penny: And they really think that's the normal thing, don't they?
>
> Heidi: They obviously just follow on you know … they follow each other don't they. They follow the lead of their friends and think 'oh well that's what I should be doing' I suppose. (FG4N)

As Heidi's remark suggests, however, in relation to sexual mores parents were not perhaps as certain of the influence of the media as compared to factors such as 'peer pressure', as they might have been in relation to media violence.

Many also considered how the media might 'normalise' forms of conduct and sexual feeling, due in part to the nature of the televisual flow – as Lynda commented, 'because it's brought into your house twenty-four seven, it becomes part of life' (FG2S). Relatively few objected to the ideological content of programmes – although Sylvia (FG8S) recalled earlier feminist politics and objected to what she saw as the offensively sexist language (the description of women as 'birds') in *SM:TV Live*. For most, the central focus was on the morality of personal conduct. Jan expressed her concerns in these terms:

> The only thing I've ever felt might have an influence on younger couples is maybe on the soaps. I don't watch very many, but my children do from time to time. And every soap somebody is having an affair with somebody else's husband or somebody else's wife and sometimes I think – I suppose more often than not they get found out. But it happens so often and it'll – whether they're just keeping an interesting story line to keep the viewers, the ratings, up, I don't know, but I sometimes wonder … if kids just think, 'but it happens all the time, it's part of everyday life, so maybe it's not so wrong', you know and I think that's the only concern that I've ever had, that maybe they're trying to make it that it is part of everyday life. (FG3N)

Similarly, Carole remarked of our extract from *Jerry Springer*, 'I'm sleeping with my sister's man': 'They will think that it's the normal thing wouldn't they? I mean, I look at it and I think they're pathetic and laugh, but would the children actually look at it like that or would they look it "oh, they've both got the same man and … oh I can go out with my sister's boyfriend and it's the normal thing to do because they're doing it on the telly and every one's watching them and cheering"' (FG1S).

As both Jan and Carole acknowledge, there are oppositional ways of 'reading' television. Jan notes that there are moral messages in soaps, at least insofar as storylines end unhappily and those having affairs 'get found out'. They can also be read as the product of wider institutional pressures to maintain ratings rather than as reflecting real life. Carole is able to demonstrate her own critical distance from the scenes in talk shows by dismissing them as 'pathetic' and mocking them. But while both parents here argue that *they* are able to identify such processes, it is crucial to their argument that other audiences are not. In fact, as we saw in earlier chapters, there was very little evidence that the children responded in the ways that are attributed to them here: like Carole, they too were able to dismiss the guests on talk shows as laughable; and like Jan, they were well aware of the pressure for ratings in soap operas.

Nevertheless, as this implies, debates about media effects are always also debates about the dissemination and distribution of media, and about the competence of different audiences at reading or decoding them (cf. Hunter *et al.* 1993). Children, especially, are readily assumed to be ethically 'immature' and to lack the specialised knowledge necessary to protect themselves from the deleterious impact of the media. Stuart was one of several parents who stated this explicitly (FG2S): 'No, I think kids would read into it different ways as an adult would read into it. They might take it the wrong way or it might influence their tiny little minds, cause they're only children. And I think you can corrupt them more than anything'. This construction of children as particularly vulnerable is crucial to sanctioning practices of regulation and censorship – and, as we will see, it also shapes the ways children respond to those practices.

Parental views on regulation

All the parents we interviewed were familiar with external forms of media regulation such as the watershed or video classifications. However, they challenged their adequacy on a number of grounds. Some argued on the basis of practicalities, pointing out, for instance, that in larger families it was often very difficult to prevent younger children seeing material that their older siblings had a right to watch. In some cases siblings shared bedrooms with televisions, and in other cases older children connived with the younger ones in allowing them to watch material their parents would (they claimed) otherwise have prevented them seeing. Parents also admitted that they were vulnerable to children's various tactics of persuasion.

Meanwhile, some parents challenged the logic – more than the principle – of the regulatory systems themselves. For instance, the watershed was often perceived as reflecting anachronistic assumptions about the domestic routines of households (such as that all children under 16 are in bed by nine o'clock). Many remarked that it was inconsistent, untrustworthy or pointless: that it should be set earlier, or should be later, that its boundaries were being pushed by advertisers or by producers. Many parents had concerns about video classifications, often being unable to understand the logic of some decisions (around *Spiderman, Jurassic Park* or *Harry Potter*, for instance), and engaging in sophisticated debates about how they might have been reached. As previous research has also found (Buckingham 1996), they argued that it was – or anticipated that it would be – impossible to enforce the regulations as strictly as the age bands suggested. Most agreed that by the time their children were 12 to 14, it was much harder to impose their will and simply forbid them from seeing material.

Such criticisms should not be taken as a demand to drop regulation, however. Indeed, all the parents we talked to claimed to supplement external regulation themselves. In many cases, they focused on quantity rather than quality – invoking the dangers of eye strain through watching 'too much telly', or not wanting children to be tired for school the next day, for example. Many also acknowledged that in large families they got 'more slack' with the younger children. Nonetheless, parents would regulate content in a wide range of ways: for instance, by reading television and film guides, consulting teletext, previewing films or reading magazines, talking to other parents and friends to get a sense of film content before allowing cinema trips, making on-the-spot decisions to send their children out of the room or to switch over, sometimes even editing films and music themselves before passing them on. Some employed overt means such as removing television aerials (!), others more subtle psychological tactics such as not engaging in arguments over controversial texts or artists (Eminem was often cited here), in the hope that their children would soon forget them. They frequently did this in the name of maintaining their personal values against those of a broader society conceived as inhospitable to them. However, they also argued that their own children were more mature than the regulations permitted, or that only they knew their particular needs and vulnerabilities. Josie and Paul, a couple who fostered sexually abused children, provided particularly dramatic examples of the need for such individually tailored understanding and insight when they described how for such children, a perfectly innocuous scene – 'a Mummy and Daddy kissing, or a Daddy kissing a little girl good night' – could trigger days of 'horrendous behaviour' (FG5N). Their experience served as a reminder of the need for sensitivity and awareness of children's relationships with media, but also of the impossibility of making the media completely 'safe' for children.

In their accounts, parents may well have presented themselves as more thorough, rational and deliberative than they actually were, but two immediate points are relevant. One is their attitude to authority – they claimed that they had the authority to supplement regulations precisely because they knew their children best. (Being a parent was sometimes seen as a prerequisite to having any authority about media content at all, as Ray (FG2S) intimated when he demanded angrily to know whether a producer of *Grange Hill* had children herself.) Secondly, we live in an age where, as Nikolas Rose remarks, ideas of freedom have come to 'define the ground of our ethical system, our practices of politics and our habits of criticism' (Rose 1999b). It is therefore not perhaps surprising that we guard against anything that seems to undermine our autonomy. Accordingly, parents here treated regulatory systems as a guide rather than as gospel. However, Rose goes on to argue that in our concern to construct what we do as the result of free choice, we overlook the many ways in which we are urged to govern ourselves and take on those strategies willingly as a mark of self-control. In this sense, parents' views here should be taken as a measure of the *success* of governmental strategies, not as their failure. They demonstrate how widely disseminated the techniques of self-management have been, and how they have instilled in many the desire and disposition to be self-governing.

'Pedagogical' parenting

It was notable that relatively few parents represented their regulation of children's access to media as an act of prohibition. When some did, other parents often expressed covert disapproval, perhaps through teasing or pointing out inconsistencies. For instance, when Carole (FG1S) related how she had ripped out a page of her ten-year-old daughter's magazine because it discussed contraception in response to a letter from a 12-year-old, April suggested jokingly that she was 'for it' because she had bought her daughter a magazine 'over her age'. Such responses may have arisen in part because other parents felt defensive, or unable to maintain such control themselves. However, it seemed also to be because many advocated an ideal of parenting that we might call 'pedagogical': that is, they preferred to enhance children's own reflective capacities through debate and discussion, rather than insisting – in a more hierarchical way – on parental rights to impose moral values. Parents' accounts here implicitly drew on 'progressive' or 'child-centred' approaches to education and child-rearing (cf. Walkerdine

1981) – approaches which are also reflected in the ideal of the 'concept-oriented' families, mentioned above.

For instance, Sandra (FG3N) described discussing with her 12-year-old daughter the *Grange Hill* storyline that we had also showed our research participants:

> In the past when I've watched *Grange Hill* with her it tends to be me who's raised it as a question to carry on discussing. I've waited 'till the end of the programme and said 'what did you think about that?' (...) Just discussing whether – because she's a daughter, she's a female, so we were discussing whether she thought the female had done the right thing and what she should have done any differently. I can't remember how exactly how the discussion went. I started it off and she took the lead and gave her views and opinions. (...) I think I made a conscious effort to try and discuss with her because I didn't have the opportunity as a child to discuss things with my parents and I decided I was going to try and raise things with her or answer from being a very young age. Whenever she asked questions about sex, I always tried to answer them in a way that I thought she'd be able to understand at whatever age she was.
>
> Sara: And do you think that having things on telly sometimes makes it easier to raise issues that maybe you wouldn't think of raising?
>
> Sandra: Yes, 'cause that issue wouldn't have been raised in the house unless we'd seen it on television.

Soap operas were particularly highly praised by many other parents, for putting a 'moral angle', for 'answer[ing] a lot of questions for a lot of young people that parents wouldn't normally approach with them' (Imogen, FG3N) or for raising issues that parents could discuss with children. This applied particularly to mothers who would often be watching soaps themselves anyway. Imogen commented:

> Well, my children tend to give their opinions. You know, 'I think she's right doing that' or 'I don't agree' or whatever, you know. And they tend to mull it over and think about how they would react in the same situation. So I think that's good in lots of ways. And then they can talk to me and say 'well I wouldn't do that mum' or 'she's wrong for doing that'. And they can see the obvious kind of moral lesson in it or whatever.

Sandra and Imogen's accounts are significant for the emphasis they place on the parents' seeming non-intervention ('I've waited 'till the end ... ') and on the centrality of the child. It is Sandra's daughter who 'takes the lead' and Imogen's children who volunteer their 'opinions', often on the basis of their identification with exemplary figures ('because she's a female [too]'). But they do so in an environment of supervision, provided partly by the parent (the mother) who gently oversees, guides and monitors, and partly by the television which provides the occasion in which such exchanges can take place.

One intense debate arose when two fathers, Stuart and Ray, argued that the portrayal of issues in soap operas was either unrealistic or something children did not 'need to know' about and hence that they should not be allowed to watch. Others in the group objected:

> Yvonne: I think that anything like that is an opportunity to explain and have a discussion with my children. (...) They'll say 'oh that man head-butted someone else' and then that's 'well that's not the right thing to do, you know, why shouldn't you do that?' and that's how, everything that happens, if there's anything they ask a question about, we discuss it. And if they ask, I tell them the truth. (FG2S)

In fact, the 'truth' or accuracy of representations was less at issue here than the circumstances of consumption. Yvonne emphasises the importance of social interaction, arguing that the television is potentially a source of moral enlightenment in the right context of reception. She simultaneously endorses the 'pedagogical' view of 'good' parenting – as equal and open discussion, guided by the parent whose 'honesty' (truth-telling) and moral example are prime values. As we saw in the previous chapter, such accounts may suggest a view of female responsibility for children's ethical development. Fathers appeared more likely to opt for authoritarian modes of controlling children's viewing. However, fewer fathers than mothers participated in our groups overall, and whilst this is itself revealing it means our evidence on this point is limited.

One consequence of parents' discussion of the social contexts of reception was to shift the object of concern, from unskilled children to culpably neglectful parents who failed to discuss programmes with their children. Thus, Ray responded to Yvonne by referring to an (imagined) audience that failed to supervise:

Ray: You've gotta understand, I dunno what the percentage is but 95 per cent of children are probably sitting there watching that television programme on their own, because their parents are either doing something else or are not even in the home. And there's no one there to sit there and explain to them and all of the sudden all the things that we've spoken about (...) are things that are coming into them, being absorbed by them with no one telling them right or wrong. So in the end (...) it becomes a part of life.

In this way, Ray was able to maintain his belief in the need for stricter centralised controls on viewing, whilst conceding that discussion might act as a filter for otherwise unwelcome views.

As we also noted in the previous chapter, many parents felt on particularly insecure ground in relation to media material that did not seem to allow such discussions, such as that outside the watershed (for example, *Club Reps*) or on cable and satellite. Since only older children tended to be viewing this material, however, parents often defined it as a question of personal preference and decision-making which they should leave alone; and in some cases, they made a tactical retreat from the main living room (which was generally the only set with cable or satellite access) in order to allow their children to watch undisturbed.

Negotiating pluralism

We might see the kinds of debates that went on in our groups as arising from the dilemmas of negotiating a changing value system. Consider the following exchange, which took place between two parents who both identified themselves as committed Christians:

Lynda (FG2S): It's very difficult ... to stand as a parent in front of a 14-year-old who is extremely eloquent – and we get on really well and we do just have debates because we like arguing (...) – and there's a situation going on about 'I believe this to be right or I believe this to be wrong'. Now when you're having that discussion with your child you can stand there with your hand on your heart and know that you are telling them the truth as you believe it to be. 'These are the correct moral standards. This is how it should be' blah blah blah but when you then read a newspaper, pick up a magazine, turn the radio on, turn the television on and you have completely contrary suggestions being put down – you doubt and you doubt yourself (...)

Ray: Are you saying you have doubts, or your children have doubts?

Lynda: I doubt that I have stood my ground. I doubt that I have the right to stand my ground because the square box in the corner is telling me that's it's ok for guys to kiss guys. It's ok for women to be in bed with other women. It's ok for this guy to go promptly into bed into that bed past the and do it behind the bike shed –

Ray: – But that box is lowering your standards.

Lynda: No it's not lowering my standards, but it does cause you to doubt. And when it's not just the box it's the newspapers you read, it's the radio stations you listen to, wherever you go, and it's talking to people in the playground. (...)

Ray: (...) When it goes back to morals in the media and the television, then I'm perfectly competent in, in what I, the sort of moral standards that we set in our house I believe are right.

Lynda: You never once question –

Ray: No. No.

Lynda: Lucky you. You are a lucky man. (FG2S)

Ray's style of parenting confidently imposes a fixed set of rules and principles – not only about media consumption but also about sexual standards (he also intended to withdraw his children from sex educa-tion classes at school, which he described as 'some bureaucrat' telling his children what to think). He blamed television – which he referred to as 'absolute rubbish', 'absolutely awful' and 'un-educational' – for society's ills and saw it as a threat to his ability to control his children's social and sexual knowledge. Lynda's parenting style may differ partly as a result of family circumstance: her children are older than Ray's, and many parents of older children recounted how they had been ousted in arguments or could no longer impose their will. But she also puts forward a position that is closer to the 'ethical' one sketched out by Rose, mentioned in our introduction to this chapter. She claims that her doubts result from her openness to the pluralist values of the society around her, which come not only from the media but also, significantly, the lives of those around her – including other parents, the 'people in the playground'. There is a good deal of rhetorical power in her enumeration of the 'messages' she claims to identify in the media; they help construct a self-image as part of a beleaguered minority. Yet her conclusion that Ray is 'lucky' is ironic and serves as a challenge to him as well. It suggests not only that doubt is the necessary condition of most people in contemporary society, but that it can be an ethical position in itself.

Some in our groups went further than Lynda. Apart from some who claimed strong religious faith, participants generally did not see their lives in terms of certainties and moral conformity. Instead they emphasised the importance of their children being able to make happy, healthy choices, to be their own people, to seek their own satisfactions, and recognised that their choices might be different from their own. Indeed, the composition of our groups illustrated contemporary social pluralism, including members of religious communities who objected to the stereotyping of Christians or the undermining of the traditional family, lesbian mothers who wished the media would reflect the diversity of the sexual cultures they inhabited, and fathers who wanted to see more images of caring, non-normative masculinity.

This context perhaps provides the backdrop for the debates about lesbian and gay sexuality that occurred in the groups. As we noted above and in Chapter 1, surveys have found evidence of a general cultural shift towards greater tolerance on this issue. In our groups there were some strong expressions of homophobia from some fathers, as we have already observed. However, for many parents (particularly heterosexual mothers), sexuality became a kind of 'litmus test'. When they sought to show how they were doing things differently from their own parents, or wanted to exemplify their philosophy of parenting, they frequently turned to issues of sexuality. Jacqui (FG5N) remarked of her son:

> when he says, 'what's that?' or 'what's that?' I'll explain. When he watches something on TV, though he's only four, he still knows. (...) and he's seen two men kissing: 'Ooh, what they doing? Ooh, look at that!' do you know what I mean? I've explained, 'it's two men that like each other that's what they do, so it's nothing' – I'm not going to put ... make sure that he doesn't have no phobias.

We would argue such views served different – albeit related – purposes for parents as compared with the older middle class teenagers discussed in Chapters 4 and 6. It helped them develop an identity formed in opposition to an older, repressive morality. Some stressed that the latter had made questions of sexual orientation taboo in a way that they would not repeat with their own children. Hazel, for instance, claimed to value fictional representations for helping her explain things in the world around her children, and illustrated this with an example about sexuality:

> One of my husband's aunts is a lesbian so then that [a lesbian story-line in *EastEnders*] was a way of them seeing it in a different light, rather than thinking 'why is she always with a woman? (...) A man's always with a woman, why has she always got like a girlfriend with her?' and we used that to explain to them, because the programme went into it, didn't it?' (FG1S).

Others emphasised how responses to lesbian and gay representations on screen reflected broader questions about the relations between children and parents – honesty being, as noted, a crucial value:

> Clare: My older child can question. You know, you've got your likes of your Lily Savages and things and it's got to the point where 'is that a man or a lady mum?' and you're like er – So that can be hard. Well, I just answer them honestly.
>
> Lynda: That's right. I think if you're honest I don't think you can go wrong.
>
> Helen: (...) Something was on the telly, something to do with two ladies I think. And she asked me, you know, 'was that the right thing to do' and my answer was 'well, you can't help who you fall in love with'. If she falls in love with – not that I want her, you know, not that I'm gonna say that's what you've gotta do – if she falls in love with a lady then I'm not gonna see that as a bad thing.
>
> David: Yeah. Yeah. Yeah.
>
> Helen: Because to me it's not. And I explained to her that two ladies do, can fall in love and they're lesbians, it's not a … I mean that's not a big deal but I can't see how seeing that on the television is gonna turn you gay which is the argument. I can't see how that can. You either are or you aren't. I don't think you might have a try if you think you –

Clare: My dad's brother was gay. I mean he died when he was 33 and I didn't find out he was gay until ten years later. I didn't know. Just, Uncle David had his friend and that was it. They shared a flat but I mean we was not aware of it me and my brother. (...) We never questioned it either. (FG2S)

Sexuality here, as for the teenagers discussed in Chapter 4, is perceived as something that you 'are' rather than the product of social arrangements and definitions. However, these mothers are aware of the pain that previous generations' hypocrisy have caused; and their responses are quite striking considering that until only relatively recently, parents were encouraged to feel guilt if their children were gay, and to scrutinise their potential role in 'turning' them that way. Mothers here emphasise the importance – for both themselves and their children – of being 'honest' about and accepting of this identity. Sexuality is defined then as a question of self-determination, being 'true to oneself', understanding what one 'is' and living accordingly, and respecting the identities of others. Honesty and personal freedom rather than following moral codes, equality rather than hierarchy within the family, seem to be the pre-eminent ethical choices here. Again, we might see this as illustrating how debates about sexuality have intensified and multiplied, taking on broader meanings about the future shape of society (cf. Weeks 1995).

The consequences of parenting ideals

Some consequences of parents' adherence to pedagogic models of parenting should be noted. Since regulatory practices construct the media as a potentially dangerous object requiring strict control, those parents who suggested that they actively wanted their children to learn about the world through the media did so in a tone of taboo-breaking. It seemed to be hard to articulate in the focus groups the pleasure that the media may well have brought them as adult audiences, despite our attempts to make it possible. Another consequence is the enhanced parental responsibility and sometimes sheer hard work that this style of parenting involves. For those parents who objected to sexual content in the media, each encounter with the media was represented implicitly or explicitly as fraught with risks, requiring research in advance as to content or decisions on the spot about when they might have to turn the sound down, turn off, turn over, encourage their children off the sofa, out of the room, to bed ... They were acutely aware of how they might be judged by others, sometimes refusing to allow children to watch videos with friends only for fear of how other parents might react. Many parents noted how much more confined their children's lives were than theirs had been and how little space they had for playing outside. To the extent that what children watch on television is available to be known by parents who care to research the viewing guides, or that their paths through the Internet can be traced, children's lives are potentially brought under a considerable degree of scrutiny, compared to the relative invisibility of outside play.

Moreover, regulation brought its own dangers in drawing attention to issues of which children might otherwise be oblivious. One example here is innuendo: as we saw in discussions of sexually suggestive advertisements or music videos (Chapter 5), children were often unaware or confused by their connotations, raising the question of whether such material therefore really affects them. When Latisha (FG9S) censored a 'suggestive' shampoo advertisement, she drew her children's attention to innuendo that might otherwise have been missed. We also showed children an extract from the children's magazine show *SM:TV* that had caused many complaints from adult viewers at the time, in which presenter Cat Deeley called a guest, the model Caprice, a 'scrubber'. Children frequently had only a hazy idea of what this might mean, and their definitions were extremely varied: 'someone who picks up stuff off the floor and keeps them'; 'a thing that you rub on the top of the table'; 'they do the work and the other person doesn't'; 'toilet scrubber'. Even those 'in the know' ('a ho' and a slapper') argued that it was not a very strong word. Parents in our groups were divided over whether the word would mean anything to their children. A parent who had accompanied her children to a recording of the show related how at certain moments the producers had asked the parents to join the audience because the children were failing to get the jokes and provide the requisite background laughter. Parental regulation or censorship in this context actively renders the world of television a more, rather than less, sexualised space for children. It exemplifies the argument that discourse about sex in modern Western society displays the inseparability of knowledge and pleasure, 'examination and excitation' (Hunt 1993; Hunter *et al.* 1993).

Moreover, if parents are responsible for their children to such an extent, they also bear a greater burden of responsibility for what they perceive as their failures. Some parents compared regulating media with feeding children, aptly drawing attention to another issue that is surrounded by ambivalence and guilt for many mothers in particular.

Thus, some parents in the groups described their shame and humiliation when they felt they had not lived up to standards that were both imposed from outside and taken on as their own. For instance, Tina (FG2S) related that her daughter had become upset because she thought that her parents' divorce meant her father would go to prison as had Trevor on *EastEnders*. Tina's tone suggested she had failed twice – firstly to be able to offer her children the stable family life she had wanted for them, and then again because she had not been there to talk to her child about the television she was watching (teachers had had to relay her daughter's anxieties). 'If I was gonna be a responsible parent', she remarked, 'I should have really sat down watching it with her, shouldn't I?'. As others in the group were quick to point out, it was impossible for parents to be as omnipresent as they might wish, and the Internet and friends often made their own measures irrelevant. However, the ideal of parental responsibility made a sense of failure almost unavoidable. In an emotional moment during another group, Vikki (FG5N) expressed shame and shock that her daughter was pregnant at 16 despite her efforts to be open with her. As we have seen, teenage pregnancy is generally viewed as inherently bad and is often blamed on parents for failing to provide the 'right' information and 'proper' guidance that would prevent it. It took Josie (a mother of four and foster carer) to challenge these notions and reassure Vikki: she remarked briskly that public hysteria about teenage pregnancy was misplaced, that she herself had longed for a baby at the age of 13, been happily pregnant at 17 and had been 'a good mum'.

Therefore, whilst we have identified potentially new values and ways of thinking that seem to legitimise a wider range of sexual identities, we should also recognise the sometimes burdensome effects of shifting ethical responsibilities onto individuals. An insistence on individual autonomy allows little space for considering broader structural issues that limit one's control over the circumstances of one's life, and makes it harder to acknowledge the unconscious processes at work in social and family interactions.

'So over-protective': children's views

Children worked hard in our interviews to counter the 'discourses of vulnerability' adults apply to them (MacKeogh 2001), by constructing their own counter-discourses of parental inadequacies or over-protectiveness and by demonstrating their own competence and maturity. Thus they argued firstly that parents were 'out of touch' and unaware of how much they knew: many echoed Krystal's (S, 14, D) argument that 'parents would *die* if they knew half the things kids talk about!'. Secondly, they emphasised the gulf between the older generation and theirs: Neville (N, 14, P) argued that today: 'You get more freedom (...) 'Cause they used to not get any freedom at all (...) When they were young they didn't really get to do much 'cause they were told not to, and they obeyed'. Finally, parents were held to be incompetent in relation to media, lacking understanding of new technology, and even the basic media literacy necessary to follow plots. Eve (N, 17, P) remarked 'That really bugs me about my parents, that they will sit there and go "Well you know, don't kiss him. Just kill him!". I say "Mother, there will be no story if she just killed him then!"'.

As MacKeogh argues, such versions of parental lack of know-how allow children to present themselves as 'media savvy' by contrast (MacKeogh 2001). We saw in Chapter 3 how children frequently construct themselves as 'sex savvy', which also shaped their arguments about parental regulation of sexual media. Kelly (N, 14, P) remarked: 'my mum always goes "you shouldn't be watching that" and I always say "but it's not as though I don't understand what's going on". I mean if I was little, like say ten or something, and you don't know the true facts about life, then maybe you shouldn't be watching it but I do, we do understand. So I don't see why we can't'.

At the same time, the 'over-protective' argument enabled older interviewees, in particular, to recognise their parents' concerns as touchingly benevolent, even if misplaced. As Jon (N, 17, P) remarked of his father: 'I think he's just laying rules as all good parents do, they've gotta set standards and they expect you to abide by them'. Darren (S, 12, P) even alleged that parents censored sexual material simply because they were 'copying' their own parents. As we saw in Chapter 8, some went on to turn the tables, arguing that in fact it was they who had to protect their parents from their actual levels of knowledge and sophistication. Others were more forthrightly dismissive and impatient, such as Alicia (N, 10, P): 'They're mums and dads, they're like *eighties* kind of thing, oh God! (...) They think it's all rude and they think I shouldn't be knowing about this until I'm about 13 or 14 or something like that. (...) They wanna keep me a child forever!'

Yet while media representations were generally held to be personally acceptable or harmless for our participants, they were evaluated in terms of 'others' for whom they might be dangerous or beneficial. However, children were sometimes hazy about what the feared 'effects' of seeing sex on television might be, proffering vague explanations such as that it would 'fill our minds with dirty stuff' (Theo, S 12, P). They were familiar with the notions of 'copying what you see', but this applied less easily to sex than it might do to violence, for example (especially for those to whom the very idea of sex was anathema). Jonah (N, 10) explained in his diary how sex on TV was different from issues such as violence: 'When I see killing on TV it makes me feel a bit freaked out because sometimes you imagine it happening to you and what pain you could be in. But when people kiss on TV it doesn't affect me because I've seen my mum and dad kissing'. When we asked for examples of possible effects, younger children could often only find examples of swearing and violence instead, although Nerys (P, 10, G) suggested that music videos might make girls 'start to wear no clothes', and older participants did argue about the media 'glamorising' sex or prostitution (see Chapter 5). In all cases, however, effects were invariably displaced onto children younger than themselves.

Nonetheless, children were aware that not regulating TV is tantamount to admitting to being a bad parent and would be viewed negatively by others. Clint (S, 10, P) explained that his mother didn't like him watching sexual material because 'she just thinks you're gonna go round at school like and talk about it and everything', which would mean, Leo added, that 'your mum and dad aren't very nice people'. All our participants knew the classification categories for videos and most knew how the watershed functioned, even if its actual definition was obscure – 'I just pictured a shed!' Jessica (S, 14, P) admitted. The existence of such measures enabled them to understand why parents were censoring material: 'They're on earlier than they should be and they're too rude for us to watch them all, and mum and dad come in and either turn it off or turn it over' (Jake N, 10, P). When Theo (S, 12, P) remarked that his parents let him watch 'mild sex (...) but not actually doing it', his use of the BBFC's own classificatory terminology is revealing.

Like the parents we interviewed, children were generally hostile to external regulation. As we have seen, people who actively complained about particular representations were dismissed as 'opinionated middle aged women', 'old ladies who are so moany (...) wasting their pensions using the phone and complaining because ages ago they didn't have stuff like this. And now they're jealous!'. They were quick to point to what they saw as anomalies in classifications, particularly in relation to computer games, but also films. Unlike parents, however, they referred not just to classifications that seemed too low, but to the false expectations a higher classification could create (as Chantel N, 14, G remarked of *The Full Monty's* classification, in a distinctly disappointed tone, 'you think you're gonna see the full monty!'). The older children asserted that they were old enough to watch such material, pointing out that at 16 they could engage in heterosexual sex and so should be allowed to see it. Some rejected any regulation at all, on the basis that it should be 'your choice' or pragmatically because regulations had little practical force anyway. A few demanded greater regulation, although inconsistently. For instance Clint and Leo (S, 10, P) claimed that sex in *EastEnders* was 'wicked', but also that it should be on later (when they would themselves undoubtedly find a way of watching it). Some drew parallels between their active decision-making in other areas of their lives and their rights to do so in relation to the media. Neville (N, 14, P) pointed out that young people were being invited to take responsible decisions about their lives at relatively early ages – his example was selecting subjects to study, which required developing a sense of what life would hold in the future beyond school. Externally imposed regulation came to seem anomalous where they were being encouraged to see themselves as active meaning-makers and decision-takers elsewhere. To the extent that the idea of regulation suggested that they were 'unfree', they saw it as an affront.

Throughout this book, we have argued that the young people we talked to set great store by the notion of being independent, autonomous beings. Yet like parents, in their rejection of regulation as necessary for themselves, they overlooked the productive role it played in their identities and media practices. Regulations helped mark out material that was desirable or where they would expect to find more graphic material. Wayne (S, 12, P) remarked that they were useful as a guide to content – 'if you look away (from a scary video) you'll have wasted £3 for nothing'. Todd (S, 10, P) proudly enumerated his collection of 'over-age' videos: 'I got like twenty 12s, one 18 and four 15s'. They had also developed a fair degree of media literacy that made them aware of what to expect of a programme from its title, scheduling, credits, and so on, and thus to cope with its potential sexual content. For instance, Keira (S, 10, P) described how she had reminded herself that a particular storyline in *EastEnders* would not end with a baby's death because 'they wouldn't do that for the little people'. Dale (S, 14, P) remarked of Sky's *Dream Team* that 'it's on about eight o'clock so you don't see that much'. They understood the fictionalised nature of portrayals, for instance that actors 'are allowed to kiss but they are not actually having sex, making a baby. They are allowed to kiss though' (Rory, N, 10, G). If they did encounter sexual material later in the evening they were aware that it was 'for adults' and that they were encroaching on their territory. Lysa (S, 10, P) who listed as one of her hobbies 'watching films over my age limit', described watching a Channel 4 programme on 'Sex Gods and Goddesses', which featured 'people humping on the back of a fire engine, naked':

> Lysa: I thought it was okay, but as it was like, it's on like twelve o'clock at night, there wouldn't be so many like little children running about the house.
>
> Sara: So you kind of knew that it wasn't kind of appropriate for kids to be watching.
>
> Lysa: Yeah. I know when it's not appropriate, but I still watch it.
>
> Sara: And so do you have a different attitude to it if you know it's not supposed to be appropriate for you?
>
> Lysa: Yeah. If like I know it should be appropriate, I'm not expecting like loads of sex and stuff, but if I know (...) I expect that there's going to be something so I'm not really surprised when I see it.

Such knowledge of conventions came to seem self-evident, which fed into their lack of sympathy for people who complained. As Tom (N, 17, G) remarked of *So Graham Norton*:

> I think the whole show is about sex and if you tune in at that time in the evening and watch that kind of programme I think you know what you're getting. You can tell from the credits when it's all like the numbers in 'phone booths and things (...) It's just a bit of light entertainment and I don't think it should be frowned upon just because the topic is about sex mainly.

Similar remarks were made in relation to other shows such as *Club Reps*, with participants commenting that whatever they felt as an individual about its content, it was appropriately screened at that time of night.

As this implies, regulation provides at least some of the terms within which children think about their relations with the media. To this extent, they have a stake in preserving its categories. Regulation gives children a norm against which to calibrate their own developmental levels – albeit mostly discovering that they are in advance of the stages that seem to be set out for them by regulations. Bea (N 10, P), for example, described how she bought girls' magazines because she was 'fast at growing up'. Growing up, in her account, is not something that happens to her, but something which she can achieve – and her media consumption is a measure of her speed and success in doing so. We might call this the 'Just 17 principle', according to which media companies target the age-based aspirations of their audiences: despite (or because of) its title, *Just 17* is a magazine whose primary readership is among girls aged between 11 and 14.

Some even anticipated a time when they would be strict with their own children and shocked by what they watched – which Jon (N, 17, P) described in a tone of cheerful resignation as the 'festering of getting old'. The putative 'other' audiences for whom regulation *was* necessary served to underpin their claims to be mature and competent. For instance, Ethan (N, 12, P) acknowledged that the guidelines were useful, referring to them as 'good rules for your children', Joseph (S, 12, P) commented that 'if there's not a Watershed you don't know what time the kids should not be watching'. These formulations – 'the kids', 'your children' – suggest that in discussing regulation both Joseph and Ethan temporarily assumed an 'adult' position.

Children were also able to rehearse for adulthood by practising censorship on younger siblings. Thus, Will (S, 10, P) was of the view that, although children of his age needed to know about 'such things' at quite a young age, its down side was that younger children (below seven) might get to see it. He solemnly reported that his five-year-old sister hadn't seen 'it' (that is, sexual material of one sort or another) but had got 'very close to seeing it'. Fortunately, he reassured us, 'I always manage to get the control off her'. For Will, seeing material over his age was a mark of adulthood; but so too was regulating material on behalf of even younger viewers. Conversely, younger siblings complained about older siblings 'telling on them' for watching programmes they were 'not supposed to'. In discussing regulation, therefore, a pro-regulation position allows the speaker to adopt an adult position (much as for parents it allowed them to present themselves as 'good' parents).

Some took a libertarian position on parental regulation: Seamus (N, 14, P) argued that 'it's not really their (parents') choice what they want their kids to see because it's not their life. 'Cause the kids might feel a different way than the parents do'. However, many upheld parental rights to regulate children's viewing. This may in some cases have been simply expedient, in that parents did allow them to watch more than they believed they were 'officially' allowed to. But they often painted a picture of being genuinely happy to receive guidance; as Noelle (S, 12, P) remarked: 'I think my mum should tell me if she thinks it is [suitable] because she's been my age and she's been older and she knows what's better for me'. Children often presented a picture of relative harmony; for instance, where rules could be bent if adults were watching later programmes with them, making the occasion something of a treat. Rebecca (N, 10, P): 'Me and my mum normally like watching the same things. So when there's a programme on that we've been waiting for for ages then I'm allowed to stay up late and watch it (...) If it's after quarter to ten and I'm not going to bed she changes the ... She like tells me not to look 'cause they're doing more dirty stuff'.

Mindful of the notion that the good parent is the regulating parent, children were careful to explain any laxity in a positive light, arguing that they themselves were exceptionally mature, that their parents trusted them, and so on. They clearly stayed up late (in many cases later than their parents may have realised). Mia (S, 12, P) argued that she was able to watch as late as she liked – including staying up for *Club Reps* – because her parents trusted her: 'if your parents let you stay up that late, then that means they feel comfortable about you watching the later programmes', she reasoned. However, her parents, who took part in the focus groups, said that she was not allowed to watch that programme as it was past her bedtime. It may be that Mia had a different interpretation of the implicit understandings of family routines, rather than that she was consciously subverting them.

There was evidence that parents also suggested actual strategies by which their children could cope with material with which they might be uncomfortable. Bea and Rachel (N, 10, P) described how they had persuaded their mothers to let them watch *Bridget Jones's Diary* at a birthday party:

Bea: Yeah, my mum said I could watch it as long as – she said, you can watch it but if there's anything that you don't wanna watch or something like that ...

Rachel: Yeah if you don't want to watch bits in it then you don't have to. You can just go out of the room or you can turn around or you could go in the bathroom or whatever.

Bea: Or you can start rummaging in the drawers.

Regulation was often done co-operatively – Alma (S, 10, P) described feeling embarrassed when *Footballers' Wives* was showing 'a bit too much': 'My mum said "do you really want to watch this?" I went "no" and my mum just turned it over'. In other cases, however, they directly challenged parental prohibitions:

> Seamus (B, 14, P): There's nothing wrong with watching it so … they can't tell me what to do!
>
> David: [laughs] And they take that, do they?
>
> Seamus: Just going to have to. [laughs] I just come back in … 'What's wrong with it? Why can't I watch it? What's wrong with me watching it?' And they'll just, don't say anything. And I just go by and keep it on.

They also described various strategies they had evolved for evading parental scrutiny, recounting scenarios in which they pitched their wits against their parents to watch the forbidden material they desired. For instance, Caitlin (N, 12, P) exploited her grandmother's deafness to watch *Sex and the City* when her parents were out; others would watch with older siblings or at friends' houses; they would capitalise on differences between their parents to persuade one to let them watch what the other would not. Lysa (S, 10, P) recommended plying adults with Baileys Irish Cream to encourage them to relent over such issues; while Bea (N, 10, P) had found simple emotional blackmail effective in persuading her mother when she was reluctant to let her take *Bridget Jones's Diary* to a party: 'I sort of say like, "yeah but *everyone*, you'll let the *whole* party down" … '. They would disguise what a text was really about, for instance by hiding cases that showed classifications. They would watch disapproved material from behind settees, on staircases, or upstairs on another television, swiftly changing channels when they heard their parents approaching. As Kelly (N, 14, P) and others pointed out, this last tactic had its limitations: 'Change channel, put something like the News on. She always goes – she knows that we don't watch the News!' As David Buckingham has pointed out (Buckingham 1996), children are not powerless within the family, although they may also relish exaggerating the amount of power they do have. It is clear from our interviews with parents that they were aware of some of their children's subterfuges in this respect, but preferred not to pursue the matter.

The children were, overall, keen to present themselves as self-regulating. In the case of sexual material, many younger children in particular often chose actively not to watch it and were very definite about not wanting to see what they referred to as 'full frontal views' or nudity. For instance, Theo and Darren (S, 12, P) commented that although 'it's kind of all right, when they're on beaches' it was less so 'when they're on beds, like proper doing it (...) when you actually got a camera on them the whole time'. When they did seek it out, or even came across it inadvertently, they often gave the impression that they fully expected to find it repellent.

As has been seen in earlier chapters, the children had very definite ideas about what they 'needed to know' and employed a range of strategies for coping with sexual material they thought was 'too much'. For instance, Theo (S, 12, P) claimed that when sex came on, even when watching on his own, he would 'just face the other way and just relax'. Courtney (S, 12, P) recounted that her mother had switched off a notorious masturbation scene in *American Pie*, remarking that 'I didn't disagree with her because I knew why she was turning it off', but adding that in any case had she been watching it on her own 'I wouldn't just like be staring at the TV and watching it, full, full frontal view, I'd just probably turn away or something like that'. Other responses included rejecting the text – for instance not watching a programme, changing channel either for the whole or part of the programme, viewing with a cushion to hide behind, covering their eyes, leaving the room, distracting themselves and so on. Others described how they could remind themselves that it was fake – that if two characters kissed, for instance: 'It's not like they're really going out, is it?'. Occasionally young people proved to be sterner censors than their parents. Krystal (S, 14, P) described watching Tom Cruise in *Magnolia*: 'and he's a motivational speaker and he says "respect the cock" and I was like "excuse me!" Aye! I turned it over and my mum says "what are you turning it over for" and I said "well cause it's not suitable for me" and she says "but I want to watch it" and I said "well I'll go to bed"'. Similarly Noelle (S, 12, P) remarked of *At Home with the Braithwaites*: 'it was just like showing how like people like can be lesbians and that. And I think that I shouldn't be watching this! I think maybe my mum or dad should've watched this a couple of times!'

Conclusion

All the parents whom we interviewed, and who were described to us, were concerned to regulate or to mediate their children's viewing of sexual material. Their grounds for doing so, and the strategies they adopted, varied considerably: they drew on diverse understandings of the nature of childhood, and of parenting itself. There were different views about what children did and did not 'need to know' and about the balance between preserving their 'innocence' and preparing them for the realities of adult life. Few parents represented their regulation of children's media use as a purely prohibitive act, undertaken without discussion: most were inclined to adopt a more democratic or 'child-centred' approach, placing an emphasis on choice and self-reflection. Most parents acknowledged the dilemmas and contradictions here, and recognised what they saw as their own failings. In all cases, they took externally defined rules seriously; but they also sought to supplement them in the light of their own unique understanding of their children's needs. However, this should not be taken as meaning that the regulatory systems in place are inadequate or flawed. On the contrary, our research shows how successfully people are managing their practices of freedom, coming freely to carry out the 'routines of social citizenship'. Regulatory strategies are based on a contract between the state (or the media industries) and the consumer: they address audiences as responsible, caring parents, prudent mothers or ethical individuals capable of exercising self-mastery, discipline, foresight, reason and self-control. Our interviewees had come to (or at least hoped to) take on those identities, especially where they connected with their own aspirations, desires and self-images.

Similar perspectives were also apparent in children's own accounts of how they managed their media use. In many cases, their parents had successfully helped them to develop strategies for coping with the media and for understanding them in particular ways. As we have suggested, the media themselves might also be taken as pedagogical in this respect: practices of regulation (such as the watershed or age classifications) and scheduling, the conventions of different genres, the identifiable address to different audiences, all teach young audiences what to expect from the media, in ways that they learn very early in life. The media provide languages and techniques of self-understanding and self-mastery as well as 'content' concerning love, sex and relationships.

Yet if parents and children gain in autonomy, they also take on responsibility. For parents, there is a definite price to pay for this, not least in the unending nurturing and surveillance that is required of them. Everyday life comes to be governed by the requirement that it be the occasion for personal growth and self-improvement. As we argued in relation to innuendo, regulation risks paradoxically constructing a more sexualised world, drawing attention to what might otherwise be overlooked or not understood. It also depends upon the construction of a pathologised or stigmatised audience, the 'bad parents' who fail to maintain the correct standards of involvement in their children's viewing, or of self-control in relation to their own media consumption. Whether or not such parents exist, the fear of being seen as one of them acts as a powerful cause of guilt and shame: in this area, as in so many others, parents may be left feeling that they can never be 'good enough'.

For children, this emphasis on self-regulation also presents them with additional choices. What it means to be a child is now something that needs to be constantly defined and reasserted and worked over, rather than something that can just be taken for granted – and sex becomes another terrain on which that definition has to occur. Rather than being kept away from such matters, children are now confronted with the question: do I really want or need to know about this? What is it appropriate or necessary for me as a child – or a child of a certain age – to see or to know about? These are questions that are no longer capable of straightforward answers, if indeed they ever were.

10
Conclusion

Qualitative research of the kind we have reported in this book is rarely conclusive. Indeed, part of the aim of our study was precisely to open up the discussion of issues that, in our view, have often been prematurely closed down – not just in the public debate, but also in academic research. It is perhaps inevitable, therefore, that we should end with more questions than answers.

Accounts of qualitative research often pay close attention to the dynamics of data gathering. The relationships between researchers and their 'subjects', the ways in which claims and counter-claims are played out in interviews and focus groups, the extent to which particular methods or questions tend to determine the kinds of responses that are received – these are familiar concerns for researchers, that have been raised at several points in our discussion. What is often harder to account for, however, is the process of analysis – and particularly of writing. In this research, we made use of computer software that allowed us to index and collate material relating to particular issues, and hence systematically to compare and contrast our data. But in writing, we have inevitably had to select, to generalise, to summarise and to interpret. We have had to discipline a mountain of data – several thousand pages of transcript and other material – into a manageable and (we hope) reasonably coherent account.

In the course of the research, we have came across several issues which we did not initially expect to address. Reading 'between the lines' of our transcripts and diaries, we can identify questions that are in need of more systematic exploration than we have been able to give here. Thus, at various points in our analysis, we have touched on broader theoretical concerns about sexuality and subjectivity, about the changing nature of gender and childhood identities, about the relations between the public and the private, and so on. These are issues that require further theoretical investigation and debate; and we believe that empirical studies of this kind should make an important contribution to this.

However, this research also takes place against a background of intense – and perhaps increasing – public concern. Indeed, part of our aim in the research was to enable children and young people to 'speak back' to these concerns – to have a voice in a debate that is about them, but that is often conducted without any attempt to solicit or explore their views. As we have indicated, this aim did to some extent determine and constrain the kinds of things they felt able to say; although it did not preclude a range of perspectives from being expressed. In offering our contribution to this debate, therefore, we would like to offer a very brief summary of what we see as the key findings of our research. We have self-consciously confined ourselves to the following ten points.

General findings

1. Whether or not they choose to do so, children frequently encounter sexual material in the media

All of the children in our sample were able to identify media material that was relevant to our theme of 'love, sex and relationships'. As we have seen, there is some disagreement among researchers about whether the amount of sexual content in the media is increasing; although the majority of people seem to believe that it is – including the 16 and 17-year-olds in our research, looking back on their 'younger days' a mere five or six years previously. The children in our study were encountering such material not just in 'adult' TV programming, but also in children's programmes, movies, advertising, pop music, magazines and newspapers, and on the internet. However, relatively little of this material contained 'explicit' representations of sexual activity; and much of the sexual content was in the form of verbal references.

2. The material children do encounter is quite diverse in terms of the 'messages' it is seen to contain

The children sometimes found it difficult to identify the 'messages' about sex and relationships that were contained in this material; and the messages they did identify were by no means uniform or always straightforward. In some instances, sex was clearly perceived as an enjoyable and desirable activity for young people; but the children also identified many instances where the media appeared to be informing them about the dangers and problems it represented, particularly at a young age. They certainly did not perceive the media to be encouraging them to have sex prematurely, or to be promoting a purely 'recreational' approach to sex; and in many instances, the predominant tone appeared to be one of moral warning. The modern media offer *mixed* messages, and often explicitly require consumers to make up their own minds about sexual issues.

3. Children value the media as a source of information relative to other sources, such as parents or the school

The children were generally very critical of the sex education they received in school, arguing that it was too narrowly focused and too moralistic in its approach. Many also found it embarrassing to be taught about such matters by their parents. By contrast, they preferred media such as teenage magazines and soap operas on the grounds that they were often more informative, less embarrassing to use and more attuned to their needs and concerns – and, in some respects, more morally neutral. In practice, the children often combined different sources of information, and used the media as a pretext for discussion with peers or parents. However, the easy availability of such information does not mean that learning about sex has somehow become scientific and rational. On the contrary, it is still surrounded by shame, embarrassment and ambivalence, in which romantic aspirations co-exist with a knowledge of sordid realities.

4. Nevertheless, children do not necessarily trust what they find in the media: they are 'literate', and often highly critical, consumers

Children are not the naïve or incompetent consumers they are frequently assumed to be. They use a range of critical skills and perspectives when interpreting sexual content; and this develops both with age and with their experience of media. Some of these are quite generalised, and relatively superficial – as in the criticisms of how sex is used in advertising, or to sell newspapers. However, the children's responses to sexual imagery in advertising or music videos displayed a well-developed understanding of how such images are constructed and manipulated. Likewise, their judgments of sexual storylines in soap operas and dramas showed a complex awareness of the conventions of narrative and characterisation. In a range of media genres, the children were making sophisticated, multi-faceted judgments about the relationships between fiction and reality. They were also able to make thoughtful contributions to debates about media ethics and regulation; although (perhaps surprisingly) there was little sustained critique of sexism in the media.

5. Children (and parents) are aware of media regulation, but reserve the right to make their own judgments

All the children and parents in our research were aware of regulatory systems such as the watershed and film classification, and used these as one source of information when deciding what to watch. In general, they agreed that such guidance was necessary – albeit primarily to protect audiences (such as younger children) whom they deemed to be more vulnerable then themselves. This was felt to be particularly important in relation to material that would be seen in more public settings, such as on advertising hoardings, or on television before the watershed. In some instances, children positively rejected material which they decided was 'too old' for them. However, they often resisted or rejected parents' attempts to decide on their behalf, on the grounds that they were old-fashioned or patronising. Most parents were inclined to avoid an authoritarian approach, and preferred to negotiate with their children over what they should see; although in some instances, this seemed to make their job more difficult, rather than easier. Perhaps particularly in relation to sexual material, both parents and children seek to define themselves as self-regulating, autonomous audiences.

6. Children do learn about sex and relationships from the media, but this is not a straightforward or reliable process

The children often rejected overt attempts on the part of the media to teach them about sexual matters, and they were sceptical about some of the advice they were offered (for example in problem pages or talk shows). They were particularly resistant to the use of drama to convey pre-defined moral messages. They seemed to engage more effectively with texts where they were encouraged to debate issues and make up their own minds. For parents too, more 'open' texts like soap operas provided useful opportunities for them to promote their own moral frameworks. Both children and parents wanted to be addressed as individuals who were capable of making their own choices, rather than as the recipients of moral instruction; and it may be that this is more apparent when it comes to sexual material than to other forms of media representation (such as 'violence').

7. Younger children do not necessarily always understand sexual references or connotations

Despite the children's claims, they did not necessarily know 'everything' about sex: they were far from being the precocious sexual sophisticates imagined by some conservative critics. Younger children's partial knowledge means that they often ignore or misinterpret many references to sexual matters, particularly where these are in the form of comic innuendo or 'suggestion' (as in the case of music videos). Younger children are also less aware of the cultural conventions through which sex is *signified* in the media: what older children might perceive as sexual, younger children may perceive as merely 'rude'. To this extent, the media have only a limited power to impose sexual meanings: in order to be meaningful in the first place, they must fit into a framework of existing knowledge – and this knowledge is acquired gradually, from a range of sources, not just from the media.

8. Morality is a key concern in children's interpretations of, and debates about, the media

The children made judgments about sex, not in the abstract but in the context of 'love and relationships'. They were very concerned about the decency or propriety of sexual behaviour or sexual images, particularly in public settings; they debated at length the motivations that led characters to engage in sex, and the consequences of their behaviour for others; and they were often critical of forms of sexual behaviour that they perceived as excessive or 'perverted'. Their moral position was often premised on ideas about the importance of self-fulfilment; but there was also a strong emphasis on the need for trust, fidelity and mutual respect. Here again, there was very little evidence that the children were being morally corrupted, or led towards a kind of amoral cynicism, by the media. Indeed, they often appeared more 'moralistic' (and in some instances, more 'prudish') than many adults.

9. There were some striking differences between boys and girls – at least in how gender was 'performed' in relation to the media

The children themselves perceived there to be considerable differences in boys' and girls' perspectives on these issues. Their views constituted a kind of commonsense wisdom, according to which (for example) girls were inherently more open or emotional than boys – although our research provided only partial support for these ideas. We found that girls were more ready to express sexual desire in relation to media images than boys, for whom such responses may have seemed 'politically incorrect'.

Boys' responses to media images of men were often characterised by a form of insecurity or 'homosexual panic', which was sometimes reinforced by directly homophobic strategies on the part of parents. The public visibility of images of homosexuality seems to problematise or relativise what it means to be heterosexual – although it is questionable whether it leads to greater tolerance of 'perversities'.

10. The influence of the media depends heavily upon the contexts of use, particularly in the family

The media become meaningful in different ways in different contexts. How children use or read a text in private may be very different from how they speak about it with peers, where there may be considerable pressure not to 'take it too seriously'. Children use media consumption as an opportunity to rehearse or police gendered identities – as when boys use pornography to harass girls, or older children use their knowledge of media to display their sexual sophistication. Different styles of parenting – which we have defined as more or less 'pedagogical' – also result in very different responses to sexual material, and very different ways of coming to terms with it. Parents can 'model' or reinforce particular responses to sexual material, and hence particular sexual identities for their children. The media do not have an autonomous ability either to sexually corrupt children or to sexually liberate them.

Issues for further investigation

In analysing our data, we often debated how far our findings might have been different had we conducted our research 20 or 50 years earlier. We could certainly point to much continuity between previous decades and the present. For instance, the discourses about the differences between the sexes on which our interviewees drew have been in circulation for many years, although the emphasis on their evolutionary basis may reflect the current fashion for such approaches. 'Gay chic' as well as homophobia both have a long history, and the former was certainly visible in the popular media from the sixties and seventies onwards, through stars such as David Bowie, for example. Similarly, women and young girls have been the target of advice from magazines since the end of the nineteenth century; and such magazines have also long suggested that personal problems may be solved by consumption of one kind or another. At least since its postwar 'invention', youth been defined partly through consumption; and the concerns about the corrupting effects of the mass media and consumerism we described in Chapter 1 are by no means new. Finally, as we have argued at many points in the book, the children to whom we talked were not in any clear sense the sexually knowing, precocious and confident beings that moral panics about the 'death of childhood' often assume them to be.

Nonetheless, it is worth sketching out what in our findings might be seen as specifically contemporary – and particularly as symptomatic of the neo-liberal 'consumer cultures' that have emerged in industrialised societies over the past couple of decades. To what extent do our findings point to the emergence of new understandings of the self, or of human subjectivity? Is the new visibility of sexuality indicative of a new way of defining our relationship with our 'essential' or 'inner' selves? To what extent does it represent a new form of social regulation – or indeed of self-regulation?

Our speculations here have been informed primarily by the work of Michel Foucault, and by Foucauldian analyses of government (e.g. Rose 1998; 1999a; b). 'Government' here refers to the heterogeneous tactics, strategies, calculations and programmes that have sought to regulate the conduct of human beings in advanced liberal democracies. Government aims to harness the personal goals and aspirations of individuals to broader political objectives such as increasing national wealth, health and productivity and enhancing social order and stability. Rose argues that, rather than imposing power on individuals, liberalism as a form of government has sought to produce self-steering citizens, who are capable of bearing a 'regulated freedom'. In the process, the modern human being has been defined as a unique individual, possessing an autonomous self that is capable of being worked on through various governmental 'technologies'. One of the most significant of these technologies of the self is the practice of confession, which in the nineteenth century was secularised and extended to institutions such as the school (Hunter 1994). As we argued in Chapters 1 and 6, the public discussion of sexuality in the media can also be understood as a form of confession, through which individuals are implicitly taught to govern their own conduct, albeit with the guidance of 'experts' such as therapists and psychologists.

According to this analysis, then, neo-liberal regimes have 'rolled back' the boundaries of the welfare state, not in order to remove power but to further entrench it at the level of the individual. They govern less through the formal institutions of the state, and more through forms of 'expertise' that seemingly lie beyond it – for instance, in the 'caring professions', in the media or the family – that encourage action on the self, by the self. An example here is the recent redefinition of the unemployed as 'jobseekers', a strategy of 'responsibilisation' that constructs those without work as active, choosing, autonomous citizens who can take charge of their own lives (Dean 1998). Another might be the popularity of self-help literature, which similarly encourages readers to act on themselves to improve their lives (Rimke 2000). The emphasis here is on the exercise of personal autonomy – rather than on the operation of the state – as the means of ensuring individual well-being.

These analyses are certainly thought-provoking, but they rarely explore how such shifts might be taking hold at the level of the individual. Of all our interviewees, perhaps only Ed (P, 17) could be said to be 'living the life' of the exemplary neo-liberal individual as it has been imagined in some writings on consumer culture. As we discussed in Chapter 4, through his diary and in interview he produced a self-consciously stylised image of a hedonistic self, fashioned though consumption – an image from which he was simultaneously ironically distanced. He moulded a 'new' masculinity, with an openness to fashion and other trappings once considered feminine or unmanly pursuits – although, as we noted, this appeared to be dependent on a relatively high degree of disposable income. In many ways he represented a rare limit case – an indication, perhaps, of the possibilities for self-identity inherent within media or consumer culture, not all of which were mobilised by our young participants.

However, there were more widespread trends in how young people presented and discussed themselves that may indicate the emergence of new understandings of the self. One of these is evidenced by the *intelligibility* of our request that participants write a diary or scrapbook. Many responded to this by telling 'the truth' about themselves – for instance, revealing unsolicited information about their own sexual lives. Those young people, discussed in Chapter 2, who pondered what they had 'learnt' about their own views and the media through writing the diary, demonstrate how modern individuals are urged to take themselves as an object of self-knowledge and as a subject of 'work on the self', through constant self-examination. The fact that their writing echoed the genre of the 'school project' illustrates the extent to which education also makes use of the technology of the confession – although the fact that this task was somewhat more amenable for girls than boys suggests that there may be a gender aspect to this process as well.

Modern citizenship, it has been argued, requires (indeed, demands) active participation; we must want to contribute and play our part, albeit in clearly circumscribed ways. In this respect, we noted in Chapter Two the readiness with which many interviewees were able to construct themselves as 'having opinions' about the media and other topics. Yet public opinion is not a social fact. The particular practices and 'technologies' of opinion surveys and polls have played a role in 'making up' people as citizens in this way. By contrast, the lack of confidence of some of the working class young people in our sample in presenting themselves in this context suggests that the competencies and capacities required for this modern form of citizenship may be unequally distributed.

None of our young participants presented themselves as dependent for moral guidance on the authority of religion, traditional morality, or established experts such as teachers (in the case of sex education), even where they came from strongly religious family backgrounds. However, all the young people to whom we spoke were involved to some extent with the secular expertise provided by 'pedagogical' media texts, such as magazines and soap operas. As we have suggested, these texts constitute their audiences in ethical terms – that is, they invite them to engage actively with the dilemmas and issues they portray and to take responsibility for their responses and views. As we have shown, young people repeatedly expressed particular preferences for more open storylines that appeared to allow them to 'make up their own minds'.

Yet audiences' scepticism about more overtly 'pedagogical' texts does not necessarily imply that they are immune to them. The fact that young people were almost unanimous in claiming that they did not read the advice on problem pages, but only the letters, for example, does not mean that they have no influence. Problem pages may be less significant for the solutions they offer than in the ways they define certain kinds of behaviour as problematic in the first place, or encourage readers to imagine themselves – for instance as individuals in control of their sexual identity and conduct. Similarly, many young people spoke of completing the quizzes in these magazines – which, albeit in frequently parodic or joking ways, are designed to yield information about the self for the purposes of self-assessment and judgement. Such media may help to habituate audiences to the rituals of assessing their own desires, attitudes and conduct in relation to criteria set out by experts. Again, it is less relevant that they often rejected the conclusions the magazines reached for them: they nevertheless echoed the discourses of such magazines as they spoke of working out 'what kind' of a person they were, where their desires lay, and of the importance of reaching 'their own' decisions about matters of sexual conduct.

All our interviewees were sceptical about centralised forms of regulation, although they were more prepared to accept the authority or rights of their parents. They provided ample evidence of the ways in which they had learned to manage their media consumption. To some extent, we can see this as evidence of the success of a process of 'responsibilisation': children today have been bound to become self-regulating media consumers. However, these responses were also to some extent shaped by the wider public debate. Children are aware that they are positioned as innocent, as especially vulnerable, or as media-incompetent, both in the domain of public debate (and media regulation) and often in the family. Their response is to emphasise their knowingness, be it about sex or the media, and thereby to construct a (powerful) counter-position to the (powerless) one that is marked out for them. When Will (S, 10) describes how he will 'find out' about sex through 'doing research' (Chapter 3) he positions himself very much as an autonomous, calculating entity in control of his personal quest for enlightenment and information – and this position was, we would claim, relatively typical. This preferred self-image significantly complicates the business of research – and indeed of education – in this field.

We might also analyse our findings about the meaning of lesbian and gay sexualities in the light of these arguments about new understandings of the self. As we have observed, 'being gay' signified very differently for different groups in our sample. For younger children, boys in particular, 'gay' served as a catch-all term that denoted a feared lack of masculinity that was to be avoided at all costs. However, for the older middle-class teenagers discussed in Chapters 4 and 7, and the mothers discussed in Chapter 9, it was brought into the ethical domain (that is, the sphere of work on the self). Sexuality was still seen as an essential category of being – something that you 'are' rather than a choice or a changeable position. However, these groups emphasised the importance of being 'honest' about and accepting of this identity in order to achieve fulfilment and happiness. This, it seemed, was the primary ethical choice, rather than concerns about whether it was 'right' or 'wrong'. Nonetheless, the fact that none of our young participants were prepared to admit to any such non-normative feelings or conduct themselves indicates that this choice is not yet a simple and straightforward one.

In our interviews with (admittedly self-selecting) groups of parents, we also noted signs of an emerging consensus that 'good' parenting should involve harnessing the self-regulating capacities of children rather than imposing norms and standards of behaviour. This suggests a new accommodation or settlement between children and parents, in tune with the less hierarchical approaches that now permeate other areas of social and working life. However, we noted how this could sometimes prove burdensome for parents. Parents also felt more at home enacting this supervisory discipline in relation to texts such as soap operas, whose conventions and approach were familiar to them. They were much less confident with those texts (usually outside the watershed, such as *Club Reps*) which appeared in some ways to exclude them, or not to offer the same opportunities for moral debate. This is not to suggest that young people were being 'led astray' by these programmes: they still seemed to offer opportunities for them to reflect and make ethical choices. However, it should caution us against the idea that the media necessarily provide a 'level playing field' when it comes to ethical debates, particularly between parents and children.

A further issue here is whether there has been a shift to a greater diversification in gendered identities in modern societies. In Chapters 4 and 5 we noted some aspects of girls' self-presentation that appeared relatively novel, particularly where they claimed to be actively desiring. However, their identities are at best hybrid (Jagger 2001). They are still concerned with traditional characteristics associated with normative femininity, such as women's ability to care, listen and nurture. They appear still to be subject to pressures around the perfectly shaped female body; and both boys and girls used aggressively sexist language to belittle certain women whose sexuality was deemed to be excessive (such as the model Jordan). Meanwhile, boys were less willing to assert their desires (albeit perhaps only in the context of our interviews). Both boys and girls referred to masculine physical ideals, encapsulated in references to the 'six pack'; and it could be argued that 'working out' has acquired specific meanings in recent consumer culture, as a symbol of moral worth and success, suggesting willpower, self-discipline and 'making something of oneself'. However, traditional ideals of masculinity – such that men must always-already 'know everything' – appeared for some boys to militate against adopting the persona of the 'incomplete' self, requiring further work, that makes governmental strategies appear to be necessary in the first place.

The emphasis our interviewees placed on their self-governing capacities may help explain the particular dilemmas of regulating sexual material. Media regulation, we have argued, actively constitutes the meanings of media texts. In particular, it invites audiences to consider texts in terms of their social acceptability – for example, as when an age classification on a video implies that it may be inappropriate for younger audiences. However, sex appears more problematic as an issue here than does violence. There is a long-established tradition of research into so-called violent media that focuses on their 'social harm'. Whilst it is certainly contentious (Barker and Petley 2001), it is nonetheless well-known and often attains the status of common sense wisdom in popular debates. In previous research, David Buckingham found that children were aware of these arguments (for instance, about the 'copycat' effect or 'desensitisation' to violence in real life) and fully able both to rehearse and to challenge them (Buckingham 1996). However, it was notable that our interviewees – both children and parents – were much less sure of themselves when discussing the possible harmful effects of sexual media. Their statements were often confused and seemed unconvincing even to themselves: for instance, young children and even some older teenagers speculated that nudity might make children want 'to wear no clothes', whilst parents seemed undecided about whether promiscuity was the effect of the media or of 'peer pressure'.

One possible explanation here might be that sexual media material has been increasingly drawn into the domain of personal ethics, as an occasion for individuals to scrutinise their own desires, conduct and responses, rather than that of social harm. For this reason, it may be harder for regulatory bodies to obtain the degree of consensus that is necessary to win legitimacy, at least when it comes to controlling sexual material. To this extent, current moves towards relaxation of these rules – particularly in relation to contexts where such encounters are deliberately chosen rather than imposed, as in the distinction between billboards and magazine advertisements – would seem to be in tune with public views.

Finally, our analysis of these issues causes us to reflect critically on our own position. As we have noted, our research had a 'performative' aspect. In discussing with children and parents the state of the media and requesting their opinions about forms of regulation such as the watershed – and now in reporting our findings to a wider public – we raise awareness of what is already being done and contribute to its legitimation. Participation in our project helped guide children and parents in the roles and responsibilities of citizenship (such as that of having opinions and being prepared to 'express' them).

Nor are we outside the operations of power ourselves. Through our research we produce a 'knowledge' of children that will be used in the government of citizens, as it feeds into policy decisions taken by regulatory bodies. Our ultimate aim may seem a liberal one. We have pointed to children's insightfulness, to their ability to contribute to public debates about matters of morality and ethics, and to their competence as media consumers. Our conclusion, in effect, is that children should be considered in a new light, as active consumers rather than only the passive objects of interventions from above. This might be taken as proposing that the definition of the modern citizen and the privileges of self-government should in certain (limited) ways be extended to young people to a greater degree than at present. This might be seen as a form of 'empowerment' – a transfer of power to individuals who were previously denied it. Yet it might also be seen as a matter of simply extending the technology through which government creates self-regulating and responsible individuals.

Certainly, there are costs to this process. Our interviewees spoke frequently of the structured inequalities of power they experienced (although not in those terms); for instance, when girls described forms of harassment by boys, or when boys both enacted but were also critical of the divisiveness and aggression within homophobic male culture. They were also aware of the limits of their capacity to manage their own lives, caught as they were between conflicting pressures. Yet the discourses of voluntarism, autonomy and individuality that are so dominant today provide little space for other explanatory frameworks that might offer different ways of making meaning of their lives. If children are to be allowed to enter the sphere of modern citizenship, they must also conform to its norms and rituals; and these impose burdens which, we would argue, will be heavier for some than others.

Towards policy

Finally, what are the implications of this research in terms of cultural and educational policy? What general recommendations might we have to offer to media regulators, or to those concerned with education? Obviously, research is only one of the factors to be weighed in the policy equation; and for various reasons, children's perspectives on these issues must be set alongside those of adults. However, there are a few points here that we feel are justified on the basis of our research.

1. The function of regulation

Media regulation – for example, in the form of the watershed or of film and video classification – did serve useful functions for both the children and the parents in our study. In general, however, existing forms of regulation appeared to be somewhat more proscriptive than either group felt was necessary. Most children claimed that they were perfectly able to cope with material that was 'over their age'; and most parents seemed quite willing to go along with this, allowing them to watch videos that were classified as older, or to watch programmes after the watershed. Hardly anybody seriously claimed that the regulatory regime was too lax, or that it should be much stricter. Among parents, this might be seen to induce a degree of guilt – a sense that they would never be able to live up to the ideal that seems to be implicit in the system; while among children, it obviously holds out the potential enticement of 'forbidden fruit'. Alternatively, it might lead both groups to the conclusion that the system is too unrealistic, or simply out of step with modern life; and a system that is frequently flouted may ultimately enjoy very little credibility. Certainly, there were few parents or children who claimed to follow the system completely, or to the exclusion of any other considerations.

As we have implied, proscriptive regulation is becoming harder to sustain in the context of more diverse and mobile societies. In areas such as sexuality, it is increasingly difficult to identify a moral consensus; and, as we have argued, debates around sexuality are increasingly characterised by an emphasis on individual autonomy and self-reliance. The emphasis in media regulation is accordingly moving away from censorship towards a 'consumer advice' model – albeit, in some instances, extremely slowly. In our view, the primary function of regulatory bodies in this respect should be to provide information to consumers, and to assist them in making informed decisions about what they would like to watch or read. Given the ease with which material of all kinds can now be accessed via the internet, it seems quite inconsistent to sustain a mandatory system, whereby people can be prosecuted for providing material in one medium (such as video) that can be readily obtained in another. In media, as in most other areas of children's lives, parents need to be involved in this process; and parents should have the power to permit or prevent their children from doing things (or at least be given some support in attempting to do so). But the case for a wholly advisory system – as now exists in several other countries – seems increasingly hard to deny.

2. The practice of regulation

There are two more specific issues relating to media regulation that arise from this study. The first is that of the 'publicness' of different media. Both children and parents made different judgments about particular texts depending upon how and where they might be encountered. What was acceptable in a magazine, for example, might not be acceptable on an advertising billboard; what was acceptable on television at 10.30 in the evening might not be acceptable at 6.30. In this respect, they supported the kinds of judgments that are routinely made by regulators themselves – as the case of the Opium ad (Chapter 5) demonstrates. Extending this to the internet slightly complicates the issue, since the internet is not a medium of public display; yet it is worth recalling here the children's complaints about the sudden appearance of pornographic images on their computer screens. We would suggest that the issue here is not so much one of 'publicness', but of the likelihood that people will encounter material *involuntarily* – or at least without adequate prior knowledge (or warning) about it. In a sense, this argument follows from our point above about the need for 'informed consumers'. It is not, of course, to suggest that we need to be told everything in advance; simply that, at least in some areas, people have a right to be alerted to the possibility of encountering things that might offend them.

A second point here follows from our observations about children's moral debates around the media (point 8 above). As with debates about media violence, there is often a tendency when discussing the issue of sex in the media to rely on simplistic measures or rules – according to which certain acts or body parts are ruled acceptable or unacceptable under any circumstances. The ten-year-olds in our study seemed to adopt a similar approach, for instance when assessing how much of a model's body was exposed; but the older children clearly recognised that sexual meanings depended upon the context. Measures of the 'decency' of particular acts represent a very crude way of assessing their meanings, if not a positively unreliable one. As with violence, judgments about media content need to take account of genre, modality and context.

Neither of the points we have raised here will be particularly novel for media regulators. However, they illustrate that regulation is bound to rely on assumptions about the competency and knowledge of media consumers. These are assumptions that, in our view, should be constantly revisited in the light of empirical research.

3. Education

There is a wealth of evidence in our research that young people are using the media to learn about love, sex and relationships – and indeed, that they are positively choosing to do so in preference to other sources. This suggests, first, that the media could serve as a valuable resource for sex education, albeit of a more 'informal' kind. However, there are some obvious dangers here. As we have suggested, there are considerable limitations in attempting to use the media in overly didactic ways – for example, in using storylines in soap operas as a vehicle for warnings about the dangers of under-age sex. As we have argued, the media are likely to be much more effective in this respect if they are used as a means of generating discussion, rather than as a surrogate form of propaganda. The value of the media in this respect is precisely that they appear to offer a forum for debate, both in schools and in homes; and there is certainly room for both teachers and parents to be given more advice about how this debate can be encouraged and promoted.

Secondly, our research suggests that the media should be a much more central focus for formal sex education classes than currently tends to be the case. Sex education teachers might use media of the kind we have considered in this book as a focus for analysis and debate – and indeed as a basis for young people to produce their own media representations. However, there are dangers for teachers in setting out to disabuse young people of the 'false' messages we imagine they derive from the media – particularly if we then seek to replace these with the 'true' messages that (we imagine) we alone can provide. In this area, perhaps more than many others, young people are likely to prove resistant to any overtly didactic approach: although they might respond well to being independent 'researchers' of their own media practices. As with media education in general, we need to begin by recognising the complexity of young people's media experiences, and the extensive 'media literacy' they already possess.

References

Ang, I. (1985) *Watching Dallas: Soap opera and the melodramatic imagination.* Translated by D. Couling, London and New York: Methuen

Ang, I. (1996) *Living Room Wars: Rethinking Media Audiences for a Postmodern World*, London and New York: Routledge

Baker, C. (1997) 'Membership Categorization and Interview Accounts'. In *Qualitative Research: Theory, Method and Practice*, ed. D. Silverman, London, Thousand Oaks, New Delhi: Sage

Barker, C. (1998) '"Cindy's a slut": moral identities and moral responsibility in the "soap talk" of British Asian girls' *Sociology* 32 (1): 65–81

Barker, M., and Petley, J., eds (2001) *Ill Effects: the Media / Violence Debate*, London and New York: Routledge

Barnett, S., and Thomson, K. (1996) 'Portraying sex: the limits of tolerance'. In *British Social Attitudes, the 13th Report*, ed. R. Jowell, J. Curtice, A. Park, L. Brook, and K. Thomson, Aldershot, Hants: Social and Community Planning Research

Bennett, T. (1983) 'Texts, Readers, Reading Formations' *Bulletin of the Midwest Modern Language Association* 16 (1): 3–17

Block, L. d. (1998) 'From Childhood Pleasure to Adult Identities' *The English and Media Magazine* (38, Summer) English and Media Centre: 24–9

Bourdieu, P., and Passeron, J.-C. (1977) *Reproduction in Education, Society and Culture.* Translated by R. Nice, London: Sage

Bragg, S., and Buckingham, D. (2002) *Young People and Sexual Content on Television*, London: Broadcasting Standards Commission

Brown, J.D., Childers, K.W and Waszak, C.S. (1990) 'Television and Adolescent Sexuality'. In *Journal of Adolescent Health Care* 11 (2): 62–70.

Bryant, J., and Rockwell, S. R. (1994) 'Effects of Massive Exposure to Sexually Oriented Prime-Time TV Programming on Adolescents' Moral Judgement'. In *Media, Children, and the Family: social scientific, psychodynamic, and clinical perspectives*, ed. D. Zillmann, J. Bryant, and A. Huston (183–95), Hillsdale, New Jersey: Hove, UK: Lawrence Erlbaum Associates

BSC (1999) *Annual Monitoring Report No. 7* London: Broadcasting Standards Commission

Buckingham, D. (1987) *Public Secrets: EastEnders and its Audience*, London: British Film Institute

Buckingham, D. (1993) *Children Talking Television: the making of television literacy*, London and Bristol, PA: Falmer Press

Buckingham, D. (1996) *Moving Images: Understanding Children's Emotional Response to TV*, Manchester and New York: Manchester University Press

Buckingham, D. (2000) *After the Death of Childhood: growing up in the age of electronic media*, Cambridge: Polity Press

Butler, J. (1990) *Gender Trouble: Feminism and the Subversion of Identity*, London: Routledge

Butler, J. (1991) 'Imitation and Gender Subordination'. In *Inside/Out: Lesbian Theories, Gay Theories*, ed. D. Fuss (13–31), New York and London: Routledge

Collins, J. (1990) *Uncommon Cultures*, London: Routledge

Collins, J. (1995) *Architectures of Excess: cultural life in the information age*, London: Routledge

Connell, I. (1991) 'Tales of tellyland: the popular press and television in the UK'. In *Communication and Citizenship: Journalism and the Public Sphere*, ed. P. Dahlgren, and C. Sparks (236–53), London: Routledge

Connell, I. (1992) 'Personalities in the popular media'. In *Journalism and Popular Culture*, ed. P. Dahlgren, and C. Sparks (64–83), London: Sage

Connell, R. W. (2000) *The Men and The Boys*, Cambridge: Polity

Cowie, E. (1990) 'Fantasia'. In *The Woman in Question: m/f*, ed. P. Adams, and E. Cowie, London: Verso

Cunningham, H. (1995) *Children and Childhood in Western Society Since 1500*, London: Longman

Dean, M. (1998) 'Administering Asceticism: reworking the ethical life of the unemployed citizen'. In *Governing Australia: Studies in Contemporary Rationalities of Government*, ed. M. Dean, and B. Hindess (87–107), Cambridge: Cambridge University Press

Donald, J. (1992) *Sentimental Education: Schooling, Popular Culture and the Regulation of Liberty*, London: Verso

Donnerstein, E., Linz, D., and Penrod, S. (1987) *The Question of Pornography*, Glencoe: Free Press

Dovey, J. (2000) *Freakshow: First Person Media and Factual Television*, London: Verso

Dyer, R. (1993) *The Matter of Images: Essays on Representations*, London and New York: Routledge

Epstein, D., and Johnson, R. (1998) *Schooling Sexualities*, Buckingham and Philadelphia: Open University Press

Foucault, M. (1972) *The Archaeology of Knowledge*. Translated by A. M. Sheridan, London: Tavistock

Foucault, M. (1984) *The History of Sexuality: an Introduction*. Translated by R. Hurley, Harmondsworth and New York: Penguin Books

Frazer, E. (1987) 'Teenage girls reading Jackie' *Media, Culture and Society* 9 (4): 407–25

Friedberg, A. (1993) *Window Shopping: Cinema and the Postmodern*, Berkeley and Los Angeles: Oxford: University of California Press

Frosh, S., Phoenix, A., and Pattman, R. (2002) *Young Masculinities*, Basingstoke: Palgrave Macmillan

Gamson, J. (1998) *Freaks Talk Back: Tabloid Talk Shows and Sexual Nonconformity*, Chicago: University of Chicago Press

Garner, A., Sterk, H. M., and Adams, S. (1998) 'Narrative Analysis of Sexual Etiquette in Teenage Magazines' *Journal of Communication* 48 (4): 59–78

Gauntlett, D. (2002) *Media, Gender and Identity: an Introduction*, London: Routledge

Geraghty, C. (1991) *Women and Soap Opera: a study of prime time soaps*, Cambridge: Polity Press

Gray, A. (1992) *Video Playtime: the gendering of a leisure technology*, London and New York: Routledge

Greenberg, B. S., and Busselle, R. W. (1996) 'Soap Operas and Sexual Activity: a decade later' *Journal of Communication* 46 (4): 153–60

Grindstaff, L. (2002) *The Money Shot: Trash, Class, and the Making of TV Talk Shows*, Chicago: University of Chicago Press.

Hanley, P. (2000) *Sense and Sensibilities: public opinion and the BBFC guidelines*, London: British Board of Film Classification

Hendrick, H. (1997) *Children, Childhood and English Society. 1880–1990*, Cambridge: Cambridge University Press

Hermes, J. (1995) *Reading Women's Magazines: an analysis of everyday media use*, Cambridge: Polity

Hill, A., and Thomson, K. (2000) 'Sex and the media: a shifting landscape'. In *British Social Attitudes, the 17th Report: Focusing on Diversity*, ed. R. Jowell, J. Curtice, A. Park, K. Thomson, C. Bromley, and N. Stratford, London, Thousand Oaks, New Delhi: Sage and National Centre for Social Research

Hitchens, P. (2002) 'The failure of sex education'. In *Teenage Sex: What Should Schools Teach Children?*, ed. E. Lee (49–61), London: Hodder and Stoughton

Holland, P. (1983) 'Page 3 speaks to women too'. In *Screen* v 24/3/May–June, pp. 84–102.

Hunt, L., ed. (1993) *The Invention of Pornography*, New York: Zone Books

Hunter, I. (1994) *Rethinking the School: Subjectivity, Bureaucracy, Criticism*, St Leonard's, NSW: Allen and Unwin

Hunter, I., Saunders, D., and Williamson, D. (1993) *On Pornography: Literature, Sexuality and Obscenity Law*, Basingstoke: Macmillan – now Palgrave Macmillan

Jackson, P., Stevenson, N., and Brooks, K. (2001) *Making Sense of Men's Magazines*, Cambridge: Polity

Jagger, E. (1998) 'Marketing the self, buying an other: Dating in a post modern, consumer society' *Sociology – the Journal of the British Sociological Association* 32 (4): 795–814

Jagger, E. (2001) 'Marketing molly and melville: Dating in a postmodern, consumer society' *Sociology – the Journal of the British Sociological Association* 35 (1): 39–57

Jenkins, P. (1992) *Intimate Enemies: Moral Panics in Contemporary Britain*, New York: Aldine de Gruyter

Jones, K., and Davies, H. (2002) 'Keeping it real: *Grange Hill* and the representation of 'the child's world' in children's television drama''. In *Small Screens: Television for Children*, ed. D. Buckingham (141–58), London: Leicester University Press

Jowett, G., Jarvie, I., and Fuller, K. (1996) *Children and the Movies: media influence and the Payne Fund controversy*, Cambridge: Cambridge University Press

Kehily, M. (1999) 'More Sugar? Teenage magazines, gender displays and sexual learning' *European Journal of Cultural Studies* 2 (1): 65–89

Kuhn, A. (1988) *Cinema, Censorship and Sexuality, 1909–1925*, London and New York: Routledge

Kunkel, D., Cope, K. M., Farinola, W. J. M., Rollin, E., and Donnerstein, E. (1999) *Sex on TV: content and context. A biennial report to the Kaiser Family Foundation*, Menlo Park, CA: Kaiser Family Foundation

Kunkel, D., Cope-Farrar, K., Biely, E., Farinola, W. J. M., and Donnerstein, E. (2001) *Sex on TV (2) A biennial report to the Kaiser Family Foundation*, Menlo Park, CA: Kaiser Family Foundation

Landry, D. J. (2002) 'Sex education: a view from the United States'. In *Teenage Sex: What Should Schools Teach Children?*, ed. E. Lee (1–15), London: Hodder and Stoughton

Lees, S. (1986) *Losing Out: sexuality and adolescent girls*, London: Hutchinson

Lees, S. (1994) 'Talking About Sex in Sex Education' *Gender and Education* 6 (3): 281–92

Leichter, H. J., Ahmed, D., Barrios, L., Bryce, J., Larsen, E., and Moe, L. (1985) 'Family Contexts of Television' *Educational Communication and Technology Journal* 33 (1): 26–40

Levine, J. (2002) *Harmful to minors: the perils of protecting children from sex*, Minneapolis, London: University of Minnesota Press

Livingstone, S., and Bovill, M. (1999) *Young People, New Media*, London: London School of Economics

Lowney, K. (1999) *Baring Our Souls: TV Talk Shows and the Religion of Recovery*, New York: Aldine de Gruyter

Mac an Ghaill, M. (1994) *The Making of Men: Masculinities, Sexualities and Schooling*, Buckingham: Open University Press

MacKeogh, C. (2001) 'Taking account of the macro in the micro-politics of family viewing – generational strategies' *Sociological Research Online* 6 (1): U109–U126

McNair, B. (2002) *Striptease Culture: Sex, Media and the Democratisation of Desire*, London: Routledge

McRobbie, A. (1991) *From Jackie to Just Seventeen*, London: Macmillan

McRobbie, A. (1996) 'More! New sexualities in girls' and women's magazines'. In *Cultural Studies and Communications*, ed. J. Curran, D. Morley, and V. Walkerdine (172–94), London: Arnold

Measor, L., Tiffin, C., and Miller, K. (2000) *Young People's Views on Sex Education: education, attitudes, behaviour*, London: Routledge

Millwood Hargrave, A., ed. (1992) *Sex and Sexuality in Broadcasting*, London: John Libbey Media

Millwood Hargrave, A., ed. (1999) *Sex and Sensibility*, London: John Libbey Media

Millwood Hargrave, A., Halloran, J., and Gray, P., eds (1996) *Young People and the Media*, London: Broadcasting Standards Council

Modleski, T. (1982) *Loving with a Vengeance: mass produced fantasies for women*, London: Methuen

Moore, S., and Rosenthal, D. (1993) *Sexuality in Adolescence*, London: Routledge

Morley, D. (1986) *Family television: cultural power and domestic leisure*, London: Comedia

Morley, D., and Silverstone, R. (1988) *Domestic Communication – Technologies and Meanings*. Paper read at International Television Studies Conference

Mort, F. (1996) *Cultures of Consumption: Masculinities and Social Space in Late Twentieth-Century Britain*, London: Routledge

Mort, F. (2000) *Dangerous Sexualities: medico-moral politics in England since 1830*. 2nd edn, London: Routledge

Munt, S. (1998) *Heroic Desire: Lesbian Identity and Cultural Space*, London: Cassell

Newitz, A. (1997) 'White Savagery and Humiliation: or a new racial consciousness in the media'. In *White Trash: race and class in America*, ed. M. Wray, and A. Newitz (131–54), New York and London: Routledge

Nimmo-Jones, G. (2001) Personal communication: (doctoral research in progress, Institute of Education, University of London)

Nixon, H. (2000) '*Dawson's Creek*: Sex and Scheduling in a Global Phenomenon' *English and Media Magazine* (42/3): 25–9

Nixon, S. (1996) *Hard Looks: masculinities, spectatorship and contemporary consumption*, London: UCL Press

Osborne, T., and Rose, N. (1999) 'Do the social sciences create phenomena?: the example of public opinion research' *British Journal of Sociology* 50 (3): 367–96

Palmer, P. (1988) 'The Social Nature of Children's Television Viewing'. In *Television and Its Audience; International Research Perspectives*, ed. P. Drummond, and R. Patterson (139–53), London: BFI

Parrott, W. G., and Harre, R. (1996) 'Embarrassment and the threat to character'. In *The emotions: social, cultural and biological dimensions*, ed. W. G. Parrott, and R. Harre, London: Sage

Penley, C. (1997) 'Crackers and Whackers: the white trashing of porn'. In *White Trash: race and class in America*, ed. M. Wray, and A. Newitz (89–112), New York and London: Routledge

Pfeil, F. (1995) *White Guys: studies in postmodern domination and difference*, London: Verso

Phillips, R., and Watt, D. (2000) 'Introduction'. In *De-centring sexualities: politics and representations beyond the metropolis*, ed. R. Phillips, D. Watt, and D. Shuttleton (1–17), London and New York: Routledge

Plummer, K. (1995) *Telling sexual stories: power, change, and social worlds*, London and New York: Routledge

Potter, J., and Wetherell, M. (1987) *Discourse and Social Psychology: Beyond Attitudes and Behaviour*, London: Sage

Radway, J. A. (1987) *Reading the Romance: Women, Patriarchy and Popular Literature*. British edition ed, London and New York: Verso

Richards, C. (1998) *Teen Spirits: Music and Identity in Media Education*, London and Bristol, Pennsylvania: UCL Press

Richardson, L. (1998) 'Writing: A Method of Inquiry'. In *Collecting and Interpreting Qualitative Materials*, ed. N. K. Denzin, and Y. S. Lincoln. Vol. 3, Thousand Oaks, London, New Delhi: Sage Publications

Rimke, H. M. (2000) 'Governing citizens through self-help literature' *Cultural Studies* 14 (1): 61–78

Rose, J. (1999) 'The Cult of Celebrity' *New Formations* (36): 9–20

Rose, N. (1998) *Inventing Ourselves: Psychology, Power, and Personhood*, Cambridge: Cambridge University Press

Rose, N. (1999a) *Governing the Soul: the shaping of the private self*. 2nd edn, London and New York: Free Association Books

Rose, N. (1999b) *Powers of Freedom: reframing political thought*, Cambridge: Cambridge University Press

Sedgwick, E. K. (1990) *Epistemology of the Closet*, London: Penguin

Sedgwick, E. K. (1993) 'Queer performativity: Henry James' *The Art of the Novel*' *GLQ: A Journal of Lesbian and Gay Studies* 1 (1): 1–16

Segal, L. (1993) 'Does pornography cause violence? The search for evidence'. In *Dirty Looks: women, pornography, power*, ed. P. C. Gibson, and R. Gibson (5–21), London: British Film Institute

Shattuc, J. M. (1997) *The Talking Cure: TV Talk Shows and Women*, London: Routledge

Signorielli, N. (1991) 'Adolescents and ambivalence towards marriage: a cultivation analysis' *Youth and Society* 23 (1): 121–49

Silverstone, R. (1994) *Television and Everyday Life*, London and New York: Routledge

Sinfield, A. (2000) 'The production of gay and the return of power'. In *De-centring sexualities: politics and representations beyond the metropolis*, ed. R. Phillips, D. Watt, and D. Shuttleton (21–35), London and New York: Routledge

Stallybrass, P., and White, A. H. (1986) *The politics and poetics of transgression*, London: Methuen

Strasburger, V. C. (2000) 'Getting teenagers to say NO to sex, drugs, and violence in the new millennium' *Medical Clinics of North America* 84 (4): 787

Tatchell, P. (2002) 'The ABC of sexual health and happiness'. In *Teenage Sex: What Should Schools Teach Children?*, ed. E. Lee (63–79), London: Hodder and Stoughton

Thompson, K., and Sharma, A. (1998) 'Secularization, moral regulation and the mass media' *British Journal of Sociology* 49 (3): 434–55

Valocchi, S. (1999) 'The class-inflected nature of gay identity' *Social Problems* 46 (2): 207–24

Walkerdine, V. (1981) 'Sex, Power and Pedagogy' *Screen Education* (38): 14–24

Walkerdine, V. (1997) *Daddy's Girl: Young Girls and Popular Culture*, Basingstoke and London: Macmillan now Palgrave Macmillan

Walkerdine, V., Lucey, H., and Melody, J. (2001) *Growing Up Girl: psychosocial explorations of gender and class*, Basingstoke: Palgrave Macmillan

Wartella, E., Scantlin, R., Kotler, J., Huston, A. C., and Donnerstein, E. (2000) 'Effects of sexual content in the media on children and adolescents'. In *Children in the New Media Landscape*, ed. C. v. Feilitzen, and U. Carlsson, Goteborg, Sweden: UNESCO

Way, N. (1997) 'Using feminist research methods to understand the friendships of adolescent boys' *Journal of Social Issues* 53 (4): 703–23

Weeks, J. (1995) *Invented Moralities: Sexual Values in an Age of Uncertainty*, Cambridge: Polity Press

Weis, L., and Carbonell-Medina, D. (2000) 'Learning to Speak Out in an Abstinence Based Sex Education Group: Gender and Race Work in an Urban Magnet School' *Teachers' College Record* 102 (3 (June)): 620–50

Wells, P. (2002) '"Tell me about your id, when you was a kid, yah!" Animation and children's television culture'. In *Small Screens: Television for Children*, ed. D. Buckingham (61–95), London: Leicester University Press

Whatling, C. (1997) *Screen Dreams: fantasising lesbians in film*, Manchester: Manchester University Press

Winship, J. (1985) 'A girl needs to get streetwise: magazines for the 1980s' *Feminist Review* 21: 25–46

Wolpe, A. M. (1988) *Within School Walls: the Role of Discipline, Sexuality and the Curriculum*, London and New York: Routledge

Index

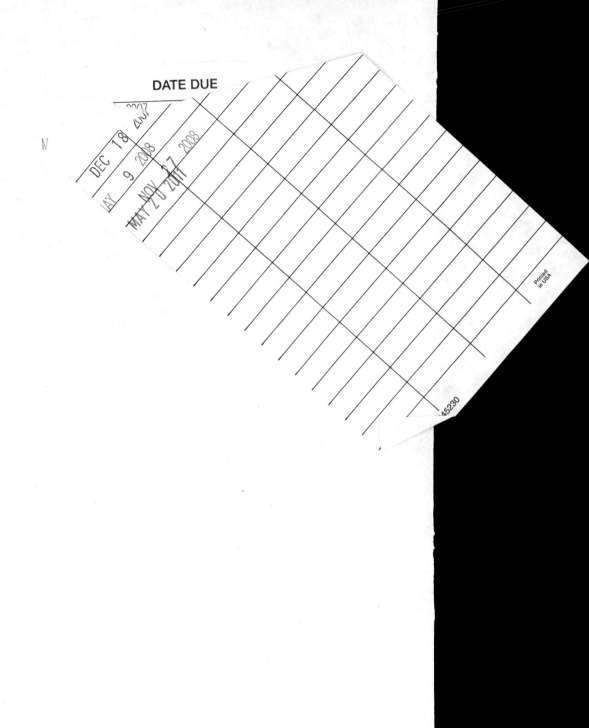

DATE DUE

DEC 18 2007

MAY 9 2008

NOV 27 2008

MAY 20 2011

Printed
in USA